Crazy Normal
Normal Crazy

Keeping Sane,
Inside and Out,
Outside and In,
with a Positive
Mind Set!

Annette Monckton

AAZZ MAD AAZZ MAMA Inc.

First publication Feb 2013 – self-published by Annette Monckton

Second Edition June 2013

Copy right © Annette Monckton, 2012

All rights reserved. No part of this publication may be reproduced, stored in a retrieval system, or transmitted in any form or by any means, electronic, mechanical, photocopying, recording or otherwise, without the prior written permission by the author Annette Monckton or nominated associates.

The above also applies to templates, processes, logo, commercial ideas and innovations contained in this book.

The Library of Congress

United States Copyright Office

Monckton, Annette,

Crazy Normal, Normal Crazy!

Keeping sane, inside and out, outside and in, with a positive mindset!

ISBN   978 0 9874787 0 2

Cover design by Greg Anderson from Ten West Creative (www.tenwestcreative.com)

Photos by Annette Monckton

Printed and bound by LuLu Publishing

I dedicate this book to a number of people:

- To my loving, caring supportive husband Mick and my gorgeous beautiful children where love holds no boundaries!
- To my great dear friend fighting the toughest ride of her life and her family.
- To all my friends & family that cared, loved, supported and assisted me & my clan.
- To all my new diverse, intelligent, creative, artistic, and amazingly talented friends from P-Block.
- To those who have been wrongfully judged, inhumanely persecuted by a system that has no compassion for the human spirit. (Mick's dedication he wanted to add and most deservingly so – thanks darling you read my mind – great you're tuning onto my mental channel.)
- And finally for all who are living an enjoyable, loving, happy, caring and enriching life and who are helping others in need.

Love to all, thanks

Mama xx

Contents

Acknowledgements 1
Foreword 2
1. Hang On – help is on its way! 6
2. Knowing me, knowing you! 27
3. Me in a nutshell - one bloody big nut too! 57
4. Full Moon/Full Circle 128
5. The day & the night – Dancing on the ceiling! 147
6. P-Block Mates 173
7. P-Block 196
8. Aftermath 257
10. Opening a can of worms 295
11. Talking about a revolution 320
12. If I could turn back time! 345
13. Hopes and Dreams 353
14. Que Sera' Sera' 362

Acknowledgements

- For all the good times and challenges that I recently put my darling Husband and beautiful children through, thank you for your continued support and the endless love! I know it provides a stronger base/foundation for our future.
- To my great dear and close friend who through her life has indirectly created the opportunity for others to live a better life!
- To Janine from the Tattslotto booth at the local supermarket for her initial support and guidance.
- To Luisa and Darren for their support and professionalism in setting up the Social Media Service, editing and assisting with the business development. Great to have you on my team and thank you very much!
- All (especially those that rode my wave unknowingly and were there to support me on my journey) my family, friends (past & present) and ex-colleagues who inspired me to be the person I am today!
- Mental Health Legal Aid – Melbourne, Victoria (Hilda – you know who you are!).
- Chief Psychiatrist Office – Melbourne, Victoria
- Dr. Stephen Newman – for not judging me and allowing me to be myself.
- A huge thank you to Greg Anderson from Ten West Creative (www.tenwestcreative.com) who created the logo, book cover, business cards etc. for the book and business. He was very professional, helpful and creative, far exceeding any of my expectations.

Foreword

Wow.....Where does one start when you have taken a trip inside your mind and explored boundaries you never dreamed of and those sub-conscious dreams became reality in a bizarre mixed up world that we live in, currently deemed as perfect! Earlier this year (2012), I said to my husband that I could have managed the MYKI project with my eyes closed (the Victorian Government's plan to implement a new train system that was continually failing), unwittingly I've now realised that I and anyone else who reads this book has the potential to achieve a whole lot more with better vision/foresight.

Since my journey of self-discovery, I've learned more in the last 20 weeks than I could have possibly imagined and can visualise changes like no other. However as I'm mindful and insightful with a very open mind, I'm also conscious of not setting an expectation so as I don't disappoint you. I would prefer you to empower yourself to draw your own conclusions.

Over my 39 years, I've endured many challenges so I was mentally prepared for what has recently transpired and what is about to unfold. What I didn't expect was to end up in a psychiatric ward at Southern Health – Monash Medical Clinic in Clayton on the 18/7/2012, with every possible human right being denied.

The trigger for this monumental time in my life was due to a dear and close friend Rose, who was pregnant with her third child, being diagnosed with a rare form of breast cancer. My friend had also been suffering with chronic fatigue syndrome (including depression) for 7 years when presented with this devastating news.

When you clear your mind of some emotions, expectations, fears and inhibitions it makes for an easier journey (release the beast of burden). Death is a reality or we would all live forever and be walking around with dinosaurs! Therefore I've written this book to help me, hopefully help Rose and ultimately help others. How quick I made the transformation, what I uncovered and what boundaries I explored have been mind-blowing! (No wonder I flipped my lid!)

Before you board my train (train of thought), I'm a simple person with a complex mind. In fact, we all have a complex mind; we all think and act differently. Our life and the world would be pretty boring, if we were all the same! (No rocket scientist needed for that analogy!)

Most people don't like change and fear stepping outside their zone. I don't and thought it would be beneficial to share my thoughts on this given my recent experience. Some parts of this book may be difficult to interpret and that is expected because they are matters of a complex mind!

With that in mind, I've always called it as I see it and will do the same as I write/type. I will discuss personal matters from my past and highlight opportunities encountered on my recent journey of discovery.

Some people, particularly family and friends may find aspects of my life hard to accept or believe because they currently think they know me, which is right on the surface! How could they make determinations if I didn't share more of the inner me?

Even my husband said "It amazes me how you think, I thought I knew you!" My reply was "You did, but now you know me a bit more!" This is based on true experiences and events. I guess I've written my own "This is your life" – my first 39 years to-date, go me!

I will also refer to recent news/changes and connecting them back to my open perspective - thought processes, to enable or assist others to view matters in a different light.

In most cases, I have used actual names and it's irrelevant which names have been changed. However no names were changed for the people that treated me medically. You'll probably notice that the tone of language will change as well and you may find parts of this book offensive.

No apologies required because this is me! Just thought I'd be courteous and provide a warning! This is "normal" for anyone riding the wave of life! I say that with tongue in cheek, because what is normal, when we are all different especially with regards to your thoughts and the thoughts of others?

Perception can be quite harmful and deceptive because people only see and hear what they want to! When you take the time to enter your mind and assess who you really are and what you are about, it's natural that you become more aware of others.

For me, it has created an opportunity of power, not the special powers the doctors were referring to, but the power of your mind and how to view matters differently! No one can buy or find this mindset in any book, you need to explore your inner-self, if you so wish.

I'm providing the insight and strategies if you're interested. Hence I have thrown some of my cards (I love black jack and poker) on a turning table (just for the record/s) for the benefit of others......... (While I'm on a roll and because I love to sing) I was on a train bound for somewhere, when I met up with some doctors, who didn't want to listen to me! (Thanks Kenny – the Gambler is one of many favourite songs!)

Throughout this book, I may repeat myself; there may be a number of reasons or purposes why and here are a few:

- I think it is important or I need to link an experience/event to another.
- With a skill set in training, repetition is vital to getting some points across. This is not meant to serve as a training guide for the average reader but more importantly to highlight to the doctors (and other academics) who I have encountered, why I, on some occasions re-iterated items that were important. (Assuming they plan to identify their own flaws or weaknesses through failure of listening and understanding me, turning their blindness into a positive.)
- I may be venting, therefore dealing with some unresolved emotions, at that point in time, as I type.

I will also refer to myself as Mama, when I feel like it! It's not because I have a multiple personality disorder but I thought it would make for a more fun light-hearted read!

Okay heading to the track (I love a punt too!), I've had an epiphany at the optimum level, a reality check like no other, some have a mid-life crisis. Throughout life, I've often performed my little reality checks, for example after a major change or when I have attended a funeral. They all served a purpose for that period in time.

This one however was very different and never in my life, have I been more compelled, determined, passionate, excited, inspired, focused and motivated to share my story, in order to help others – sharing is caring!

Even when faced with difficult situations outside of my control, I have remained positive and I never lost sight of who I essentially was. However, I did and I am continually changing as time evolves, because this prevalent insight and outlook is developing for me. The change is more about how we think and react. The core essence of me has not changed and you are probably thinking how? This will be explained in great detail as you learn more about me.

Like any departure, it is slow to gain some momentum!

All aboard ……… welcome to my train of thought……… no ticket required, wishing you a happy enjoyable read!

1. Hang On – help is on its way!

Since my mid-twenties, I've always talked about writing a book and was often encouraged by many because of my antics. The first book I intended to write was to be titled "Trials and Tribulations of Love". In my mid-thirties to late, it was "Families chucked through the Blender" (relating to experiences of a blended family), "Violate me for the sake of health and baby!" and "Bringing Trash to the Trailer Park" (my experiences at the caravan). I don't think I will get around to writing these books because I perceive this one to be the "Mama" of all books (with the potential to write a couple more).

Given that my epiphany of all time was triggered by Rose, I'll start there. Rose has always been a great close friend; very loving, caring, supportive, independent, funny and private.

She was with my husband when he chose my engagement ring. In fact, Rose was part of the plan when he proposed. Mick proposed at the Colindina Caravan Park, in the parking lot. It was near the beach but I couldn't see it behind a big sand dune! He wanted it to be a surprise and it was! It didn't matter where it was, he was declaring his love and it was private, simple and sweet. He proposed on New Year's Eve 2005, before our night of partying and drinks. Gee that was a laugh, because I was so eager to wear that ring, two sizes too small, that nearly every patron at the pub ended up having a crack at releasing it! Anyway we tried ice, butter, twisting & turning, soap and cold water in between many drinks and repeating it again and again! One blue bruised finger and some cheap entertainment, more than an hour later I was free!

Of course Rose was in my wedding party and was pivotal in making sure it went without a hitch – organisation was another one of her specialities! We took road trips together. We had great times down at San Remo and Ocean Grove, especially when we had access to the green "Thelma and Louise" convertible. We shared heaps of drunken nights and always managed to get home safely.

Just an example of some of our shenanigans, one time she pissed herself laughing when we pulled up to the San Remo bottle shop! I blurted "I just burped a fucking Ronald!" after a Macca's feed of course. Now that I think of it, it was the same weekend; we were having a drink and punt after fishing. (Can't fish with "Annette" – too boring for me! I don't see much joy in just hanging around! Ha ha ha) We got a little excited and quickly ran out of cash but low and behold, I pulled a trifecta and we were back in business. In fact real business, we ended up in lock down and playing cards with some other patrons and the owner, Mama cleaned up and we went home with $500 in our pocket! One guy was also lucky, not that way (even though I was single), he accidently put on a $100 bet on a horse and was forced to pay! It won so we happily scored free drinks too. Just reminiscent of the times of the past, like in the movies, it was a great night!

For my thirtieth, Rose and Lu brought me 30 stubby bottles of Smirnoff double black as my cake – best cake ever! Rose was always considering others and their needs (including the need to drink!). We've known each other for 17 years and have mutually talked about life, men, work, babies, hopes and dreams, you name it.

I could go on but you get the drift, she is a very special sister! You don't have to be related by blood, just like out of the goodness of your heart, we adopted each other! We didn't need to say it but that's how it is! I'm very lucky because I have many sisters and love them all!

So on hearing her devastating news, it did impact me. No doubt about it. However, as we talked about things leading up to the day she was officially diagnosed, I knew beforehand because I had completed my own research (not at great detail at that stage but enough to know the details of the potential diagnosis). The World Wide Web provides information and I knew how to interpret details accurately – I didn't need to be a doctor nor do I claim to be one. I just wanted to know and understand the situation at hand so I could effectively support her, as any sister would.
She was diagnosed with Inflammatory Breast Cancer (IBC). Just so you are aware, IBC is a very rare invasive breast cancer which

affects 1-2% of women in Australia. There are six types of breast cancers and this type starts at a stage III – IV, four being terminal. Unlike all other breast cancers, this starts in the vessels and there is no apparent lump, although they can develop as the cancer progresses. Symptoms are similar to mastitis and unfortunately the cancer can go undetected compromising length of life.

Now those that know me, appreciate how I cruise through life regardless of most situations for the following reasons:
- If it's not life threatening or changing, there is no point stressing over it.
- If it is outside my control, why worry?
- If I can't remember what I stressed about one year ago, it won't matter soon.
- If it hasn't eventuated, it may not happen so why put myself under pressure and
- Most importantly, I always try to remain positive and view situations from different perspectives.

Stress does serve a purpose for a short time. For me, stress is short lived, it is wasted energy. Where there is a will, there is a way. Except (and there is always an exception) when facing the inevitable, catching a plane to a better place (my interpretation on how I view death)!

When I received the official text message from Rose, my heart sank. I felt compelled to give her my 100% support. I knew time was of essence and her mindset with the news, in addition to having chronic fatigue syndrome (which triggers depression in some cases because you aspire to regain what you have lost, but your body doesn't allow you to function as you did), as well as being pregnant wouldn't make for an easy journey. I wasn't stressed, I just threw myself into how I could make the ride more enjoyable, if she needed or wanted my help. I was very mindful of letting her deal with the circumstance as she pleased because after all, it was her journey. However it was a motivating force for me.

What did I do? I just did what I would normally do for any other friend or family in need. On Thursday 14/6/2012, I purchased a foot massage voucher, four boxes of tissues, two slabs of coke, chocolate, a Tattslotto ticket and a card. (I don't know why I bought four boxes of tissues, I guess they were on special! I was strapped for cash but I don't put a price on things that are important to me).

Rose had expressed no visitors, understandably so, I was doing a drive by. Car running, I parked the car on the neighbours side, crept through the garden and dumped the goods. I was sprung! I hadn't seen Rose peering out the window and she was happy to see me. I was thrilled to see her and gave her a big "Mama" hug.

It was a great opportunity for her, her husband and me to candidly talk about things. I let them express what had transpired the day before and actively listened. There were no tears and it was all matter of fact with a few laughs. I'd throw my odd comment about what I knew, for example, for IBC breast surgery isn't an option in the first instance. Rose felt comforted by this because of what others had said. She commented that I should be a doctor. (She didn't know (nor did she have to) I was up all night – not unusual for me when I'm passionate/determined or drunk!)

I found it interesting that other people were unintentionally adding to their "mental burden" by asking Rose inappropriate questions or telling her what to do. For example; you should remove your breasts! You have to have the baby now (at 29 weeks)! I was privately thinking to myself whether people realised they were actually causing more distress by asking her these questions? I knew they were asking them out of love and care but essentially it was an indirect way of exerting control over a person who was already very vulnerable. Rose already had enough to deal with and her doctors were there to assist with respect to her treatment.

Before I continue, Rose had mentioned the physical changes to her GP (of many years) four months earlier. He was dismissive of the changes and she trusted him. When the symptoms advanced, he still wasn't convinced it was anything untoward but arranged an ultra sound. To his credit, it is very rare, hopefully this creates more awareness. The sonographer advised that all appeared clear. The GP decided to refer Rose to a specialist and she did not expect to hear what he had found. She had to endure invasive tests unexpectedly on that day. The level of expectation was very low, trust was high so the impact of the news hit harder. What made matters worse, she now needed to trust another doctor with her life after those events – any person's level of confidence would be one of huge trepidation. Effectively, by doing my own research, I was more aware of what to ask and discuss. This allowed me to be more sensitive, therefore being a more effective support person.

On Friday 15/6/2012, I attended Yvette's daughter's 4th birthday. Yvette is a sister of almost 30 years, believe it or not! She'd have more stories on me than me, because she didn't drink as much as me! Yvette is very loving, caring, organised, supportive, kind, private and generous – just like Rose really! Anyway Rose was attending that night with her daughter and Aunty. She had previously requested that no one mention the recent news. We were there to celebrate a party at a kids centre! We all had a great time! During the evening, I snuck out to swig a drink (tough week, plus I was heading to a friend's 40th. Bad Mama – I wasn't really, I only had one and it takes me too many to have any effect!) We enjoyed watching the children running around, admired their painted faces and took photos! Also dealt with the odd incident or sook! Basically everyone had a great time and all were emotionally in check.

Now after I had the swig at the kids party, when I returned the conversation led to when did you have your first drink. I laughed, Yvette was there, and it was Kay's 16th birthday party. Yvette's dad dropped us off and my dad was picking us up. I think I was only allowed to go because Yvette was going – I was ruled by an iron fist from the Middle East. Anyway, I had a blast, a new dress and finally had a chance to flap my wings! (Did you think I was going to type bits??) No sweet sixteen kiss for me, I was too busy running riot laughing, talking, dancing, singing and drinking! Yvette didn't, she was worried, and she knew what my dad was capable of. I don't know who supplied the alcohol, obviously that wasn't important then or now. Quite frankly I didn't care, I copped that many beatings one more wasn't going to kill me! Anyway, I made mention that I had got away with it but I never knew if it was because I acted well, Yvette was with me or my dad was in denial.

Clearly I survived and you're probably thinking where the hell is this going, well I need to tell you a bit more before I get to that - sorry!

On Saturday 16/6/2012 (4 days after Rose's official diagnosis), I told my son Max that I would be shaving my hair off. His initial reply was "Oh no Mum". I proceeded to explain that Rose was very sick and the medication will make her feel better. However sometimes it affects other parts of the body and Rose may lose her hair. Before I continued, Max said "Oh Mum, you're doing it to show her not to be scared!" I was so proud of my caring, thoughtful and intelligent son.

I took Max to a birthday party, where I caught up with some school mum's. I had arranged with Jacky to shave my hair the next day at the football clinic.

After that party, I returned home and looked up places that sold organic items. Rose had mentioned that she was eager to consume as much healthy products to boost her immune system. I decided to drive to the other side of the city to buy organic items for juices. I spent an hour in this small shop and tried to obtain as much information on products I never buy. I nearly had a cardiac arrest at the counter, $260 later for a small box of goods that included magic chocolate bars, vegetables, fruit, super powders and oils. I thought to myself, this isn't healthy for the pocket?

I felt guilty because I couldn't sustain this for Rose, if I wanted to. If this was your best chance, it would not be sustainable on most household budgets. Again it was important to Rose at that time and I happily accommodated without her knowledge. There was no expectation for me to and I know I didn't have to but I wanted to provide the best.

When I dropped off the bars and provided some information, she was so surprised and grateful that I had thought of her. That made me happy knowing she was happy, every bit counts. (Luckily her Aunty covered the bill as I was short for a house payment.) By this stage it was 7pm so I grabbed dinner and proceeded home.

Yvette and her husband (Little Mick) were over to help make the juices and unwind. We finished the juices around midnight, if the kids weren't around we would have finished by 9pm but you get that, all part of the fun. I also wanted to prepare a sign for the big day.

It's amazing how creative you can be, when at the last minute you put your mind to it. I used two new top bed sheets. I never use the top sheets because I always get tangled in them and makes for more washing, so no loss for me. I cut out a message that said "We R here 2 support U!" At 3am after finishing the sign and during the night, a whole bottle of well-deserved bourbon, I retreated to bed!

Only 20 minutes later to be woken by the most ghastly cough, it sounded like my second child was taking his last breath! FUCK ME! It was very scary! Yvette and I were up as soon as we heard the first bout! We immediately called an ambulance and gave him some Prednisolone (treatment for opening the airways). Harley coughed most of it out, so it didn't even go down!

He wasn't taking much air in. I was extremely stressed at that point! What amuses me, the person on the emergency line advises that an ambulance is on their way (approximately 30 minutes to get to our house) and to call back if he deteriorates! Why would I do that? They have already advised you on what action to take, if no assistance is there, how is diverting your attention to making another call when your child is turning blue or has stopped breathing, going to be of any assistance? Just thought I'd point out the inconsistencies as they come to mind or maybe there is a reason and someone can explain this to me?

As soon as we got into the ambulance, Harley was treated with adrenaline because his airway was significantly restricted. Harley recovered quite well and was actually a pain in the rectum. He was full of beans. No sign of the sudden attack and a sleep leading up to it and I had about 10 hours in 3 days.

I was extremely happy that he was better but once he was good, I was cursing my husband Mick. Especially knowing that it took Yvette twice to practically nudge him out of bed and here I was tired in a damn hospital when I could have been catching up on some sleep.

Oddly, I'd even forgotten that I had been drinking and I didn't feel the effects – normally I would have been pumped with energy. I think it was because I focused on what I was doing that night or maybe it was the shock of Harley that scared the "piss" out of me!

As I was entertaining Harley at the hospital at 4-5am Sunday morning, a teenage boy and his mother arrived. For some unknown reason, my attention kept being drawn to her and her son. After a smile and a few fleeting glances (you try to respect other people's privacy even though you have none), I said "You look familiar, are you Kay?" I had not seen Kay since school, and had only mentioned her the night before. By sheer coincidence, her son and mine ended up in the same hospital at the same time? Hmmm does this sort of stuff freak you out?

Kay's son was in extreme pain, on morphine and vomiting. Kay was pregnant with her 4th child and was feeling weak and faint like. (Harley was settled by this stage.) I asked if she wanted me to assist and gently rubbed her son's back whilst keeping it together myself. (I have a very sensitive stomach. I vomit just looking at dog spew/dribble or the unfavourable smell of something toxic!)

Anyhow, we cleaned up the mess, of course there were no nurses to assist at that time, actually most times because they are so under resourced or filling out too much paperwork! Once her son recovered from the attack, he apologised. I said "You never have to apologise for being sick. Plus I think you were doing me a favour because I might have to assist a friend soon and that was good training!" He told me I'd make a good mum one day. I half chuckled, the drugs must have got him! Because I was thinking I am a mum and my son is over there!

When I returned home to pick up the kids, Max said "I'm a bit scared for you Mum" referring to my hair. I replied "I'm not scared, it's for a good reason!" Max thoughtfully said, "I know but you look beautiful, I love your hair but it will grow back. I love you mum!" My heart melted.

I managed to get to football on time for the big shave! I was excited! I had never done anything that extreme with my hair. It was going to grow back, all sweet on my account. My family (except Lexi my youngest), some friends and others had a turn at shaving my hair off! I didn't expect to get so much joy from a haircut! I loved watching the kids' faces and the expressions on the adults.

What I was finding difficult was all the positive praise! I shaved my hair in support of Rose, I had a choice and she didn't. She also hadn't really explained much to her daughter (if anything) so I thought it would be an opportunity to show her it was fine to have short hair and create that opportunity.

I loved the spirit of the community wanting to donate but at Rose's request (she is very proud and doesn't like the fuss), we politely declined donations. Rose did not attend but was heading to my house that afternoon. Oh I almost forgot, the girls planned a surprise for me too - the smallest of tails! I loved it and still wear it proudly today!

When I returned home, I typed up a little pack for my dear friend. It contained a couple of photos of the past, some photos of the big chop, juice recipes, an important reminder (for hope) and benefits of the Hari Mama Krishna cut.

VERY IMPORTANT REMINDER

I personally will not accept to have done enough until you are sitting on my deck in 40 years' time and we are talking about our grandkids and the good old days!

You are more than a sister and I know that you will be forever grateful but I also know you would and have done, just as much for me!!!! So here is my way of saying thank you and you're one of my best and dearest friends! I love ya Rose! xx

Benefits of the Hari Mama Krishna Cut

- Every day is a good hair day – we save time as we don't have to do it!
- Don't have to clean hair up off the bathroom floor, drains etc.
- We won't find a stray in our tooth brush or in our food!
- No need to wash hair, save money on products!
- We don't have to dye our hair!
- Our kids can't pull our hair!
- Can have a different style or colour for different days or occasions. Blonde one day, brunette the next. If we get kicked out of a pub, we can get back in. Also on special occasions, we can support the day e.g. Australia Day – wear gold/green wig, Anzac day – in honour of our aging war heroes, we can wear a toupee.
- No one will mess with us! Fook who would be game!
- We won't get any knots or tangles and no-one can put chewy in our hair!
- We can march at the Mardi Gras!

Best of all!
It's an experience – it will grow back and we can have fun freaking people out in the meantime!

Rose shed happy tears on her arrival. I came around the corner of my kitchen singing Hari Hari Krishna. For fear of shock, her family did warn her, but she couldn't believe that I did it. It was nothing for me and the moment of happiness that it brought both of us, I will cherish. She loved the pack too.

Rose had caught up with all her family prior to visiting us and I asked her how her day went. She had a good time but made a subtle comment about her dad not being able to look at her or really talk. I was concerned, as I knew Rose was carrying a great deal of emotional baggage along with the pressures of managing a family, finance, children, and health. She didn't need to be feeling the burden of others. In the same token, how could she know what she wanted or needed with the enormity of matters on her mind? I know if I was presented with the same issues, it would be very hard to clear the fog and identify what is essentially important and what becomes secondary or what is irrelevant. For me, with an uncomplicated mind, would be to determine what I wanted on my journey.

Prior to Rose leaving on the Sunday, I also asked if she wanted a hand on the Monday, her reply was "if you want to". Now I took this as a yes, because I had read previous cancer patient stories of how they don't like asking for help. I also assumed she didn't know what she wanted and I could do something.

That night I considered what approach to take, do I say something to her Mum and Dad or let it go? I assessed the risk and consequences. I determined that her parents would understand where I was coming from, as it was an attempt to help their daughter. I wasn't making it my business. I had promised her the best support. I saw an opportunity to free some of the inhibitions and fears.

So I gave Rose's parents a call around 7am Monday morning (6 days since diagnosis) and highlighted to Rose's mum that Rose's dad needed to deal with the situation and face his fear (not in those direct terms but I'm keeping this short because it is of a private nature). She understood and later thanked me. Rose was totally unaware what I was doing, she didn't need to know.

Unbeknownst to me, Rose had also spoken about this with her husband and Aunty on the Sunday night. Rose had called her parents a couple of hours after me. Consequently, Rose's parents were able to effectively support their daughter and son-in-law at the doctors. Both her mum and dad felt better. Why? They felt better because they faced part of their fears, had more knowledge and instead of thinking of what may eventuate; they were able to focus on the here and now – day to day, more or less! Rose and her husband felt more relieved. ("Heads up" for the next chapter!!) For every action, there is an equal and opposite reaction – fear (negative emotion) and relief (positive emotion) creating a balancing effect for all (simple and logical).

One of my soul brothers (who is Rose's brother) and his wife, popped in that Sunday after Rose had left. I provided them with some more information because they were unaware of the seriousness. I really hated being the bearer of bad news and I was torn. My intent was to create awareness to ensure the family was sensitive to Rose's situation (I was mindful of not making matters worse by saying too much). How could they support Rose effectively, if they didn't truly appreciate what the problem was?

Like most families, there are always moments due to past behaviours or miscommunication. As there was a ripple or rip in the wave, I tried to smooth that out so it inadvertently freed Rose. She would get the family support she needed, without further distractions. Sometimes you just got to do, what you have to do! There is no right or wrong, it's about how it is explained, executed and how the person chooses to react. It always comes full circle and I think I managed this quite well.

My mantra to keep me focused was:
Give me strength, to have a good day, to get the job done and to be the best that I can be today!
Living in the moment!

Monday morning after organising Max and Isaiah for school, I dropped Lexi and Harley off to Carmie's house. Carmie is a very spiritual loving, caring, generous, happy and supportive friend. We catch up at least once a year for our annual mother's group Christmas party and the occasional visit during the year.

I know my babies are quite adaptable and knew Carmie would be fine. I did not feel guilty for leaving my children in her care even though she was practically a stranger to them. If the situation became too difficult, I was only 10 minutes away.

I know Carmie would have been apprehensive for the same reason. Carmie couldn't believe how good Harley and Lexi behaved and played. (You do not need to substantiate how good a friend is based on how much time you spend with them. For me, it's quality, not quantity because we are all on our own journey – well that's the way I look at it!)

Before I left Carmie's, I had an emotional conversation with her. In fact, she is probably the first person to experience that raw emotion for me, (talk, see and hear). Not even my husband, family or friends of many years have seen this side of me. Others have always considered me emotionally sterile. I generally dealt with matters at the point in time which has allowed me to move on and enjoy my life. Therefore I was just in check with being happy, looking at the positive and have an attitude that "some else is worse off"!

We both opened up about life. I was telling her how I felt guilty and overwhelmed by the positive comments and praise for shaving my hair. I didn't know how to deal with all the positive comments. This was because it was at Rose's misfortune at a heart wrenching time of her life. Carmie and I discussed how life just doesn't seem fair at times but we also recognised that we should make the most of it and enjoy.

I arrived at Rose's around 10.30am, and she had already left for her appointment. Her aunty and sister-in-law were home. We were discussing Rose's situation and how to support her. We were all talking in code, because Rose's 4 year old was unaware of what was happening. I respected that, it's not my family but I thought to myself the sudden change in events with doctor's appointments, physical changes, sickness, stress, people coming in and out with food, unexplained wasn't going to help her daughter or Rose. In fact it was going to make it much harder.

When a child is in their comfort zone, they feel safe i.e. at home. When things dramatically change around them, they become more apprehensive. In turn, this affects their behaviour. They become more demanding because they feel threatened. If you don't explain the situation, how are they going to understand and deal with their own emotions, feelings, fears and anything else on their very intuitive minds? You are not in their mind so you can't fix these for your child. Essentially by not accepting changes, we are neglecting their needs as parents. (Irrespective of this situation, we change by the day physically and mentally without even realising as we learn and grow). Effectively parents need to provide guidance based on the core traits of each child as they progress

Back on track, Rose's sister-in-law made mention of not doing too much and I appreciated where she was coming from. When she started the conversation with "you are probably not going to like what I'm going to say", I thought, damn right! Who would? You've already told me what you're thinking! I know what she can be like and hence I knew there was a hidden agenda.

Rose's sister-in-law on the surface is friendly, supportive, giving, caring and appears happy. However some of her personality traits are questionable. I assume because happiness is based on material possessions. I'm not her, so I can't claim to know for sure but past actions and behaviours suggest this. She caused more division in the family whether intentional or not.

The ripple that I was attempting to smooth was the friction between mother, daughter, brother and sister-in-law! (At its simplest form!) We all ignore it, most live with it but we struggle to deal with the complexity of all types of dynamic relationships. Why? Essentially most still haven't found what they have been looking for! What makes us tick? We buy into the charade of expressing what is good or bad/right or wrong for others when we don't even know what we want or need for ourselves.

If we were happy, we wouldn't be worried about entertaining what other people are doing in their life. We would be celebrating their good times and supporting them in times of need unconditionally (without passing judgement). Undoubtedly, it appears that we do but not at the depth to be satisfied in life. Of course, there are many that live a happy and satisfied life and it has nothing to do with how much money you have or have spent, speaking from my own experience.

Rose's sister-in-law felt threatened by me. I could tell by her tone, how she was instructing me to do things and observing her behaviour. For example: telling me what needed to be done with the photos a friend of mine took, of my experience, shaving my hair. They weren't even my photos. She didn't have the right! I didn't say anything, I bit my tongue!

We all had to consider Rose and did not want to add to her stress. She didn't want my photos posted on Facebook. I understood but it was actually my experience, my hair and there was no mention of her. Does having a serious illness give you the right to dictate what others can do? I knew her mind set and wasn't going to be selfish and make an issue of it. Again there is no right or wrong but how you react.

My friends had mentioned the shave on Facebook so others were interested. In the end, I blocked those directly connected to Rose and allowed my photographer friend to post some photos. I never said anything and just let it go, it wasn't important in the scheme of things. I satisfied my friends' curiosity that hadn't seen me or were interstate or overseas and didn't make it an issue.

I assumed Rose's sister in-law wanted to redeem herself for her past actions, wanted recognition for her assistance or sincerely wanted to help. No one was to blame for family disconnections but more so each individual needed to acknowledge their poor behaviour and the consequences of those actions or make a change for the better. (Not that I said anything to anyone, but these were my observations).

When Rose was suffering with chronic fatigue syndrome, it was her sister-in-law that caused her a great deal of emotional pain. When there is hurt, there is always an underlying anger or why else would you be hurting? (Vice versa) On the flip side, if someone has hurt you, there is a sense of betrayal (feel & think). I always offered Rose advice on how to manage the situation to help. So I knew her sister-in-law's support may not be as effective as Rose required, particularly with the friction between Rose's mum.

She also wanted control for whatever reasons. I didn't have a problem with that but I knew I had to be careful. I had to appease in order not to displease. I ended up heading out to the shops, as it would have appeared non-beneficial and counterproductive for me to stay. In addition, I don't like being told what to do. Neither do my children for that matter! Who does? I normally use the following for my children, "Wouldn't it be a good idea? Have you thought about this? What other options are there? Let's compromise?" Promotes active thinking!

So my day at Rose's (whilst she was out) wasn't wasted because I spent a good couple of hours talking to Janine at the Tattslotto booth. Rose's aunty had mentioned in conversation that she had been suffering from breast cancer too.

Janine is a beautiful lady and was happy to talk to me, in between customers. She openly gave me some valuable advice on how to support Rose. Janine mentioned that cancer is like a chain, as soon as one person gets it, another person has it. She said most people like to share stories. She found that this was great because they were still standing and living a healthy life. Janine also said that people sometimes treated you differently like you became the cancer which I thought was interesting.

Her views on the matter were very positive. It appeared that cancer wasn't consuming her and she was still living her life. Great attitude to have managing such a nasty disease!

She shared some personal details of her life. I had instantly made another friend in that hour or so. You could tell Janine honestly felt for Rose. I still head down there to catch up with her and see how she is going. I hope to get to know Janine better in the future.

I headed to the ladies and ended up bumping into Rose, her doctor's appointment went well from her perspective. They were increasing her chemotherapy. She was told her toes and finger nails could be compromised and that she may feel a little lethargic. I said "that's good it went well". I know why Rose was thinking it was good because more chemo meant more chance, I would too. I didn't say but I did think to myself, why set a low expectation again (referring to possible side effects of treatment)? Do these doctors consult each other or understand what they are doing? Or don't they have time? What slips through the gaps as a result?

I returned to Rose's home and had a brief chat with her mum and aunty. I started working on a plan. The purpose of the plan was to assist with managing the change. Rose said she didn't want anything to change and to keep everything as normal as possible.

Not that I said anything but this was unrealistic, all changes need to be managed. Cancer was a part of her now everyday life. With everything on her mind, she would find it difficult to think or obtain any control. I thought by preparing a guide, it may help in some way. I had done this before for her a year prior and it seemed to have helped. Something was better than nothing and I thought I could end up using it myself. I know Mick could have used it when I was in hospital. It was a generic plan.

Another reason was to identify what was important for her. The plethora of booklets, leaflets and guides (not pertaining to the medical side of the disease) was overwhelming for me to look at, let alone read. (I didn't read them). One of the pamphlets was "sex and cancer". I'm thinking my poor friend is pregnant and has just been bowled over and is given that with all the other stuff, in a folder as big as a phone book. That would be the last thing on my mind. What is wrong with today's world?

Rose's state of mind was already at full capacity (as previously mentioned) and she now had a great deal more to process. Why not keep it simple? Offer a plan, one that could be tailored and have additional information on request. People know what they need to ask for, they can think for themselves even if they have a lot on their mind. That's how they are able to deal with the situation. From my perspective, this was a case of too much and little benefit. Work on the practical to disregard that, so you are able to focus on more important matters.

By this stage the family left for dinner, they went to Rose's mother-in-law's house. I hadn't quite finished at 5pm, so I arranged for Mick to collect the kids and we did a car swap. Only Mick parked in the drive way and I told him to move it because I knew Rose wouldn't appreciate it there. The car wouldn't start. Mick was bleeding, tired and hungry after a good day's work. I told him to settle down as the stress wasn't going to fix the situation. He was fuming. Gee it was funny trying to roll the station wagon up the curb, especially when I was laughing. As I was working on adrenaline and my mind was more open, little things didn't matter so much.

When Rose returned at 7.30pm, she was clearly unhappy. I didn't expect to be there nor did she give me a time to leave. Irrespective of this, I couldn't get home. I asked whether it would be possible to get a lift home and sort the car out the following day. She snapped at me. I didn't say anything and let it go. I couldn't even call a taxi as I had no money. Her aunty had roadside assistance, so we used that. (Her aunty would have driven me, but I live in the sticks and it would have been hard to find her way out in the dark). Her aunty had said that Rose's mother-in-law had a turn, it was similar to a stroke. No wonder she was stressed, how much can a friend endure?

A week had not even passed, this all occurred in 6 days. I had approximately 16 hours sleep in 6 days. Most people fall in a heap or go to sleep. I've been able to do this throughout my whole life. School assignments and university provided great practice. I always procrastinated and performed better under pressure. I can keep going because my body allows me to, hence the rush of adrenaline.

It's like when you're tired and you feel drunk, only at a higher level – maybe a second wind for you and blast for me!

Now I never once compromised my own family in any way, we just did things a little differently. Instead of washing clothes every day I did a couple of loads when I could. We had more than enough clothes. We never missed a meal or activity like reading books.

As a direct result of diverting my attention to helping a friend, I had no time to nag and the older boys (Isaiah & Max) pitched in. Marvellous!! By default, instead of relying on me, they empowered themselves to think and do things. I noticed that Harley was more bearable, normally my very demanding and stubborn 3 year old had almost changed overnight.

Why? The little things that normally do your head in were less important. It wasn't because I was compromising their time, health, attention, play etc. the normal household boundaries were more relaxed, for example: I didn't fuss over the kids running in and out making a mess. Harley would get the broom and sweep, instead of disempowering him, I thought what a good little boy. He knows I'm busy and even he is helping. I'll clean the bigger mess up later, it wasn't a problem!

These little things in life only become a problem, if you allow them to. There was little expectation, so of course the adverse effect; there was little frustration or anger. I found I was more productive and we had a happier home!

The first major opportunities I identified on my journey were:

- Knowledge lead to a better understanding
- Miscommunication leads to misinterpretation
- Acknowledgement and acceptance assists in dealing with complex life problems
- Expectations affect our emotions and in turn influence behaviours and reactions
- For every action, there is an equal and opposite reaction resulting in a cause and an effect (physical) / reason and purpose (mental)
- Change is inevitable and there are benefits to managing this more effectively in our lives

Chugga chugga chugga, we have a great deal of ground to cover! Hang on, help is on its way as this train is heading to new territory! Well for me anyway!

2. Knowing me, knowing you!

Monday night the plan was finished but I didn't think Rose was ready nor wanted any assistance of this type. However I couldn't sleep, as I was working on some other strategies. After a quick Google search to determine whether there were philosophies at the depth I was exploring, it appeared that there weren't any. I was excited by the notion that I was developing something new and raw. Wholly Mama, I accidently found something that made me tick! (Separate from my husband and children).

Life Plan

Purpose: to regain some control when circumstances are unknown

Objective: to determine what is important to you

Support: determine those you would like to support you and your immediate family. Maybe nominate a key contact for friends, if you are unavailable so they can keep others updated or know when to drop off food.

Communication: obviously family and friends want to help and care for a loved one. They want to be informed and know what can be done to assist. You also need to be mindful of what is communicated as it could have an impact later. Sometimes this can impede on you or others. We all have great intentions however we are not mind readers either. It may be beneficial to set boundaries so you don't become more stressed during a difficult time. For example: no visitors after 5pm, explain that you will communicate when you are able to etc.

Tasks: When dealing with a crisis, ascertain what components of your day-to-day tasks can be managed by others, if required. This should provide peace of mind when things occur outside of your control. This allows you to focus on more important aspects in life whilst trying to keep balanced.

For example:

What	When	Who	How	Action
Bills need to be paid or if running a business: print and mail invoices	Monthly	Nominate who will manage on your behalf	Determine method: Bpay, cash, cheque	Show them what they need to do and how to perform the task
Ensure children attend their activities	Weekly	Determine who as required	Prepare a schedule of commitments	Confirm a back-up person in the event someone is unavailable

Life Matters: Write down what is important in your life in order.

For example:

- Spending time with the family, picnics, beach, holidays
- Attending appointments
- Preparing in the event you become too sick and want to leave loved ones special memories, gifts, notes or films. (I have and know friends that have done this who are not ill. It provides a sense of comfort and it also serves as a journal of events captured at that time, e.g. milestones, memories of holidays etc.)
- Build trust funds in your children's name and sort out finances
- Work – number of hours required to live the life you choose

Consequently some friends don't know how to react in difficult situations. I know it was difficult to find information on how best to support my friend in need, so I prepared some other guides.

Communication Tips

- ❖ Be yourself, the person is still the same, has the same personality, attitude, beliefs and values.
- ❖ Still ring, talk and text as often as you like.
- ❖ If you don't call or act normal, any person in any circumstance would think you don't care or are insensitive. Are you a true friend?
- ❖ Don't be offended if you don't receive a reply to a message or call.
- ❖ If you are unsure of what to discuss, it may help to check with a supportive friend/family member.

Other helpful notes: Instead of asking how are you going, ask how the day has been? Most people live life day-to-day in difficult situations and feel very vulnerable especially when they are sick. For example: If their reply is good to "how are you?" some may inadvertently reply "oh so you're better" when the case may be the opposite. It may make them feel worse and then they may feel obliged to explain which may create an awkward or uncomfortable moment for both.

The friend in need may say it's been a bad time. It is important not to be scared or afraid of this type of response because it indicates you are a true trusting friend who can assist. (Recommend it is dealt with sensitivity, no one knows what to say at these times.) Active listening is the key and supporting their views can help, basically offering assurance. Humour often helps or it could be a matter of asking if they want to talk about it and providing the opportunity.

Essentially people need to deal with their emotions. We are all different, have different wants and needs. If people are open and honest when communicating, it will create a positive environment.

If we are emotionally challenged, it affects all those around us. (Happy wife equals happy life!) However if we don't communicate effectively, how is anyone to know? We are not mind readers, we need to talk and if we are hurt, offended, angry, frustrated, stressed etc. it needs to be dealt with as it inhibits us from moving forward and living a happy life.

Some techniques:
Think and ask yourself:

- What am I feeling? Did I contribute to the issue?
- Why do I feel this way? Consider the other side (empathy).
- Does it need to be rectified or is it that important? If it's not important, it may be a case of walking away and taking deep breaths, playing some music, spending time alone or with others for a short period.
- What do I need to do to rectify the important matter? Talk, resolve issue, make a commitment etc.
- Is what I'm feeling now going to affect my life long term?

By default, by dealing with emotions in your way and in consideration of others, it will ultimately create a happy balance for you. You can't control how others perceive or react to you – that's their choice. If you have acted with good intentions and provided an explanation, if and when required, then it removes any ambiguity.

My husband and I do have our moments normally over trivial matters. What works for us is a verbal spray and literally 2 seconds later we are back to "normal" for us. It's out and off, no grudges, anything said in the heat is not taken personally because deep down we understand and respect each other. We know we are just venting. Before we had children I would flash him a brown eye or a breast depending on what we were arguing about, just to spin it around!

If we were to contain these emotions, we would have lost the love, respect and passion because mentally we would have been bitter, stressed, frustrated and angry, creating a far bigger problem. This keeps us balanced, happy to report that there are far more happy times than the challenging. But you do need to be challenged to keep you and your relationship stimulated. I still haven't found a way to get that leg around my head, just kidding!

Understanding how to use language can avoid miscommunication, conflict and can provide a positive outcome. Just to elaborate on what I touched on in the previous chapter:

"I think you" is indirectly forcing an unwelcomed opinion and in effect indicates a person is telling you what to do *in a nice way.* The person may only be trying to care and express their concern however if they have little appreciation of the full picture it could be misinterpreted causing more angst than good. No one is in another person's head to think for them. Since my new outlook, I have been retraining myself to say, 'have you considered or factored other perspectives?' Or if I know it's not that important, I refrain from commenting and express that I understand where they are coming from. Sometimes you can't explain or prove anything if people have already established their own view of you or a situation.

Anyone that starts with "You are not going to like what I'm going to say" is negatively telling you what to do indirectly. The recipient will naturally and automatically either respond (say) or think in a negative manner. It is a no-win situation. A more positive statement to actively engage and assist would be to use a phrase like 'have you thought about or considered the impact?'

Most people in difficult situations carry an extra burden because they don't want to trouble others with their misfortune. That does not help them release the emotional pain that they are suffering. Consequently it does affect their behaviour and those around them. It is very naive of us to think otherwise. How it is managed, is dependent on the individual and those who are implicated.

Other tips when an individual faces a life changing or threatening position are:

- We do not need or have to know everything – some reasons may be that they are protecting loved ones or it is a private matter that the individual wants to manage on their own.
- Friends and family are engaged for different reasons.
- They may not need or want your help, better to ask or gauge on feedback, behaviours, and actions.
- They may not have time to accommodate others.
- You may have your own personal challenges to deal with too. (Don't ignore them as you will find it harder to deal with the situation).

When I had mentioned what I had prepared to my husband and a couple of friends, I was surprised that all commented that it was a "work" like plan. I was perplexed and explained that, although it was similar, if it could help, why is that bad? I wasn't expecting or demanding anyone to use it, I was providing an option.

The only part that I planned to provide was support, communication, day-to-day tasks in the event someone else needed to manage them and identifying what was important (not even providing any examples – I've just elaborated for the purpose of this book). I hadn't even thought about giving it to her because I knew she wasn't ready. I was thinking ahead, like I normally do!

Logically, physically and medically you can't cure an incurable disease but you can manage the "mental" journey more effectively in an attempt to enjoy your life. If you don't give yourself that opportunity then has the disease already taken control of your life? Facing your fear is part of that journey and it is difficult to accept.

Ultimately, people will only do what they want and with every right because it is their journey. Unless someone is willing to help themselves, no one can help them. However there is no harm in providing an opportunity. Sharing is caring and also helps us get through life!

I considered that my time and the plan would eventually be beneficial. In actual fact, it has provided me and my husband the opportunity to develop the guide for our personal journey. Hope it does for you! I can't say whether this would have helped Rose. I assume she would have sought advice if she needed it, like she has in the past.

Tuesday 19/6/2012, I had to be at Rose's at 9am as she had an appointment and wanted me to help her choose a wig. She also asked if I could bring my blue wig. I use to wear a blue wig out occasionally, just for fun! I remember one night at one of the old stomping grounds the "Hallam" pub, a guy asked me if my hair was real! I asked him if he wanted to check my pubes! I was only joking of course – he didn't get to see them! I always had fun being different! I guess Rose wanted to lighten the mood and we would have had the opportunity to re-live some fun memories to distract us from the main purpose.

So that morning, I searched everywhere for that wig. I could not access the cupboard door where I thought it was tucked behind. But I managed to lift the lid of the container from the opposite side. I gave it all my strength to pull out absolutely everything in that damn box but to no avail. This was 7.00am and I thought I'll just take a bag of hats instead, since I couldn't find the wig. All the hats in the costume box signified a day and it was the next best thing.

I prepared a bag and changed the younger two. I gave them breakfast, made lunches and had a shower. Ready to go, I put the kids in the car and I assumed the keys were in the ignition (it's not unusual for me to do this as I live in the country). Shut the door locked at 7.55am, only to realise the keys were inside the house.

This is with only 16 hours sleep across 7 days now! The normal me would have peaked but since my improved outlook, I seemed very controlled and relaxed. I was very alert and focused. I knew I had to be at Rose's at 9am (20 minute drive), take the boys to school and I still had to drop the younger two off at a friend's house. If I panicked all would have been stressed, angry and upset. It would have made for a bad start for the day and I would have been late. (Some may have laid blame because it is easier to feel better about the situation but it doesn't change anything! I've been guilty of this many times before!)

With that, I lit up a smoke and whilst I contemplated the next move, Isaiah checked the windows and doors around the house. I knew they would all be locked. So I grabbed the ladder and propped it up against the small toilet window. I knew I'd have no chance getting through it. It would have been like sending a parcel through the slit of an envelope opening!

At this stage, Isaiah was hyper-ventilating. He doesn't like heights and didn't like the idea of missing the bus. I gave Isaiah instructions on how to climb and which legs to enter in with. He kept saying he couldn't do it. I reassured him and said he wasn't going to hurt or kill himself. The worst he could do was land in the bowl or break the seat! It wasn't life threatening or changing! I softened the impact of him sitting on the frame, so my hand was nearly cut in half in the process. He managed to safely get in! We were on our way within 15 minutes of locking the keys inside.

I dropped Harley and Lexi off. On the way to school, Max read to me, as we didn't get the opportunity the night before. I also decided to voice record what had transpired (I left the iPhone on the dash whilst we were driving). The reason I decided to record it was so we could reflect and have a laugh of the memory at a later date!

I noticed that Isaiah was counting and asked him what he was doing, he was compiling a tally of all the things I did that morning. It was around 40 things in two hours (obviously I haven't bored you with all things) but I don't realise how much I can do when I don't think about things. Just another example of how I manage myself when there are time constraints. If I did think about them, I probably wouldn't get much done.

Isaiah has never really opened up but you can tell when things really bother him. He would never tell you and not even his dad could understand Isaiah, in order to help him. On that day Isaiah was very proud of himself and enjoyed the recording. The incident was an example of applying what I discovered during that night. I couldn't believe how instant the change and effect was on all of us.

On the way to Rose's I continued recording myself. I thought, I wondered if anyone had done this before. I knew I was working in a very relaxed state of mind because I had no sleep. I refer to it as the semi-conscious but fully functional and physically tired all the same. I kept recording as it allowed me to capture and process information. I called these recordings "brain dumps" so I could sleep and collate details later for my research and book.

In that particular brain dump, I spoke about recent events. How my mind and body were in control even though I had little sleep over the last week. Also how this allowed me to view life from a totally different perspective (because of my very "open" mind). How I have always performed better under pressure and I reflected my dynamic traits.

I reflected on how I had attended an uncle's funeral and felt privileged to have known such a great man. He was a significant positive father figure in my formative years. I marvelled at how colourful and enriching his life had been. He married his true love, had a passion for painting and served in the Army. He was a wall and floor tiler by trade. He loved gardening and cooking. Most of all he had a love of life!

Uncle George was an Italian gem, loved to party and be himself. He played the piano accordion too and loved his music. If anyone said it was too loud, he would turn it up! If anyone didn't like the extra olive oil in the pasta – he told you not to eat it! He also smoked, drank and loved a bet on the horses. You never left before midnight! His catch phrases were "Oh Shit", "What for?" or "Porko Dio" (I can still hear him say it in his tone/accent and it makes me smile! Well that's how my memory works, not sure if it's the same for anyone else because I am different!)

He always made us laugh and we always had a great time. I truly cherish the memories! All things I love to indulge in today are the influences I inadvertently obtained as a child/adolescent without truly realising or appreciating until I had my epiphany!

What annoyed me at the service (held at the Springvale cemetery) was that we had barely left the room before others started to filter in. I thought how insensitive! Are there that many dying that we don't have facilities for or are we trying to process more for the sake of profit? In fact, we were politely ushered on when flowers for my Uncle's service had not been delivered outside. How disrespectful!

I wasn't upset that I had not seen him in the last 7 years of his life as he forged a permanent spot in my heart. I also appreciated that being a proud man, he didn't want anyone to see him in such a frail state. He had previously suffered from fluid on the brain years prior but made a full recovery. The last couple of years however, his health deteriorated significantly and at the age of 83 his mental and physical capacity had been compromised. He lived a fulfilling rich life and death is inevitable so I wasn't sad! I found comfort knowing he was no longer in pain and believe when I catch that plane whenever that may be, we'll party together again!

A few weeks later, I attended a friend's art exhibition. She had spent an enormous amount of time setting up and co-ordinating this community project. I was calling her the curator and knew the event was important to her. My son Max and I admired the local artists and viewed some marvellous pieces of work. I mentioned the funeral to Veronica and discussed with her what I would be recognised or remembered for in life. I recall saying "I'm happy! I've done the corporate career thing for 20 years. I have a beautiful family and enjoy spending time with them. I also love to party and have travelled. That will do I guess!" Veronica's comment was "and you're funny too!"

I was entirely happy with that but I didn't realise how quickly a change could stir you into a whole new dimension unexpectedly. Just like they say, you find love when you are not looking for it; I inadvertently found a new purpose in life, being happier by helping others! (It was a case of be careful what you think and say, not that I realised at the time!)

Choo choo…I can ramble sometimes, but back on track! So I arrived at Rose's with 20 minutes to spare, frikkin' amazing! I had a cigarette as I could see Rose was on the phone and just waved to let her know I was there. She retrieved something from the car and I said "Hi, all set for a great day!" trying to lighten the mood knowing she was clearly unhappy from the night before. I sensed she still wasn't her normal self but I also knew she had a lot to deal with, so it didn't bother me and I didn't ask any questions. Her sister-in-law arrived and we headed off.

On the way to our first stop, the chiropractor, Rose had mentioned how she wanted to take about 8 on a shopping tour in a limo. I was thinking to myself that this was great, she had hope! I piped up and said "I hope I can come?" Rose was short with her reply and said "You don't shop" and I replied "That doesn't matter, I'll do what we did last time, you shop while I pub crawl".

Now I know this wasn't normal. Without saying it, she didn't want me there or maybe I was reading into things? Maybe she changed her mind on wanting me there for the wigs? Maybe she needed to vent because of all issues? I didn't say anything nor did it have any bearing on me because I understood her mindset. The old me, would have been hurt to some degree and taken this personally. I just sat and listened.

When we arrived at the chiropractor, I didn't feel comfortable sitting in the car so I thought about checking in with my building surveyor across the road. But I was too tired and couldn't be bothered and as it was cold, I ended up retreating back into the car.

Rose's phone rang and her sister-in-law answered. I thought she is game. You shouldn't be answering another person's phone when they haven't given you permission, more so it's not courteous. Plus we all knew Rose had message bank.

Her sister-in-law mentioned that we were on the way to shop for wigs. I knew Rose wouldn't be happy. She was still dealing with everything and tried to contain the mayhem as best she could. When Rose returned to the car, the phone call was mentioned. She wasn't impressed. Her sister-in-law gave her a brief update. Rose queried how the person knew about her plight? And asked whether anything was mentioned about where we were going. Her sister-in-law said "no, just out shopping!" that was it. Well I thought why lie? I then said "I'm sorry, you did mention the wigs!"

Obviously this didn't go down well and I could have let it go. However one of my pet hates is lying. I don't do it and I can't stand when people lie to me. It is dishonest and disrespectful. Little mistruths to avoid situations with children I view differently as you are trying to protect them or your sanity.

Rose was quiet for a bit and then changed the subject. I just kept quiet in the back until I was engaged. Out of nowhere, Rose got angry with me because I was at her house at 7.30pm the night before. I knew I was about to become a punching bag and was ready to take the punches as best I could.

She mentioned that her daughter was asking questions. I didn't realise she hadn't told her, an issue that I couldn't resolve or control. I didn't want to state the obvious and say well my car had broken down. So I said "I thought something was up so I sent you a text." Well with that, it snowballed.

I said she could have yelled at me or talked about it but she didn't want to because her daughter was still awake. She then complained that she received a million texts and didn't want to read my fucking text! She forgot that she sent a group text message advising everyone about chemo on the Monday so naturally everyone was contacting her even though the date had changed.

I also sent text messages at any time of the day because she told me that her phone was turned off at night and my intention was if she was up at night she could call me at any time if she needed to chat. I didn't ask her to read the text but said if you want an explanation it is there. I knew whatever I was going to say was making it worse. However I couldn't avoid it when answers were being demanded.

In the end, I apologised for inadvertently hurting Rose even though I know I didn't create the issue. I said this was only the tip of the iceberg and I hurt her family the day before. I guess because I was tired and didn't exactly know what I could say; I was trying to provide an insight as to what I was doing without telling her directly. Just trying to be a good supportive sister! Rose was crying uncontrollably, yet I was riding a wave with empathy.

Next minute I was accused for playing the victim by her sister-in-law. She started with "I don't know where this is coming from, you're a great person and I don't want to blow your trumpet, you have done a lot of good things!" I replied "Thanks" (acknowledging that I was listening) and her abusive response was "Fucking don't talk back". I just told her to let it out! I tried to defuse that situation, to no avail. I was basically told to "shut the fuck up". It was quite an ear bashing to say the least but I took it in my stride. The whole explosion lasted all of 5 minutes. No one was in the right or wrong. I did capture this on audio for my own benefit because I knew I was in a different state of mind and I may have interpreted things differently. There was obviously a reason and purpose for the outbreak.

It was a very quiet long ride home, as we were almost near the city. What was meant to be a fun filled day of trying on wigs ended in misery! It didn't have any emotional impact on me because I knew what was going on and in these circumstances I can naturally disconnect emotionally in order to keep focused on the main problem.

I knew Rose was still digesting what had transpired and what she had to face. I was concerned that I had inadvertently ruined her day and that she was most upset. But at the same time, maybe that emotional release helped her talk about something with someone else. I knew in time it would not affect our friendship unless I allowed that to happen.

Now obviously a few friends were concerned that I was doing too much (with good reason, they all loved and cared about me too). They didn't know the entire story or could appreciate the full picture. I wasn't doing all of this for Rose, I was doing something for me.

They noticed that my messages on Facebook had changed. The context and type of messages I was posting were not normal for me. I chatted to some about what was happening but I didn't speak of my book at that time.

My research needed to be in its truest and rawest form to hold any credibility – basic logic. I could not tell anyone until the time was right, not even my husband knew at that stage. How could they understand if I couldn't tell them? I had already articulated that family/friends would notice and I needed to manage that accordingly. But I had to engage others to determine if my theories were accurate. What was the point of developing a philosophy/strategy if I couldn't prove them? Especially in the area of psychology! I had no interest nor had or have I studied this topic in any way, shape or form. I believe this was a huge benefit for me because my mind was untrained and able to explore freely.

So I tested the waters, 19/6/2012 Facebook Post

Ok warning…so you know where I'm coming from, I'm in a semi-conscious state but I am functioning normally for me, may not be the same for you and it shouldn't be, unless you miraculously jumped into my head, for tech heads I'm in the safe mode/zone!

I'm in this state of mind for a reason

    a) I consider this to be the optimal place to be, to resolve complex challenges.
    b) I'm not in this state by choice, circumstances have led me here and my brain must process to get the job done, in the most effective way
    c) You don't have to understand, agree or care, only I can tell me how to think, feel, sense, see coz this is me and obviously you are you!

There will be times that we laugh together, cry together, disagree etc. this is normal and required to identify what we need and once we have dealt with what is holding us back, we can move forward.

Only then are we able to realise the next stage. Sometimes you may feel like you are losing control and you don't have the skills to manage or cope.

Fortunately I have been able to realise this for me, in order to highlight and manage core problems. And I know I can manage it in an effective way for me because over the last 39 years I have experienced, learned and processed what I needed then, to use when suddenly my human spirit (you can call it whatever you like) exploded in my mind.

Positive or negative, that is entirely up to you! E.g. "I know you are feeling"...HELLO when did you become me? Is what I would be thinking – negative action makes it harder to achieve goal. Positive response, take the time to ask and listen. Well this is my opinion, I don't care if it is right or wrong, nor will I need to entertain it coz my semi-conscious state knows it's not important, it is not life changing or threatening.

I have no inhibitions or fears as a result. So I am acknowledging that at the moment a lot of people are asking how I am, offering support and who are curious about me – I needed to let you into my head to do that so I could assure others that I am ok. It is part of the learning process, it's not always how we want it to be but there is a reason!

Only people that have taken the time to know themselves and read the signs when things are happening can be confident of that. I'm lucky I can move forward positively. And I hope I can do this in my natural conscious state.

As there is a lot going on from my FB posts. This has and always will continue to be my forum to express, share, manage whatever I wish to coz that is my page for me and that is my choice. ………..I have no doubt that this will eventually have a positive ripple effect!

I challenge you to prove me right or wrong and it depends if you want to take the negative path which will be harder, but you will get there, or fast track where or what it should be efficiently in a positive manner! For now, I'm taking a break and will go back to conscious state.

The reason I posted the message was to provide friends peace of mind that I was fine and to offer a subtle insight as to what I was doing without actually saying it. I was obviously also processing what had transpired that day whilst acknowledging that I was in a different state of mind that wasn't foreign to me.

There was also a purpose which was to highlight the challenges in regard to the car incident and posting photos of my experience/shave. It also allowed me to evaluate any responses for my research.

I knew I was traveling further into my mind and I had control, I was just rolling with it. Retyping this now for my book, I can see how friends would have been more concerned, I didn't entertain that at the time because I was not considering their view – reference to inhibitions alludes to that! I also knew I was putting myself out there; people would question my mental state, it's only natural when your behaviour or actions change. I had to ignore friends' feedback so I wasn't distracted or it would impact the research path that I was endeavouring.

There were many events that occurred that linked back to the plan created on Monday. Some I have mentioned, you can work the rest out, if you want too but I need to move on!

Just a slight detour first …………..I was delighted that a great friend Noelene who I have not seen in roughly 28 years commented that

"Ellen" would love my work and was happy to join me if the opportunity arose!

Noelene and I had great times together. We met at school but she had moved to another school in grade 5. We both received "can rings" as a token of love in grade 3 from David and John – those were our skinny days! We frequently visited each other's homes but over time that became less and less.

Noelene taught me about the birds and the bees! Funny because it was another 7 years before I became a lady at 17.5 years and knew how to manage a cycle by then! We watched movies like Screwballs, Porky's, and romantic comedies. We would always be dancing and singing around the house! We cooked and mucked around, I never wanted to leave the company of her and her sister! From Noelene's Facebook postings, I can tell we are 2 peas from the same pod! I can't believe how alike we are, not sure if she knows it, but hope to catch up with her in person soon!

It was no fault of our own that we became disconnected; my Dad was responsible for the less frequent visits that became none in the end. Only after mentioning that I had reconnected through Facebook, my Dad opened up.

Basically he didn't think much of Noelene's brother who was different, probably suffering depression. He also didn't like the idea that they were from a single family. My dad always taught us, "If you haven't got anything good to say about someone, don't say it!" I once pulled him up on this way before this situation, when he was grouching about someone and his reply was "I thought you weren't listening!"

It was a classic case of practice what you preach! Double standards at its finest - makes me laugh! But what did annoy me was the way he judged and I never really paid attention to that growing up! My thought was it denied me of an opportunity but I wasn't upset because I believe things happen for a reason and a purpose.

It also explained a great deal about his personality traits, good and bad! I love both my Mum and Dad very much, with all my heart and always will! Just so you know, by highlighting some negative traits or events it should not portray a person as bad. Its purpose is to support and provide examples for my theories that will come.

Ok on track again……..The FB post wasn't clear nor should it have been. I knew most would not understand what I meant, how could they if they hadn't experienced it for themselves? Some may have been confused and others were curious like my second mum (Mich's mum – more about her later – love her to bits!)

Mich's mum probed further and asked if I was ok. I replied:

Yes love, presented with an extremely difficult situation and unfortunately it is highly charged with emotions and challenges that need to evolve. Sometimes you get caught in the mix, not intentionally, but it's expected because of the nature of the beast. Just helping but sometimes when we are trying to help a person who is hit with a tsunami, realistic metaphor, there is too much to process and we have to wait for direction and you may cop a bit. I'm fine and realize it's part of the process for me. I will continue to be a friend and when I'm asked to be a supportive friend I will be there. Although today turned negative, it will pull us in the positive path when the time is right. Not personally impacted cos I understand it's not normal circumstances. Thanks for caring!

Mich's mum highlighted that it was a very deep answer. Another friend said I was jumping all over the place and one said I needed sleep. The friend that had mentioned I needed sleep had knowledge of what was transpiring and knew I hadn't been sleeping adequately.

My final response to reassure my second mum was:

I have been in a deep place but I'm back with a new outlook coz I've changed but my core, personality/attitude/values and behaviours are all the same. I'm just more positive for going through 7 life changing days. It's been great for me and I'm sure others in the future.

At that stage, I didn't realise I only had a quarter of a book. I was probably on the surface of sub-conscious, not too deep in thought/mind. (I was obviously naive to think they were 7 life changing days!)

You are probably thinking where are the strategies and philosophies? Give me time, my vault contains years of experiences and events. It's difficult to know what to include! I only started putting fingers to board on the 4th of September in my spare time! We will get there – chugging along!

Wednesday 20/6/2012 was Rose's first day of chemo, 8 days from the official word and the day after the explosion. I thought I had sent her a text message wishing her well but I must have been side tracked by the kids. I didn't realise that I hadn't pushed send until two days after. However I did send her husband a message on that day, which is quite cryptic but given that I was in a drunk like state because of the lack of sleep – this message would be a standard "normal" drunk note for me:

Hey Jude, just popping my head out of my shell, lol yesterday was a hurdle that we needed to face. I still stand strong to my words. And I wouldn't be giving Rose my best if yesterday didn't happen, even though sometimes we are going to hurt loved ones to jump mountains.

I'm here for you anytime you need me, I'm the mentalist. Lol fook can you imagine little mini mama mind fuckers attacking the world? No one needs to be sorry or understand what's going on coz they are trapped in a cloud of fog. But Mama is waiting with her trumpet (and it's on purpose I use trumpet) to lift you out when you are ready.

I'm strong, I have jumped out of the pool, because everyone has to save themselves but we can't help the main beearch lol, if we are all dealing with our demons or whatever is inside our head.

This is very fucking deep mental shit and everyone is asking what's happening to Mama?? Mama is on a train to the next stop, ensuring that things will be ok. Just felt I had to let you know that.

If it helps, I'm playing my part to support you! If you don't understand that's perfectly ok and normal, I'm not offended, I know you are not ready and still cooking the roast…All the best today, lots of love Mama who I'm sure everyone thinks I'm crazy but has actually found her mind in a sea of mess!! Who would have thought???xxxx

Surprise!!! Rose's husband didn't reply and I wasn't expecting one! I would have never sent him a message of that nature if I was in my normal state of mind. I was rolling with it and when you finish this book, you may realise it makes more sense and oddly relates to what transpired over the following weeks!

That same day, I had to take Lexi and Harley to the doctor, as they both had bad colds. Whilst I was waiting, another patient had mentioned she was looking after her grandchildren while her daughter was undergoing treatment for breast cancer. I guess she mentioned this to me because I had recently shaved my hair. I explained that Rose had chronic fatigue syndrome and was being treated for IBC. This lady was also a nurse and mentioned that there was a high incidence of people suffering chronic fatigue syndrome who developed cancer. I thought that was interesting and sure enough after a quick Google, I was able to validate her claims. It was a very coincidental chat with a stranger. I had encountered so many coincidences during my sleep deprived state!

After the doctor appointment, I wanted to buy my son Max an iPod. I asked him what was important to him during that phase, school was most important and so was receiving an iPod. He had waited 6 months for his birthday present and I promised him one that same week. Obviously I was short on cash but planned to use my GE card. Unfortunately the retailer would not accept the purchase through this facility. I had already broken the promise the day before and Max was most upset. I had explained that sometimes a change in circumstance prevents you from doing what you intended. I did say I would fulfil his wishes. Therefore I had to borrow money off a friend who I paid back 3 days later. This was the only extraordinary purchase I made during that phase.

Around that time, I also received the boy's school reports. Max had an exceptional report. However the whole time I was reading it I was mindful of whether Rose would get to have the same opportunity. As much as it was great to read my son's glowing report that filled me with much happiness and delight, I did feel the emotions of helplessness and compassion for a friend too.

From the 19th-21st of June, I entered a different part of my mind. The models for my templates that I created linked to other matters and I explored these in great detail. Obviously with less frequent sleep my body adjusted by creating more adrenaline. I entered deeper into the sub-conscious. I was certain I was going to win Tattslotto. Don't we all dream or wish for that? When I engaged Jack and Diane who we have known for 12 years, they were surprised by my sudden change and weird foreign messages.

Jack and Diane live life like us! They are a great, fun, loving, caring and sharing couple. We have spent many nights and days, kicking back and enjoying life together over the years. I met Diane through work and she is a true comedian at heart, so is Jack. Nothing is ever a huge problem and they have helped us out a couple of times. If Mick and I had to catch the plane early, our children would be entrusted in their care.

Back to the messages, some of them were related to terror attacks at the Olympics. My attention was drawn to exploring this avenue because of my theories. Primarily understanding how beliefs affect behaviours and how others perceive confronting issues. It was more plausible that there could be a terrorist attack than shaking "God's" hand but friends found my claims disturbing.

I know it is because it wasn't in my nature and they didn't know what I was endeavouring. It was also because they cared. I had previously expected this and was ignoring their concerns to progress on my journey.

I explored a tiny bit of Nostradamus's work and religion, I had never been interested in this before. I did however recall watching a program that highlighted that most religions believed that the 21/12/2012 was a significant date. I read all sorts of different theories in respect to this and found some interesting connections.

Another avenue I explored was politics and I had absolutely no interest in this area either. Main reason for me, it's all based on hypocritical practices! I know I live in a democratic society but is it when you get fined if you don't vote? I also became a historian in that phase as well.

Just another slight detour, I have only ever voted once stating "hypocrites" on the card and that was because I just tagged along with friends! I haven't filled out those government surveys because they have the information. It is an extra expense to society that provides little benefit when it takes years to collate and publish.

Why? When the same current accurate information is available at their fingertips and they do little with it!

Ok back on track, so I sent out a few alarm bells! But for me, I had completed the first phase of my realization. Essentially, I found my purpose in life by identifying, what, when, who, how and why on my journey in life. Part of the process was developing the models and strategies for others as well.

At this stage I wasn't at my peak of sub-conscious because I was still functioning normally however I was discussing extraordinary things for me – understandable when you delve deeper into your dream-state of mind! My tone and core behaviours were intact, it was more about what I said and did.

What did I do? I sent a text to Diane and two other ex-colleagues who are great friends too (Jodes and Mon), explaining that I had 97 cents in the bank and I'm sending an e-mail to the top 4 book publishers. I basically advised my friends, that if I'm on the right path with my theories/strategies, I will receive an acknowledgement with 24 hours. If I didn't, it wasn't the right time and I needed to explore more. Here is that email:

Power of a positive mindset

From:
Date: 21 June 2012 11:43:23 PM
To:
erin.crum@harpercollins.com
mary.callahan@us.penguingroup.com
intsalestmp@randomhouse.co.uk
mswinge@randomhouse.co.uk
webmanager@macmillan.org.uk
france-office@uk.penguingroup.com

Hi

My name is Annette Monckton and you have probably read this introduction line many times before. I guess this is the mindset of how we have been programmed over time, which has not always come from a positive mindset.

I don't need to tell you, that many theories and strategies have been explored because you live and breathe literature.

My initial story, which I innocently embarked on was to help a close friend in a dire situation.

Instead I ended up understanding my own psyche because I could not comprehend why people were not accepting a strategy that could help her and was so obvious to me.

This lead to my realization that my positive thought process was significantly different. As a result, I need to write a book. I need to protect my intellectual property I have obtained over the years, to manage this change, as my theory is not aligned to how we function in the current environment. It is a massive mind blowing change which will create upheaval. More so, because our current psyche has not allowed us to explore another dimension.

My journey has evolved as a consequence of a close pregnant friend with two children being diagnosed with breast cancer.

If you would like to board my train, to embark on a journey outside of the current psyche world, you can add me as a friend on Facebook, which will provide a snapshot of my unexpected findings. If you feel it is worthy of your attention, I'll be waiting for your acknowledgement as I proceed on my journey.

Kind Regards,
Annette Monckton

I also engaged a select few through Facebook privately, phone and heytell, all for different reasons, purposes, causes and effects. Some of the reasons other than for the purpose of my book were to:

- Help
- Provide hope
- Share my knowledge to view matters differently

But wait there is more, because I was so wrapped up in what I found, and whilst in a deep state of mind. I began to believe that the terror attacks were inevitable. I'm not the only one! Many thought this, so it wasn't that extreme and as a matter of fact, was talked about in the news daily leading up to the event.

What does a person do, who has found her calling and her main purpose in life is to be happy; and part of that is helping others? I sent a couple of electronic notes to the President of the United States. What? What's the problem? I'm laughing because any normal person probably wouldn't have the audacity.

Me......with an attitude that is different to most! I considered that, if the forum wasn't available then I wouldn't have had the opportunity. Secondly, if I was right and didn't say anything, who would have believed me after the event and who would suffer? Thirdly, if it was going to happen, make sure there were enough resources to manage any situations. Finally, if it didn't eventuate, I wasn't harming anyone and it made for a good story! Just 4 different ways of thinking and understanding how to assess situations differently in a different state of mind!

You are probably wondering how I ended up in a psyche ward! The best is yet to come! With that, the base or foundation that will assist you in determining your purpose, if you so wish, is below!

Scaling back the years

Firstly, I assessed what I wanted from my life if I lived another 40 years. I then considered whether those expectations would be the same if I lived for 10 years. I continued to assess whether my expectations would be the same if I had one year, 6 months or a week to live. In essence, it became obvious that I should be enjoying each day as I wished, keeping in mind what I wanted to achieve in the future. Or another way of looking at it was to determine how I could achieve what I wanted to accomplish whilst living my life.

For me, although I realised that money was essential to everyday living, it could not buy you happiness or health. For example, I could sell my house and buy a cheaper home further in the country. I could still be happy and have a smaller mortgage. I had choices of how I could manage my life better by determining different needs and wants. If I lived a week, I wouldn't want to be burdened by money. I would want to spend precious time with my children enjoying my final moments and assisting them as much as I could. I also thought of others that never had the opportunity because of tragic circumstances. My husband and I always leave the house with a kiss goodbye and a happy mood. I guess we are mindful of ensuring a memorable moment in the event of adversity. This really helped me align what was important in my life and my family's.

The Eye of the human psyche

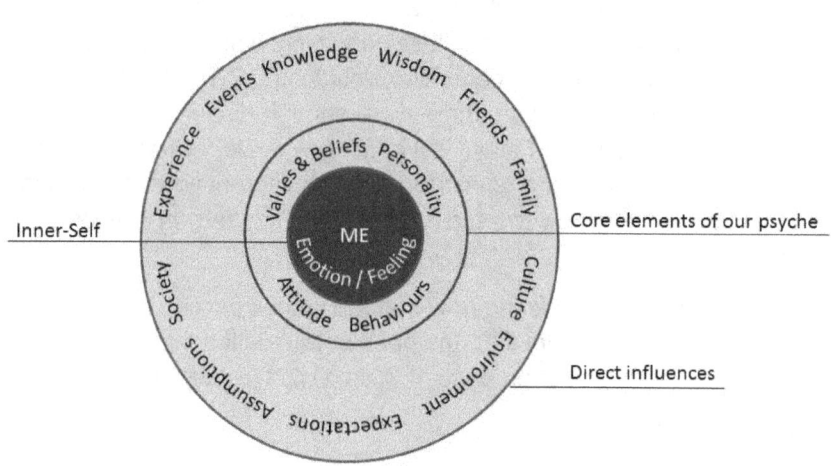

Each person is driven by a force of emotion/feeling

How you view, perceive, process information and react is fundamentally based on 4 elements:

- Values & Beliefs
- Personality
- Attitude
- Behaviours

Those elements are directly influenced by a number of factors, just to name a few:

- Experiences/Events
- Knowledge/Wisdom
- Family/Friends
- Society/Culture
- Environment
- Expectations
- Assumptions

The 4-elements work collectively and can be independently interconnected.

By understanding those elements, we can identify our strengths and weaknesses in order to find a happy balance within our lives. However you need to honestly assess yourself, both the good and the bad!

Before I get to how we do that, obviously every person requires energy to function, food, air, water and sleep/rest being the basic components for our bodies. Our mind works on a different energy level; it requires a positive and negative factor to keep us balanced when dealing with emotions/feelings. Like any energy source, for example a battery, you require a positive and a negative to create a power source. Applying logic, for every action, there is an equal and opposite reaction for energy to be created.

In theory if our personality, attitude, behaviours, values and beliefs are positive, in effect the result would be a happy life. If all elements were negative, it would result in an unhappy life. Any combination of positive and negative could affect your overall mindset and influence how you feel. For instance, if an individual is highly stressed, it may instigate problems with blood pressure and impact their heart. Our feelings/emotions are connected to how our body functions; it has been proven to a degree. The reason for specifying to a degree is that your physical matter is clearly just as important. If you lack a vital physical component, regardless of your mindset, it could be detrimental to your health, e.g. lack of food would affect your energy levels and in extreme cases can be fatal.

In light of the above, each individual has positive and negative core traits as part of their mindset. Some are more extreme than others. Some favour the positive side more than the negative and vice versa. Most of us don't recognise this part of ourselves. It may be the underlying issue to being unhappy, misguided, confused, depressed etc. Furthermore if this aspect isn't acknowledged it may be difficult to resolve such challenges.

When I analysed myself, I came up with the following models:

My "sun" dial – the positive attributes of me:

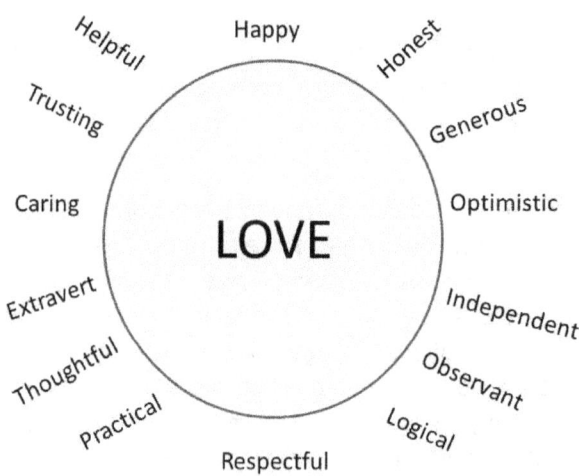

My "moon" dial/shadow – my negative attributes are as follows:

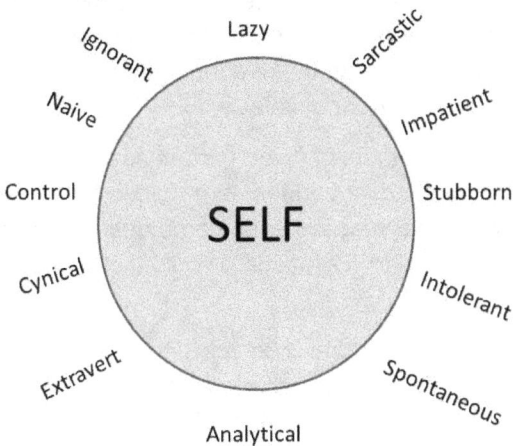

These traits essentially provide the energy for me to function. Other traits are utilised when required but these are my common ones. A summary of my psyche at a high level would be:

Beliefs: I believe in myself. I believe in Karma, what goes around, comes around! I believe that any challenge is an opportunity to learn and grow. I attempt to embrace the positive.

Values: I'm respectful and treat others how I wish to be treated. I'm mindful of those less fortunate and don't take things for granted. (However if someone is disrespectful or treats me poorly, I'm inclined to retaliate).

Personality: happy go-lucky, extravert, energetic, caring, helpful, generous, optimistic and thoughtful.

Attitude: is generally positive due to my personality, values and beliefs. However it can be influenced by the same factors as behaviours and I may be inclined to exert the "moon" dial consciously or sub-consciously.

Behaviour: is generally good but can vary depending on circumstances, e.g. factors that influence behaviour.

Your attitude and behaviours are linked and can vary significantly during the course of your life in contrast to your base/fixed traits, i.e. personality/values and beliefs. Obviously the latter can change however it requires more perseverance, control and attention because we are either born with these attributes or they are ingrained from a very early/formative age.

When I consider the 4 elements of who I am at a high level they are reflective of a positive mindset and they are unique to me. However an experience may trigger a negative outcome depending on my emotion/feeling in respect to a situation. I could therefore exert a negative energy.

Ultimately I have control over that by perceiving, interpreting, thinking and feeling before I respond with an action or reaction. In essence, this was the change I experienced as part of my realisation. I learned to view many possibilities in order to do what was right for me and create a happy positive balance or energy. For every positive action, I could articulate an equal and opposite negative reaction – basically Newton's law applied to matters of the mind and in theory linking science to the human psyche.

By understanding most attributes and knowing traits of others, I had a deeper appreciation of them. For example: If I know someone who tends to worry, I'm mindful of not complicating matters for them.

Basically the outcome of my initial realisation was that I was responsible for being myself. No one could tell me how to think, feel, act and say. If you can understand the consequences and impacts of your actions and behaviour it shouldn't matter how others influence you directly or indirectly!

I also realised that there was no right or wrong (to a certain degree) but how you respond impacts the outcome. When expectations are not met, people are disappointed. In addition, assumptions and beliefs can also misguide you. If you free yourself of fears and inhibitions you release the burden and can live a carefree/happy life. For every challenge, find the positive to re-centre yourself. As you progress on my journey you will have a better appreciation of what I mean!

Pool Effect

I made reference to this in the text I sent to Rose's husband. In principal, if someone jumps into the deep end and is struggling with their own problems (trying to survive) and others with problems or emotions attempt to assist; this could actually prevent or impede that individual from effectively helping themselves. The individual could carry the burden of others when in a fragile or vulnerable state of mind. They could be misguided because their emotions override dealing with the practical matter. Too much information may become evident and create an overload. (As per the examples I provided pertaining to change, expectations etc. in the first chapter.) The more people in a pool, the less chance of swimming and if you are struggling, those that have jumped in to help may be inadvertently bringing you down, hence why I referred to my theory as the "pool effect". People need to help themselves (or at least acknowledge their plight) before others are able to effectively help. This also became evident as a result of my realisation.

Jan - a great friend who I met through Mother's group had visited during my phase. She is very understanding, thoughtful, kind, caring and generous. She also has a very open mind. She understood my theories and accepted what I was endeavouring at face value. At the time, she did realise that I was on a path of self-discovery and that although my behaviours were odd, she recognised that they weren't extreme. This was because I had provided her with some insight as to how I based some of my conclusions and explained my sub-conscious state of mind.

To determine the core essence of one-self, I guess it is honestly considering who you are or what you want to be. For me in one word, it was happy (love is a given) and I identified that my core purpose was to help others because this made me happier. You have to acknowledge and accept your past before you can move forward. As I have always done this, I didn't give it much thought throughout my life. However it was crucial during my realisation phase to appreciate my life lessons at a greater level. This takes us to the next chapter for some of my life's experiences and memories!

Just a friendly announcement, I hope you are enjoying the journey. Please take time to stop and smell the roses. For the safety of others, place all baggage under your seat! You may find the next carriage upsetting, so grab your tissues if you are emotionally fertile! There will be more laughs than tears!

Knowing me, knowing you, was the best I can do!! ABBA is one of my favourite bands from the 70's and every ABBA song resonates with me! I love dancing queen and porta-loo too, I mean Water loo (I always change the words to suit me!).I still enjoy their music today!

KICK by INXS was my favourite album/band during my teens, as with all of Bon Jovi's music. Green Day is currently my favourite band. Every song from these artists I connect with. I love all types of music from Edith Piaf to Pearl Jam, from Bob Marley to PINK. I guess my tastes reflect my dynamic personality and attitude! With that in mind, let's chug along and explore my past! Chugga Chugga Chugga....

3. Me in a nutshell - one bloody big nut too!

I was born in April 1973 in Noble Park, Melbourne, Australia at the South Eastern Private Hospital. Ironically the hospital has recently closed their maternity section, as it was not profitable. A shame really when there is such a shortage of resources. My mum Ursula had me at the ripe age of 21 but 2 days before she turned 22.

My mum had two miscarriages before me. After my birth, her doctor at the time compromised her physically. After a botched operation, she was told she could not have any more children. Dad was livid but luckily for all of us, mum had three more. Second to me is my brother Armen, born at the Mercy hospital 3 years later which was a difficult labour. Followed by Marie who was born 5 years later and with a 10 year gap from oldest to youngest, is Anthony. The younger two were both born at the South Eastern Private Hospital as well.

My beautiful loving mum, who is 61, where love holds no boundaries, has always been a great mum. She is kind, generous, patient, caring, funny, reserved and giving; she would do anything for anyone. She had an extraordinarily difficult life. She was born in Germany in 1951 and orphaned at 3. Her grandmother and her migrated to Australia not long after but unfortunately my mother's brother was left behind (not sure of the reason). Her step aunties Erica and Herta also migrated along with Aunty Hilda and Uncle Peppo. She spent most of her time in the formative years growing up in Williamstown.

My mum never had a formal education and her grandmother died when she was 12. She was abused by a member of a church and was poorly treated by relatives around that time, from what I know.

I'm sure she had many adventures along her way, she rarely speaks about her past so I don't bring it up – too painful for her or maybe she is like me and dealt with it when it occurred. But she did tell me once that she was on camp and someone told her to chuck something in the fire. Obviously the person took advantage of my mum because she ended up starting a grass fire! Way to go mum!

My mum never had confidence in herself due to her experiences and lack of education but she held a job in the city mint prior to falling pregnant with me. She never learnt how to drive but was very independent. She took great care of us, and I can't thank her enough for the values and morals that she and dad ingrained in me! I now teach my children those same values, pretty amazing considering there was no one to completely guide her throughout her years.

When things did get a bit rough, she called on Aunty Margaret (not blood related) who was like a mum to my mum. She was another kind, loving German lady, so mum spent most of her time in her late adolescent years there.

Mum and dad met at a singles dance that my dad organized. Funny about that really, it's something that I would do but have never done – maybe because he has done it! At the time, dad was working for EMI pressing records. (For the younger generations, I'll try and explain; a record was a very thin round plastic dinner/saucer plate with a hole at the centre. When pressed with a template, it embedded the plate. When placed on a moving turntable with a needle, it would create the vibe to emanate a sound through a speaker! Hope that sounds right! Well that's the best I can come up with at 12.50am). My mum and Dad married in a simple backyard barbeque wedding 3 months after meeting each other. Dad took mum "overseas" (you have to cross over a bridge) to Phillip Island for their honeymoon and what a great beautiful place it is!

I have clear memories from around the age of 3. A friend of mum and dads who was a gorgeous Italian woman, loved to pinch my cheeks – Aunty Bridgetta. (While I think of it, we called all friends of the family uncles, aunties and cousins, just so you don't get confused.) I use to scream – she had a firm grip but I don't think it was because she hurt me, I just didn't like it! I must admit I love chubby cheeked babies too and have the urge to do the same, just a Mama thing I guess. I also remember times when my brother and I huddled, frightened and traumatised, in our room many times too from that age!

My first prized possession at the age of 4 was my metallic green banana bike with the bell and streamers. I recall my Armenian born grandmother Arfenia and great grandmother Baboo (seriously that's what we called her so I assume it was her real name) watching and clapping as I rode off down the street. I loved my grandparents with all my heart. My Dad's father had caught the plane before mum and dad met. My dad and Uncle David don't talk about him, what I do know seems to be conflicting to my Dad's view.

Baboo was a very funny, generous, happy, kind and loving lady. She would do anything for anyone and my mum loved her too. Arfenia was very protective of me, loved me like no other and was the same as Baboo except only those she was endeared to. My grandmother would always give me more money and lollies than my other siblings but I always evenly divided them up! I knew I was her favourite but I didn't work it to my advantage, I was always a fair innocent kid.

Arfenia wasn't always happy and always spoke about dying or death. Her catch phrase was "Oi Oi Oi Oiiiiiii" She was psychic and would read cards (playing cards) and tea/coffee cups. She was well known in the community. She also performed this ritual with eggs that would clear any evil spirits you have or something to that effect.

We lived on Corrigan road with my grandparents across from the Sandown race track. We would throw the eggs off the bridge in a water reserve down the street. My grandmother wore those real fox shawls with the beady eyes, wigs, bright red lipstick and nail polish. She plucked all her eyebrows out, goodness knows why and was a short lady. I guess she was a little bit out there – no wonder I was! Both were very creative and often made jewelry. I came across necklaces that were made from paper clips that were contacted when going through my grandmother's belongings after she caught the plane. They were quite stunning and colourful.

However Arfenia had a very dark side that I witnessed but it didn't change my love for her. She abused my mum to no end. I witnessed her trying to burn her with the iron. I saw her pull my mum's hair so many times that I cringe thinking about it. She pinched, punched, scratched, kicked and bit my mum countless times too. She would throw things at her as well. It was horrible for my mum and I honestly don't know how she tolerated it. I believe this was because my grandmother didn't approve or wanted to take control of bringing me up! It could have been many factors, severe depression being the main one!

Baboo passed away when I was around 5. I don't recall being upset. I guess my last memory would have been relating to that great time I had on my new bike. I'm mentioning her death just to highlight for me, at that age, it obviously didn't have an impact because I can't remember the funeral or any emotions of her passing.

Back to the steam engine, my Dad, control-ruler of the home and all those in it! He is a great man, loving, funny, kind, and generous. He would do anything for anyone too. He is very intelligent but I believe his inhibitions, fears and emotions have clouded his journey through life.

My Dad migrated to Australia on a boat with his brother, mother, father and grandmother, when he was 16. He once held about 20 jobs in 2 years in the 70's. Obviously he didn't like the jobs or was adaptable to change. He is a wall and floor tiler by trade and still does this today. Both of my parents speak English very well; however my Dad's is a bit broken.

On one occasion, I dropped to the floor rolling like I was on fire, preventing a light bladder leakage (LBL). This was because my Dad had told a 70 year old customer that "if he wasn't there on Thursday, she could suck him" - clearly he meant sack. I was 15 at the time and it still makes me laugh! I loved going to the "bitch" in summer too! (Beach-another classic favourite!)

My Dad loves to talk to people, is very endearing and friendly. He'd wear a Jewish cap when he tiled places for Jewish people for example. He'd eat crumbed snakes (it was probably eel) that Indian's cooked for him. I didn't like that day because he told us they were nuggets and waited to tell us the truth – nice hurl that one!

He doesn't drink much (one or two light beers now but did drink a fair bit in his late teens) and is a reformed smoker. At one stage, he was smoking 2 packets a day. He'd smoke in the car, the house and even the toilet before times changed. He loved his cars and we loved them too.

We travelled in style in the work/family van. Sometimes we sat on buckets/milk crates, occasionally we'd have a mattress and there was also the couch. There were also the fold down chairs at one stage but when seat belts were introduced, dad had to upgrade. Not the car, but he picked up some second hand airplane seats and installed them. We thought it was great and it was the closest thing to flying, especially the way my dad drives.

He once lost his license for dragging a cop in the 70's. In those days, if you had connections, you basically got your license back straight away. He has a passion for cards and loves a punt on the horses too! He, like myself, has had all-nighters at the "CAS" (casino) on many occasions, must be in our blood! I knew my dad's phone account number and remember that number today! From the age of 8, I would often place bets on the phone for him, if he was busy.

He is a very private respectful man and has always been mindful of what others think. He told us stories about Tehran, Iran his place of birth. Like people's fingers getting cut off, teeth of the dead sold at markets, people being murdered and bashed for their crimes by stone and fire. (I never gave my Dad's stories much credence because it was foreign to the world I was accustomed to. Since media coverage of those areas and exploring more, I have acknowledged his heritage and understand why so many suffer physically and mentally.)

My Dad is great but at times is "dark" too (like his mum). He failed to recognize his severe depression and seek help – very old school and proud. We all suffered and to some degree, we all feel the impacts now, such is life!

Now no one likes to highlight negative traits especially those we love and care about, particularly parents. It is with a heavy heart that I do this to explain my side of the story in order to help others. I will be exposing times that were bad but I did deal with those emotions and feelings at the time they occurred.

Like any other child (even at 39), my love for my parents is unconditional. With that in mind, I'd appreciate if those reading, who know my Dad particularly, please try and refrain from judging him. I view my experience as a reason for enabling me to be the strong happy person that I am. It is more painful to type knowing that I may hurt him by writing this book than actually experiencing those bad events - that's love! (Deep breath – tough stuff, gets worse before it gets better – my waters broke!)

In actual fact, I hope he doesn't read this book. He normally only reads the form guide so I should be safe. The only reason why I'm bringing these to the fore front is to highlight the positive and negative theory for me keeping balanced and how I managed to cope. Just thought I'd get in early so you have an expectation; because if you are expecting the worst and it isn't that bad, then the impact of what you will read will be less!

I attended St. Anthony's Primary school (no longer standing) and half way through grade 2, attended St. Elizabeth's primary in Noble Park North.

St. Anthony's was managed by nuns and was very old school. You had yard duty and students enjoyed ringing the hand bell at recess. I enjoyed singing, writing, math, running around, playing and buying treats from the tuck shop. I was a very quiet, polite and obedient student. One of the unusual things I remember was a slight soft hill behind the toilet block. Most students thought that there was a monster underneath or maybe it was just me! When we jumped down and the ground rose, we'd scamper off! I still carry a scar from a major crash on the gravel from one of those times. Now that I think of it, it was probably the sewerage pit! Eewww……..

An unpleasant memory was in grade 2, when I brought some presents in for friends from my Dad's tile shop, (he was one of the founders of Amberley tiles that was a successful business). I had collected textas, labels, notebooks and a little pretty flower oblong slip. My gift was an innocent act of kindness and I didn't know the flower slip contained a razor as I didn't check it. However a boy ended up cutting himself with it and required stitches.

The Nun's (who were Nazi's) marched from room to room and I did hear that they were closing in. I know it may seem odd to you but kids talk and it was the talk of the school at recess. When they finally entered our class room I knew I was in trouble. When they called my name, I actually wet my pants in fear. I tied my jumper around my waste and walked the line to the front of class. I don't know if anyone noticed that I did. I wasn't just in fear of the nun's and I don't even recall what happened with them, it was my Dad that I feared the most.

I'm not sure if I caught the bus or if I was escorted home but I know I apologised to mum. I told her that I wasn't well and went straight to bed before dad got home and pretended to sleep. I didn't want to get beaten. I escaped a beating not sure why but I wasn't going to ask. I did think to myself (all the way back then), gee I'm lucky, I thought I was in deep trouble - maybe it's good to fear and think the worst because it may not happen! I don't know how forceful those beatings were during the younger years but I know what they were like from about the age of 9.

While at Corrigan road, I also witnessed my mum getting beaten by my dad as well and a great deal of that was due to my grandmother. What my grandmother did to my mum, my dad did the same to her and us, except he didn't bite, pull hair or scratch.

As a kid, I did Judo, Ballet, Tap dancing and swimming when we lived with my grandmother. Mum would walk us to my activities. It obviously provided some time away from her place of hell. I recall walking home from ballet/tap one night when out of nowhere I released a hair curling scream and frightened my mum. She asked what was wrong and I told her someone was following us. It was my shadow; a car with lights was passing from behind. As the car got closer, my shadow got bigger so I thought the person was able to grab us! I was around 6 at the time, always aware, alert, analyzing and observing. Maybe I had to be on my toes because I was constantly watching what I had to say, do and act when growing up.

My mum was trapped and couldn't take any more! All she had was her three children at the age of 28. She did think about suicide but could not stand the thought of anyone else raising her children. (My mum only recently mentioned this to my sister after the first phase of my realization!) I guess because she loved us like no other and was an orphan herself, she pulled herself up from the depths of hell! She had no access to support or funds. She had her aunties but I assume she did not want to burden them with her troubles when they really didn't approve of my dad back then. Fuck, what would you do? This was back in 1980, 32 years ago!

We walked, I remember walking with my mum, my 2 year old sister was in the pram and my brother 4 was sitting on top. We had only the clothes we left in and whatever food that she could take, plus her bag! (I'm crying at the moment because I can't imagine how hard this would have been for my mum!) We walked from Corrigan road, Noble Park, down Lightwood Road, right through to the Springvale Road and stopped at the library, approximately 4kms. A fair walk for a 7 year old but I never complained. I guess my mum was re-assessing what she should do. She ended up ringing Aunty Herta who obviously was able to pay for the taxi ride to Mentone.

I enjoyed my break with my Aunty. She was a beautiful loving person, kind, generous and caring, who loved cooking, gardening and doing crafts. She loved knitting, crochet and decorating emu eggs too. She loved to dance and sing as well. She always had music playing, so does my mum for that matter. She was married to Uncle Oscar who died of cancer in 1980 and gave birth to Heinz.

She was also a volunteer for the Peter McCallum cancer centre and other charities too. She loved helping people! She was always on my back for smoking and drinking and I would call her Aunty Hitler, in a nice way! She was my godmother and was a positive mother figure in my life too, I loved her immensely.

She caught the plane about 4 years ago, as they carted the coffin out at the service; I laughed and almost started dancing. The "Chicken Dance" song was played!! She always requested this at weddings and it was a tribute to her having fun! A moment in time that I will always remember!

Getting back on track, Mum basically told my dad it was her or his mother. She still loved my dad! She obviously set boundaries and to a degree, things did change for her! So mid-year in 1980, we moved to Mulgrave and I was enrolled in St. Elizabeth's. I never witnessed any violence towards my mum after we moved.

I opened up at this school, I became loud and my true self. I'm not sure why I changed. I even gave some cheek back. One time, I was ordered to do 20 lines, so upon completion I handed the teacher a piece of paper that had 20 straight lines on it – fairly straight forward. She failed to mention that I had to write I must not talk in class. Clearly she didn't see the funny side. That night I had to write, 50 lines of "I must not talk in class or act smart. I must listen and do what the teacher tells me!" Double, double whammy – but it was worth it!

Some students called me Annette Step-On-A-Fart because of my surname. I never took offense, as I found it funny and gave me right of passage (pardon the pun). Once Noelene left, I pretty much bounced off other friends, didn't matter who I played with, I just had fun! (It's funny because I ask Max how his day was at school and who he played with and it's the same for him.)

In grade 6, there was an "elite" group so to speak, Samantha was the ring leader, and then there was Michelle, Lisa and Tanya. Samantha had a bladder problem and we'd help her! One would stand at the toilet door and cover, while she dried her gear. I guess she was very vulnerable at the time and needed to exert control over others. Knowing what I know now, she was probably troubled at home! I drifted in and out of the group but never really considered myself as being a part of it because I just played with who I wanted, when I wanted.

One day, there was a bitch fight, they obviously didn't know I did Judo and had been since the age of 4. On this day, the elite girls and 2 extras were ready to go a blaze! I had one down on her back in a second and they took a step back. I moved forward and took another one down and said "Do you all want to go down?"

They scurried off, all cool for me! I wasn't afraid of getting hurt because I was beaten at home! I had the skill from my passion of Judo and I didn't care what they thought, because I didn't need to associate with those types of girls. I guess even in high school, if I was teased or bullied I don't remember. Most of my memories are of fun, so obviously the earlier experience and my attitude was a tool to manage this type of situation.

There was a situation where my grade 4 teacher Mr. Baker had treated Mary poorly. Mary was a gorgeous Mauritian girl with the most angelic voice! She was always laughing and telling jokes but she also suffered years of abuse because of her weight! This teacher who had to grab a ladder hurled abuse at her and called her a fat stupid idiot. All because she got stuck up on the monkey bars and was too afraid to get down. I was disgusted at the time and really felt for her! Can you imagine your child alone taunted by other children and the teacher? (I have a remarkable memory and plan to use this event later in the book, just in case you're wondering why I brought this up! It also gives the doctor's an insight to how my brain works.)

Back to me again, I was brought up as a Catholic but it was not my choice. I only believed in myself. All mum ever wanted for us was to be happy – that's all I wanted to be too. My dad wanted us to be successful (and happy of course), he insisted all our names began with the letter "A" hoping we'd get these in school - serious! This was clearly important to him. I kid you not – I told you he was funny and that is on many levels.

My parents weren't active in practicing religion! They only complied when they needed to and that was to obtain a discount on school fees. I suspect that they wanted to provide the best education that they could afford, as any parent would.

Dad sold his share in Amberley tiles to buy our new 3 bedroom home. My parents still live in it today. It is approximately 12 squares in size and we all shared a bedroom. The bedrooms were fairly small as with the living areas but it was a great home. Our home was always cluttered and full of people. One of dad's sayings were "people come to see you not your house".

It has a reasonable sized back yard which once had a Clark rubber pool. Dad managed to pick this up from somewhere secondhand or free and we had great days playing in the pool.

When the earth was excavated to install the pool, myself, my brother and neighbours would play war games with the large boulders. The hole was there for a while before the pool was erected, like most things in our home, it was a slow process. Anyway those games came to an abrupt end real quick, when a sharp shooter (me) nearly carved my brothers eye out accidently. As mum didn't drive, she had to call on the neighbour. The injury wasn't that bad because he can still see out of that eye! Sometimes that eye does turn but I reckon it's because of the drinks he enjoys, just like his big sis! (We always had great times with our neighbours!)

Unfortunately a few years later and after many re-linings the pool died. It became a whole in the ground due to financial reasons that was effectively brought on by the 1983 recession.

My dad went into business with Heinz, my Mum's cousin and unfortunately succumbed to a sudden end like many businesses around that time. With a mortgage, a family of 6 and an additional $40k to repay, something had to give. The additional amount should have only been $20k but Heinz decided to neglect his responsibility. My dad did not what to declare bankruptcy and wanted to provide for his family. So he worked as long and as hard as he could to keep us afloat.

At the time, Heinz was a successful businessman. He had managed ski resorts and hotels. We had a couple of holidays in the snow which I thoroughly enjoyed. Heinz never re-paid my Dad and the relationship was strained. My Dad however was respectful and never made an issue, if by chance they crossed paths at my Aunty's house.

Years later Heinz ended up bankrupt and had to move into his in-laws house. Exclusive schools were a thing of the past. My Aunty lost her unit and had to rely on public housing. Heinz had to buy his and the family's clothes from opportunity shops. It was my first major insight and confirmation of Karma! What goes around, comes around! I live by it and it does keep me centered. But never wait for it, as it prevents you from moving forward! Just have faith!

Back to Dad, he worked for Telecom (Government Telecommunication Company –before privatisation) and tiled at night and every weekend. Like all government jobs, it was pretty easy going. You worked but you didn't work hard. My dad would often take naps in the truck or head to the tab for a lucky punt (he'd only spend what he could afford). He was the record holder of most absentees. He made many friends along his way but with all the pressure, he was still extremely unhappy.

I was required to fill the gap at home with all chores. I use to help mum cook, bath the younger ones, cleaning, ironing and would do the lawns; from about the age of 8. I loved helping mum but I also hated the chores especially gardening and mowing the lawns. Once my Dad came home and the lawns weren't done, before any questions were asked, I was slapped, kicked and beaten. I or mum didn't even have a chance to tell him that there was no petrol.

Another time, my brother had thrown bags of grass over the neighbour's fence and I copped the belt, kick and open-handed slap. Those hands came at a force greater than 20 watermelons hitting you at once – well not that I experienced that, but metaphorically that's what it felt like! An open slap to the face never left a bruise, only a red-rash that disappeared by the next day.

I have only had the iron out probably twice in my life since turning 18 and I only clean when I need to. I don't mind cooking but I love eating and drinking more!

There were many broken windows in our house because of us kids. Anthony once smashed the sliding door window with his arm because my sister called him acne. My brother threw a coffee table at me and it went through the window. For broken windows you got the entire special treatment (as above) plus bending over with your pants down and receiving a couple of leather whips with the belt! We all received beatings but Armen and I received more, mentally and physically because we were the oldest.

My dad often called me a stupid idiot, shit for brains and fat, he would say it a jovial way when happy and harshly when he was in a bad mood. He picked on how I walked. I was forced to walk around the house with a book on my head when dad was giving me a gestapo type lesson in deportment. Fuck they were frustrating and yes received a few beltings with that too! I get knocked down and I get up again! What doesn't kill you, makes you stronger.

When my dad was in those moods he always yelled and it is one of my pet hates today. When someone is constantly yelling, it takes me back to childhood and I feel a flurry of anger. Sometimes I find myself doing it, it's what I was use to and it is hard to break the cycle. I normally try to walk away or take deep breaths, scream back in a funny way, turn the music up or sing!

He also never really listened to what I had to say or needed because it was his way only! I sometimes get frustrated when people don't listen to me for that reason but again manage that in adult life as a result of the experience. Sometimes I will interrupt, it's not because I'm rude. I recognize it's a result of having a million views on the matter and want the opportunity. (I'm assuming some friends would be shaking their heads thinking oh that's why.)

We were always ordered to grab things for Dad or attend to his habits. I once told my dad to get his own apple from the fridge and never did that again for the reasons already highlighted. I hated scratching his hairy back or rubbing his feet, yuck! (I probably enjoyed it as a preschooler when life was easy) but not since the age of 6. I'm so glad Mick is naturally hairless and doesn't care if I don't rub his feet. I think that got him over the line, only joking!

We only had two holidays but there was one horrific one to Yarra-fucking-wonga! Great place - but not for me back then. I had completed one of those timeshare competition forms when shopping! I was only 12, SURPRISE we won! It was 2 nights at a luxurious resort. Before I got there, I wanted to die. Packing and getting on the road was an issue but it was more so the ride and what transpired.

It was a 4 hour drive and along the way, I explained I was going to be sick. My dad didn't stop and I threw up. Spew in a confined car with 6 people isn't nice but it got sorted. He cracked the shits so we weren't on any "Venga bus". Not long after, my dad's back wheel blew out and our car travelled on the opposite side. We just missed a head on collision.

Dad always stressed especially under financial hardship, me throwing up and organizing the trip (they didn't have to go but obviously decided to) and now that a tyre was required, he was about to explode!

The straw that broke the camel's back was the tail gate opening. Departing after a stop in the main street to collect supplies, I was told to shut the back of the van door. The power-lead foot that my dad is, drove off at a million miles an hour, only I hadn't shut the door properly. Bags and food across the main street!

No "panel" beating required on that trip but there were a few dints in my shell, it made me stronger! I would have preferred to stay in my room and listen to music. I can't even remember what we did on those 2 days and at that age I should have; it obviously wasn't a trip to remember! I haven't filled out a free competition since unless it was for free drinks in a bar!

Since about that age, I decided I wasn't going to cry anytime that I was beaten. I didn't want to give my dad the satisfaction that he had hurt me. I also emotionally disconnected and it allowed me to focus on what was important for me at that time. I did try and commit suicide many times around the age of 12-14.

It was around the time, when my only grandmother, passed away when I was 13 that I was at my worst. This was my first experience that I recall of someone really close to me dying. She had flat-lined on the Friday but magically started breathing again. The hospital called and as mum wasn't that great with messages, I took the call. I had to ring Dad at work. First time I heard my dad break down was hard for me. It hurt that I had to tell him the news, I hated seeing my parents upset.

The service was a combination of Armenian and English. Yvette attended as well. I only cried when I understood what was being said in English. Her casket was open. Following my dad, I kissed my grandmother's cheek, with tears streaming down my face. I then thought what the fuck, hope dad didn't pay full price for the grooming because they forgot to pluck her hormonal hairs. I then quickly thought, gees, I just kissed my dead grandma! Funny really – but that's the way I am and think sometimes!

That night I cried myself to sleep and wished her goodbye. I pretended she went on a holiday. I have occasionally thought of her during life. Sometimes a familiar smell like nail polish or taste of food would stir a memory. Sometimes it was my need for cash and sending a "grandma, if you can hear me, a win would be good now!" Since then, I always looked at passing, as a moment in time, to catch a plane to a better place, where we all meet up again!

So you are probably thinking how did I try and commit suicide or did I distract you? I didn't try it because of my grandma dying. It was again my dad and him dealing with the aftermath of her estate, on top of what he was already dealing with! I tried by holding my breath, yeah fucking laugh, it's funny! Mick had a great laugh when I told him. I only wanted to do it this way so it looked like a natural cause of death. Even though my dad was mentally and physically abusing me, I never blamed him. I just found ways within myself to cope.

During that time when it was really rough, I still had respect and a great unconditional love – so I didn't want to purposely upset him or mum if I was successful. Power of love I guess. For those that have tried witchery (voodoo dolls, spells etc.) it didn't work for me back then either – that was plan B!

Anytime we were visiting friends or family, we were given the call of duty, "You should be seen and not heard! Do not touch the table (referring to snacks) unless they are offered. Don't breathe (I'm serious) or I'll break your head or arm!" He often said I'll break your head or arms and we thought he meant it because of the tone he used and his behaviour. Today I view it in a comical way and when I say it to my kids, they laugh! So I have turned it into a positive and get a lot of laughs out of it when I occasionally use these phrases. My dad always said "Why me?" I thought the same! I'm tipping, he'll find out now. At least now I won't have to run, duck and cover!

I will try not to dwell on any more negative events, but I'm sure it gives you a clear understanding of the volatile home I lived in; and the unfortunate things that happened to me. None of us were ever abused sexually – I dislike having to write this but I need to make it clear because if it isn't stated in black and white, some readers may jump to conclusions or assume the worst.

My mum never hit us and when we were bad, we had to stand in the corner facing the wall. When we were really bad, we had to kneel on the tiles. I only hit my mum once and that was out of pure frustration because she blamed me for something my brother had done. I apologised immediately. We inadvertently gave our mum a hard time because we weren't allowed to be free to play and be children when dad was home. With all the violence, my siblings and I ended up lashing out on each other too. The only way to release the emotion, I guess! My poor mother!

Some young mum's of today think they have it hard! When there are so many opportunities available! Even though my mum still doesn't give herself credit, she is a survivor and very strong. It was obviously how it was meant to be!

Now you are probably wondering what my mum could have done? She was powerless and tried to protect us as best she could. I do not blame her nor has it impacted our relationship or my life. Like I mentioned earlier, things happen for a reason and purpose. I would not have been the person I am today if it wasn't for my parents conceiving me and the experiences I had. (Always remember where you come from! However some people that have been so traumatised may need to move on and must disconnect. There is no right or wrong. Therefore you should do what is right for you, if you want to remain balanced and happy in life!)

The support for women during that time was minimal. Financially, how would my mum have survived with 4 children? How would she obtain a job with little skills, low self-esteem and confidence? Who would have looked after us? I actually learned through her, how important it was to protect myself so I never found myself in that situation (cause and effect). I also knew how I was going to treat my children and be mindful of the poor behaviour displayed by my dad (reason and purpose).

As mentioned, I have never blamed my dad for his treatment because I don't know how he was treated. It may be culturally ingrained or his mental state did not allow him to understand that he needed help. He didn't purposely treat us this way because he did love us. He didn't have control of his behaviour. He was under a lot of pressure with the failed business. My parents, my experience, my view and I'm happy with that!

Climbing back to the happy track, there were great times too. There was always food on the table. We did wear hand-me-downs which I didn't mind because I admired those friends and their choices in fashion. Plus I felt special that they wanted to give me something.

Occasionally I did want something new. I remember getting a new pair of jeans in grade 6. I wanted Levi's because they were the "in thing" but scored the cheaper Wrangler alternative – funny because they are not so cheap now!

One Christmas, we received a t-shirt and a pair of thongs that were 3 sizes too big. I thought cool, I can surf on these when we get to the beach (sarcasm). Dad went shopping for those presents, not sure if it was a mistake or tactical on his part. My brother and I invented our own game of slapper thong, bit like 'stacks on' hand style but with thongs. When you stuffed up, you got the thong! The Aussie version of the dong!

My second best present when things looked up was my white roller skates with the red shining wheels. I had to wrap them up myself as with all Christmas presents, so I rarely had surprises at that time (birthdays were different) but couldn't wait to roll on! We spent many days at the roller skating rink and I loved every minute. The games, speed skating and the classic style dining, it was fun!

In my late twenties, I'd thought I'd re-live some memories. I headed to the rink with Yvette, Anita, Heath (Anita's husband) and little Mick. I participated in the speed skate session that day! Boy – my skills were rusty, so I started slower than in my hey-day! As I gained momentum, my confidence was restored. Until I had a blow out! Arms, legs and ass come sliding across the floor a million miles an hour! No breakages and it was very hard to stop a leakage. I was laughing that much I couldn't get up. The rink announcer kept instructing me to get off the floor, for safety reasons. So I crawled off giving my friends an even bigger laugh!

Now growing up, when we had take-out, we had it by the truck load! Dad would order us two burgers each on most occasions. I think he thought that they didn't fill us up because he needed more. I was always obliged to eat every bit because of how hard he worked and didn't want him to get angry for wasting food. We always ate at the table and didn't leave until everyone had finished. We had to eat everything on our plate. Occasionally I'd find ways to by-pass the system undetected. Obviously I couldn't get rid of enough, because it did have a bearing on my weight.

For my first 12 years I was always in proportion. I did participate in a lot of activities but when we moved, I had to give away ballet and tap. (No funds or driver!) I have always been active, sometimes overactive and sometimes very lazy. With a combination of bad habits (eating everything on the plate), decrease in exercise (from what the body was accustomed to) and boredom, consequently, my weight has fluctuated throughout my life.

I have been on every diet known to man. Weight Watchers, Sure-Slim, Lite and Easy, Jenny Craig, all powder replacements, you name it over the last 27 years. At high-school I even tried binging! My theory was to eat heaps of what you like and make yourself sick so your body would learn to hate it. It didn't happen and I hated throwing up! I also tried starving myself and clearly that didn't work either.

Just before my wedding I was feeling a bit of the emotional pain because I wanted to look great for my husband and my photos. So I tried a *dodgy* doctor, he was injecting some toxin that made you lose weight fast but I knew it wasn't a healthy option. I only used his service until I was satisfied with myself. Anyway it took me a great 32 years to *personally realise* that each time I dieted, I would put on what I had lost plus a bit more. So I was done with dieting, I was happy and I wasn't focusing on my weight. Ironically, it stabilized naturally. This was probably because I wasn't messing with my core system – my mind. I wasn't ready to make the required changes to physically do anything to slim down.

Now prior to my realization, I would never have disclosed how much I weighed but I'm busting out because I have overcome the mental burden-inhibitions. At my biggest, for my sister's wedding, I weighed around 137kgs and I was happy. At my lowest in adult life, I was 78kgs. For the last 10 years I've hovered around 110. Whilst I was pregnant with Lexi I lost about 18kgs because I was ill and put some of that back on after birth. However during my realisation, without any exercise, I lost about 25kgs in 8 weeks. I had a reduced appetite because I wasn't bored, I was focused and adrenaline was the key. Bonus for me, because I have no time to exercise at the moment, not that it's ever been a priority! (Just humoring myself!) Not sure what I weigh today and it doesn't matter. Although I do need to get some smaller clothes because I still can't fit into the skinny clothes that I have kept! Buy now or later, I think I'll wait!!

That's a weight off my shoulders! While I'm at it, I might as well confess that I have been pretty crafty over my years too. Obviously I was smart or learned to be smart! Once at my Aunty's house, my brother wanted a drink, so I poured him a cup of vinegar (I was around 9 at the time.) At around 11, I told my brother that mum had brought green cordial (mum never liked this flavor so it wasn't part of the cart) and gave him a glass of that! He didn't know the dish washing detergent bottle was broken and mum used a cordial one as a replacement. My mum gave him water and effectively, my brother became a bubble machine! Payback was a bitch sometimes – I was dishing out my own karma every time I got belted for something he did.

Another great time, was in one of the Coles New World Cafeteria's. It was a great place! As a child, I loved looking at all the food on offer and dragging my tray across the rails! People chatting with one another, talking about specials, life and what was happening around town. Pity it's not like that anymore! Anyway on this occasion, my brother and I were fighting over something and I put salt in his drink. I knew he would put the pepper in mine and I also knew it wouldn't sink to the bottom like salt did. Mum made us drink it and I was better off, as I couldn't taste the pepper! You are probably thinking how does a child know this? By experimenting, always thinking ahead or free to explore – all three for me! (I wonder how many people will try this at home.)

My mum enjoys a wine now but only started enjoying the odd glass here and there over the last 10 years. When I was about 14 (25 years ago), we were at one of my dad's relative's 21stbirthday. I was pouring my mum alcoholic drinks unbeknownst to her. I would tell my uncle Henry that mum was after a special drink when he was at the bar! Well my poor mum was plastered! She was so funny and chatting away like a little girl. I think dad was embarrassed because mum ended up hurling on the front lawn! She also lost a back tooth. No-one in the family knew that mum had a false tooth. So the next day, we all had to search the front yard for this tooth. I never said anything back then because I didn't want to get in trouble. Mum had to get a new tooth put in but at least things weren't that bad financially at that stage. I wanted mum to have fun and let her hair down! Sorry mum!

As a child, I often engaged in different activities to keep me amused, and one of them was hairdressing. My brother had a couple of nice bowl cuts but luckily Aunty Sue (our neighbour) who was a hairdresser, was able to rectify my mastery with the scissors. They say practice makes perfect and I now cut Mick's hair instead. Although he never asks me after a big night unless he wants a buzz cut! The only reason for doing Mick's hair at the moment is because it's financially required. However when I do it, it takes me back to those days and I feel like a happy playful kid! As a result, Mick doesn't mind the odd boob rub in the back (wife with benefits)!

Some other favourite past times as a young child, other than singing and dancing, were teaching and retailing. I would set up a "classroom" for my brothers and sister. I would teach them how to write and spell. I also got them to do activities. I never had any ambition to be a teacher after those early years, maybe because I didn't have the patience. I used the ironing board to set up shop and would pull out cans and stuff out of the cupboards for my stall. My brothers and my sister would buy things. We'd role play and pretend to be old or famous, innocent low cost fun!

I also had a heap of fun spending time with Aunty Nadia and her girls, Natalie, Fiona and Julie. Aunty Nadia is one of Mum's greatest friends. She is a true gem, always laughing, chatting and running around. She is 70 and only looks about 50. She is very loving, kind, generous, thoughtful and giving. She would also do anything for anyone. Aunty Nadia also knew my grandmother very well and has shared some great stories with me, often over a game of cards. (That also reminds me, I use to love building houses out of a deck of cards with my grandmother and watching them come crashing down! My challenge was seeing how big I could build them before they collapsed.)

Aunty Nadia would always offer to take me to Loch Sport as a child and I loved it. Us girls rode bikes, explored the beach and the bush. We played dress ups and kicked around. We often stopped along the way, to pick up flowers on the side of the road on the way there and home. The only down side to these wonderful trips (and I was fortunate enough to have many) was the bloody mosquitoes! These blood sucking insects, some as big as birds, would leave me looking like a leper!

I enjoyed hanging out with the girls. Natalie was always the boss and still is but she was fair! She always worried about something and would keep us in line. She still tries to keep Fiona and Julie in line today and they are in their thirties. Fiona and Julie have bubbly personalities, are very caring, loving, sharing and friendly. Actually Fiona has passed on all her children's clothes to me for my children which I'm quite grateful for! It's funny because I use to get some of my hand-me-downs from Aunty Nadia. I love catching up with the girls, reminiscing about the younger days and having a good gossip of what's going on in our lives today. Mum's friend for life and her daughters are my friends for life too! A great sisterhood – I'm lucky!

Better get cracking or I'll run out of fuel – choo choo. I'll jump right into high school. I was enrolled at St. John's Regional College in Dandenong. What was great about going to this school was I got to meet up with all my other buddies from St. Anthony's too. The transition from primary school to college was easy for me. I loved the freedom of having to catch two buses because I was just outside the zone. It made me feel independent.

Mrs. Leach was my year 7 teacher and she was as blind as a bat! I often talked in class. On one occasion after being told off for the third time, my reply was "This better be important because I'm in the middle of a conversation!" I was always jovial so didn't really get in trouble. I had to stand facing the wall at the back of the class. However before moving, I asked whether she could see me as she had taken her glasses off. I guess I was cheap entertainment for the class and I always had fun!

It was a great school, full of culture. There were the skips (Australians – I assumed named after kangaroos), the wogs (Europeans), the nerds, the elite and the in-betweens! We also had a high number of deaf students who integrated really well. Then there was me, I was a combo – managed to break through all groups! I got along with everyone!

In the mornings before school, I'd often play cricket with the boys. I only ever got to field because I was a girl but that didn't bother me. When I'd had enough, I'd just move on! The boys cracked me up, any time a bird had dumped on you, they would run around yelling "Birdman", like the cartoon character.

Like primary school, we often played elastics or hop scotch in the junior years. Occasionally, the girls would shoot hoops and I'd dabble in that too! The girls mainly gossiped, admired the boys and did arty things. There were also the pranksters – me included.

Even though I was chunky, physical education (PE) was great! Lots of fun activities! It wasn't a core elective for scores in university back then but I still undertook the subject. However that was only after dropping a science class. I passed a test in physics but then decided I was never going to be a scientist so it was pointless completing the subject.

The only thing I didn't like about PE, was the posture and fat test. Like hell, I wasn't going to stand in a room with my fellow students who were all half my size! Amanda and I bailed. We headed off downtown to Dandenong, so we *"wagged"* a class. I thought there was no chance that I would get caught, because my dad was working.

On our walk, we were puffing away on a fag, when low and behold I notice my dad's car! In shock, I almost fucking swallowed the whole cigarette! I quickly threw the smoke into the garden, so did Amanda and I waved to my dad. I thought if he does see me and I didn't acknowledge him then I would appear guilty. By the time he turned around, I gave Amanda a run-down of my plan.

I told my dad I was sick, Amanda had a free elective and offered to walk me to the doctors. Dad took me to the super-clinic in Dandenong, where we normally went anyway. Those days, mobile phones weren't common place so you were able to stretch the boundaries. I faked being sick really well and then we dropped Amanda home. I didn't take the medicine I was prescribed! Doctors aren't always right!

Another time in year 12, Amanda and I decided to venture out to the city. I was working back then so I did have my own cash. We had a great day roaming the city. We rolled down the hills on the banks of the Yarra River. We thought it would be a good idea to hire a bike. We must have been checking a group of guys out when we come flying off the bike, just short of the river. We laughed, there could have even been a slight bladder leakage. We came home covered in bird shit from rolling on the hills and bruised. It was a great day!

Amanda and I had a lot in common, weight was one of them! I spent many nights staying at her house and doing "homework". She was funny, caring, kind and generous. I remember when her parents were out once and we were playing on a "CB" radio when two guys tracked us by the frequency. I nearly decapitated myself! As I was running up the drive way looking back but heading to the garage, I forgot the roller door was only half up and came crashing down on my back! I had to roll under it while Amanda shut it secure. More on Amanda later!

Back to the books, I loved the idea of learning Italian and obtained great marks in this subject. In year 10, for one Italian test, I received 99% even though everything was right. The teacher took a mark off for not adding my surname! Obviously it annoyed me, or I wouldn't be writing about it! In year 11, Mr. Piccinali was a great teacher who was very enthusiastic and fun! I remember we had to stand up in class once, one at a time and say a sentence in Italian. You had to come up with our own. I came up with "Tu hai la faccia di l'asino". (You have the face of a donkey!). The whole classroom erupted and so did Mr. Piccinali – luckily he saw the funny side!

I think the other reason why I loved Italian was because of Uncle George's influence and the fact that we often attended the Italian Club in Dandenong. It was like an "Octoberfest" for Italians but the event was every week. Great people, food, drinks, entertainment and I always loved the music and dancing! A number of my friends from school also attended these events. My dad was also the treasurer for the club for a short period of time. Forgot to mention he was great with numbers! Funny how a non-Italian was able to contribute to a marvelous club! It was because my dad was friendly and well respected, didn't matter where you came from, he was a great person.

I was always great at Mathematics too. However in year 10, we did have a teacher that had no control and was clearly not equipped to handle students. Everyone's grades plummeted and he only lasted a term. I was also good at accounting and Yvette would always get annoyed. That was the only class we had together during high school. She still talks about how I would be chatting away and then was able to answer the teacher's question. (Mrs. Bean was a female version of the Mr. Bean too!)

English was never my forte! I disliked being told what to read and I had better things to do. I generally just watched the movie or fluked it for my reviews. Anyway in year 12, Mr. Toomey my teacher advised that I was going to fail English because I didn't hand any assignments in. At the time, if you failed English you pretty much had no hope of entering university. One weekend and 6 essays later after reading two books, Educating Rita and Brave New World (they were small) I handed my work in. Obviously I didn't sleep that weekend. I managed to satisfy the internal score. Needless to say I only passed with 53% for the year! However I ended up writing countless procedures, training manuals and communications for Coles - a major retailer.

Once a year, there was a "disco" night called the "Sock Hop". It was named appropriately because we couldn't wear shoes in the gym! You had teachers on "Pash Patrol", everyone generally had a great time dancing and mucking around. I don't recall ever drinking at these events. The school also held a performance each year. I decided to audition in year 7. I didn't get a main role for the "God Spell" play and I didn't mind either! I was out of the house. I was never allowed to participate after that, as Dad found it hard to collect me after practice.

We never had the opportunity for the interstate camps that students are fortunate enough to attend these days! I attended one Religious Education camp in year 12 and I attended two ski camps that were optional for PE. The first time skiing was the funniest! It took me about an hour to gear up and then I read a sign that said beginners put skis on after taking a ride on the chair lift. (I thought I'm not wasting any time!) Bang, crash, boom, I star fished the most gorgeous looking instructor and I couldn't get up! I was laughing and said, that's one way to get a number! I was all talk but didn't mind having a go! The other major incident, no-one told me you couldn't sit on the pommers. Well I sat on the pommer, ski hits me in the head and I think I'm bleeding only to discover it was the cold ice! I also came down the mountain about halfway with my back positioned on the skiis, right in the 3 line chair lift queue! If they didn't move, I would've knocked out at least 12 people! The best thing I can remember about the RE trip was the mud walk through the bush! The rest must have been of no interest clearly!

It was funny how Yvette went to the same school but we never hung out together but have remained lifelong friends. She was always a part of the family so I guess looking back I didn't want to play with my 'sister' at school. Tanya was a friend from primary who I bounced off predominantly until year 10 when she decided she needed to move on with another group! I was cool and I didn't care, others were dismayed. It didn't bother me so it shouldn't have bothered them. It gave me the opportunity to spend time with others – too many to mention, but they all know who they are! Some I'm still in contact with on Facebook today!

Years later, I ended up catching up with Tanya at the local football and then at our 20 year reunion! She also visited just before I had Lexi, it was good to catch up! She also dropped off some clothes and a present for Lexi too. Just goes to show how people can come and go through your life. I'm not sure if she re-connected out of curiosity but it doesn't matter, she is a great person who is very kind and caring. We haven't had the opportunity to catch up in person recently but we do on the odd occasion through Facebook.

Before I forget, Summit if you are reading this, I recall we had a bet of who would make a million by the time we were 30! I hope you did because I didn't and money has never been a driver for me! I did enjoy attending a co-ed school. When it came to boys, I did pass on the odd "crush" letter but I didn't have a "boyfriend"! It was never important to me either! I didn't even "pash" anyone at school come to think of it! I certainly made up for that later in life!

For schoolies, I went to Bali with 6 others. I was surprised my dad allowed me to go because I wasn't quite 18, I had to pay for my holiday. On the day of departure my Dad said he would refund my money and buy a car because he didn't want me to go! I didn't expect or want my dad to buy me a car and exploring was more important for me. It was a great start to traveling aboard and I had an awesome time. I loved the culture, people, weather and relaxed environment. Bartering was fun too, I'd bargain down as low as I could and then would give more! I fell out of a ute on a pub crawl and won a few drinking competitions, which put me in good stead for university! Came home with a heap of presents for the family, braided hair and a tan – a great 2 weeks spent with Lee-Anne, Shaun, Paul, Penny and can't remember who else!

Although school was important, my homework or what happened at school was of little interest to my parents. Mum was always busy with the younger ones and didn't have the academic background. Dad's distraction was work. He really didn't have a great education either! I guess that's why it was so important to him! I was told to do my homework but it was never checked. Most of the time I listened to music, I sometimes completed the work depending on how I felt. I did have varying grades (A/B's up to year 10 and B/C's in year 11/12 except English and Religious Education which were Ds) but ultimately it was about learning subjects of interest and self-ambition that made school so enjoyable and worthwhile attending, along with hanging out with my friends.

Upon completion of year 12, I knew I was destined for university! However it wasn't exactly what I wanted nor did I know what to do! I had thought about becoming an actress for the simple reason I could be anything! I did audition for the Victorian College of the Arts but obviously the structured activities didn't allow me to shine or I was shit at it!

So I made Dad happy, I managed to get into Maths & Computer Science at Swinburne University in 1991, for half a year. I didn't even know how to turn on the computer. The only subject I passed was accounting (without opening a book) and drinking! I knew my time was up when the "Dean" called me in! He did me a favour, meant I didn't have to pay fees for the rest of the year! I didn't have to explain myself to Dad because I was 18 by then!

Actually I think it was a bit of a relief for him. A few months before, it was the Easter Fest at Ethal Hall and we had to build beer pyramids. Well we didn't have to, but I wanted to partake in the fun! I was with my water skiing buddies and at one stage was anchor! Anyway we were just about done when I placed the can on the construction site and it came crashing down! Gee it was a great day but I returned home plastered (drunk). I was meant to be home to baby sit the others because Mum and Dad were going to bingo. I caught the last train & last bus and arrived home very happy! Dad yelled at me but I didn't get a hit, nearly 18 at that stage! He said "you're drunk". I replied "yes that would be correct!" It left him with nothing to say and I went to bed! Tables were starting to turn in my favour!

Just one more story for that year, I attended a water skiing trip that was out of this world. I broke the bottle of booze I brought at the shop, so had to buy another! I accidently left my bathers at home so had to ski in shorts and t-shirts. The camp fire was like a scene out of "Stand by Me" because I had a name for drinking. I accepted a challenge to scull beer from the tap. My opponent managed 12 seconds and I managed 14, I had to be sure I won. With that, we both looked at each other, when he burped, beer flew from the site to the camp fire, and mine almost went to the river! (It felt like that but it wasn't that bad – don't recommend pumping your guts with that much gas, it's unsightly!) You would think that was enough, but no! I continued to drink spirits and sculled a flask of bourbon! Everyone was counting down, 10, 9, 8, 7, 6, 5, 4, 3, 2 and they were right I couldn't remember one! Apparently I threw up and started a chain reaction! I was surprised I woke so spritely in the morning and was thankful that my friends looked after me! Unfortunately I didn't manage to keep in contact with any from that year even though Mel T was a great friend then! Would love to know what she is up to now!

One night at Mel's house, she found me in her lounge room. I was standing asleep between the curtains. I frequently walked in my sleep when I was young. Mum once caught me heading out the back door when I was planning on watering the garden. Another time, when I was much younger, I accidently stepped on my dad's privates. (We were staying at my Aunty's because she had an air conditioner and my parents were sleeping on the floor.) Although I don't sleep walk now (maybe I'm too lazy) I have been known to speak a foreign language fluently, so I have been told. (Sorry to deviate again! Mel would have a laugh over that incident, if the book ever finds its way into her hands. I nearly peed in her drawers too that night on my sleep walking adventure. I must have thought it was the toilet!!)

So with my jagged start to university, I continued to work for the remainder of the year and decided later what I planned to do! I forgot to mention I started at Coles on the 21/6/1989. One of my first great and dearest friends from that time and still is; is Mich. She is very confident, straight to the point, funny, loving, caring, generous and kind! I always had a room at her house. We would often go clubbing together and run wild!

Her Mum was great too, she fussed over us! Mich and her Mum loved to "doll" me up with make-up! I was never into it because it just didn't feel right! I felt like a clown. Anyway on one occasion, we thought it would be a great idea to tame the brows! Well when the strip was pulled and we looked it at, I thought I'd lost an eye brow! Funnily enough it was fine, nice little bit left! Hair-larious!

Mich's mum was great because I could talk to her about anything, sex included. She was one of my mum's growing up and still is! I often enjoyed the Boxing Day's we had together with all their family! I'm always remembered for my antics as well! Like turning up in a clown suit or painting the kids' faces and of course prancing around being drunk!

Mich, Michaela and I decided to dress up for Halloween for an event at the local night club once! I think we were the only 3 that had dressed up! Mich and I were witches and Michaela was a pumpkin! I loved the idea of harassing others and being incognito! I never got to "pash" anyone that night probably because I had to keep emptying the sweat that formed in the nose! No skin off my nose, just sweat!!

In 1995 at 22, I told Mich I was booking a Contiki trip to America. I planned to start in New York and end up in Los Angeles, then head to Hawaii for a real rest! Mich wasn't going to come but decided she didn't want to miss an opportunity! We had an awesome time! Bungee jumped in Florida and sky rocketed. We nearly were abducted by a black van, can't remember where that was! In New Orleans, I jumped for the ground thinking there was a gunman! It was the 4th of July and I didn't realise it was part of the celebrations in America.

I loved BB Kings, the drinks called Hurricanes (which when I think about it, seems odd given the devastation that area has endured!) and Bourbon Street! Our tour guide said you could probably only drink about 2 of those drinks! I had 5 and ended up being escorted home by fellow friends! Poor Mich came back to the room and was trying to get back in. I was so toxic that I just kept waving back at her!

I also remember catching a cab with Mich, Stefanie and Lisa and asking the driver how he managed to get a bullet hole in his windscreen. He said that he was shot at for no reason in broad daylight! We all sank into our seats. The South Africans weren't perturbed by any run down of each city because they were accustomed to this sort of violence! So it was an eye-opener for us Aussies.

Another time Mich and I walked into a no-go zone! It happened without us realising, one street block, that's it! We quickly got out of there once we felt eye's piercing on us! We also had this dude in Savannah laughing and chatting to us, until he was asked to leave the venue we were at! Upon leaving, he banished his gun and we thought wholly fuck, lucky we were nice to him! I'm grateful that guns are not part of our culture here in Australia!

In Anaheim, having dinner at our hotel, we got chatting to these high flyers for a prominent baseball team (so they said), they were in their 40-50s, I think. Anyway they loved the way we talked, what we talked about and our antics – we were blind drunk! They were planning on picking us up in a limo and taking us to spur on the boys before a game! Now Mich and I decided it wasn't a great idea and never showed up! But you didn't have to be smart to realise that if they were who they said they were, what the hell were they doing at our 3-star hotel? Basic logic and observations can keep you out of harms way! It may have been valid but not worth the risk girls!

Ok so I deviated again. I started as a checkout chick and loved chatting to my customers. If I saw dog food on the belt, I'd talk about dogs. If there were nappies, I spoke about kids, even though I didn't have any! I often threw in my own review of a product and commented on the price of things! I was generally in demand and it made the time go quick. Customers enjoyed heading to my work station over others. I did proceed to work in the office and learned a great deal. I learned a heap on payroll, cash management, book keeping and store procedures. It was great ground work and I loved the friends I worked with. I even changed prices on the weekend when the shop was shut. I often kept an eye on the prices because I had a sharp memory and even back then the fluctuations were as great as my weight! It's just more noticeable now because there is little to go around and everyone wants a piece of your hard earned cash!

Heading back to education, I decided to complete a TAFE course in Business Management 1992/93 and performed really well! It was a great transition from high school and was more personal and conducive to learning! At university, you just felt like part of a herd!

Now there was one teacher and I never expected to find myself in this position! He had talked about his travels and I innocently said I would love to check out his photos. He invited me over for lunch one day! I accepted and he planned to pick me up! I did have a car but for some reason he insisted. Well when I arrived, he mentioned that he had recently corrected exams and he hadn't done mine yet! I said "I don't need to know that!" Score it how you should! Marks weren't a priority for me! Hmm I knew I could smell a rat!

He asked whether I wanted to watch a video, thinking it would be from a holiday! Instead he put on a pornographic movie! I played cool, pretended Humphrey Bear was on and didn't look at that TV. It was on for a good half hour while I was talking shit. I don't even remember what I was talking about but when we sat down for lunch, (I just said as a matter of fact) "can you turn this shit off!'. I ate lunch and said I had to be home because Stephen and I were catching up! With that, he insisted he take me home on his motorbike! I was cringing the whole way home! Thank goodness I never came across him again! I guess being innocent and naive can be a disadvantage but what you learn from it, is the key to becoming smarter or street wise! Maybe I was just too trusting!

I met my first love Stephen in the first few months of TAFE. We had a great time studying together. Cooking, movies, playing pool (he participated in competitions) and just enjoying each other's company. Stephen was very mysterious, had long hair and had these wild blue eyes. Some often felt uncomfortable because of this stare he had, I found it intriguing! He was very reserved and quiet, which is odd because I'm not! He was very caring, giving, thoughtful, playful and kind. I couldn't ask for more in a man really, I was extremely happy in his company! Except you are probably going to laugh and I loved him like no other but we never had sex (well I guess it would have been called making love). After two years, we did dabble in foreplay but when I declared my love for him, it wasn't meant to be!

He explained that we both had university, we both wanted to travel and we should remain as friends. I was totally sweet and respected where he was coming from! In essence, I wanted to travel and do things too, if it wasn't meant to be together, I accepted that! No point forcing someone to do something they don't feel comfortable with. We still remained friends however only for a short time after!

I'm going to have to back track! Hold on to your seats, I'm throwing the train into reverse! Just realised I missed a whole chunk of me moving out of home! I moved out when I was 19, after I had saved for and purchased a second hand (used) car. Finally I could be totally free. I never looked back and always did what I chose or wanted. It was about having fun and enjoying life!

At the time, dad was furious because I was doing a fair bit around the house, like paying bills. Driving my mum around and helping with chores. I needed to break away, I was always independent. My dad said "If you want to go and live a life getting into drugs, don't expect to come back here!" Tough love, I responded with "Well if that's how you think you brought me up, then I haven't failed!" Basically turning it around on him! I left that day. I still kept in contact but didn't visit home for 6 months. Not because I didn't want to, I just didn't want to create any issues.

I moved in with some girls that I knew through another friend I met at work, Rachel. We had some great times and did get up to mischief. Rachel didn't live with us but was always around. Our first rental was in Mount Waverley.

Amanda from school also moved in too, with her man. Unfortunately with all the dynamic personalities in the household, friendships fizzled very quickly. Amanda's mum interfered and with good reason but the situation had nothing to do with me and we ended up disconnected. No one was really to blame and I never hold grudges. I'm a friend of hers on Facebook so who knows, she may feel comfortable catching up if she reads this. I guess I'm highlighting that if you had a good friendship in your life, seems silly to wipe them off!

Ok so I didn't really like the house, it had a bad energy about it! We were robbed once which made us feel unsafe. The other disturbing incident was Rachel had brought a guy home one night and he drugged me and another! No surprise as to what happened there! At the time, I figured I can't change anything even though I did feel dirty and disgusted. There was no hope of ever seeking justice nor would it have been possible. I didn't blame myself and moved on with life! Shit happens! I always made sure that I was diligent when it came to drinks as a result! You can't change what has happened but you are in control of how you react. As I have always tried to remain positive, I bounced back. I don't hold on to the past, if I did, it would not have allowed me to move forward and I would be imprisoned permanently!

We did move to Clayton not long after but I had to move back home after I wrote off my car! You wouldn't believe it, I hit a motor cyclist! I was taking my sister's boyfriend home. I didn't have my wallet, I had no shoes and my P plates weren't displayed. It was meant to be a quick trip! Anyway, I put my sister's shoes on, told her boyfriend to run back and grab my purse (the accident didn't happen that far away!) I then displayed my P plates – I think they had fallen down! The rider had to have a knee reconstruction but at least I didn't kill him 2 weeks before Christmas. I had to blow in to the breathalyzer which was clear and received a fine for not giving way! I was lucky, the rider was luckier and it was an innocent mistake!

I also learned the importance of not to drink and drive. I was guilty of this whilst on my P plates for a number of reasons. One, transport was an issue and I couldn't rely on my parents. I didn't intentionally drink and drive; I was just out and changed my mind. Two, if you had one drink then you might as well have many more because you were still going to get in trouble irrespective. Thirdly, I did have a close call myself as a result of being persuaded to drive. I guess I was being selfish and not considering others as some in that age group today! It was also the fact that when you consume alcohol (or drugs), it does change your behaviour and it impedes your judgments. As we know, this can be quite deadly (more on that later). However I did think to myself, if I could have killed someone inadvertently sober, how much worse would it have been if I was drunk? How would I feel? It wasn't a risk I was prepared to take anymore!

Anyway mum and dad were out and they didn't know my sister's boyfriend was visiting – so I was a great responsible sister - not! Even though I was just called on to help her out! Stephen came around that night and I think I smoked a whole packet stressing about what my options were! In the end, I figured it wasn't worth stressing over, I had to do what I had to do! Return to sender – address known, at least I have a home!

Moving back home was going to be interesting after being out for almost 2 years. I did get my own phone line so that wouldn't cause conflict and I was out as much as I could be. Stephen did come around a fair bit and stayed which was odd coming from a very strict background. I guess my dad had started to mellow! It didn't stop dad from constantly nagging but I put up with that. I spent more time at Stephen's house!

One great thing about moving back, it allowed me to have a 21st birthday party! I love parties, getting together with friends and family, food and music! Nothing better than having a great laugh and dance!

Stephen was at the party along with many friends from work. At that stage, I only kept in contact with Yvette from school.

I had a few friends from TAFE as well. There was this guy, Paul who had a crush on me and I didn't feel the same way. I was happy being friends. However on the odd occasion I did "pash" him when we were out (when drunk) prior to me being fully interested in Stephen. Unfortunately Paul liked me more than I thought of him and at my 21st he went the big French kiss. I was shocked, immediately broke loose and punched him in the face! I was also concerned it would ruin anything I had with Stephen. It was funny watching the video a few days later. I guess I never held back.

At my 21st, I was also frustrated that people were talking when I was trying to say thanks, so I gave them something to remember! I said "Shut the fuck up!" I quickly apologised and all was quiet! Many people were surprised, obviously dad was embarrassed but hey, it was my party, I can do what I want to!

In January of 1995, Duncan and I met at "Styliss" nightclub. I was with Mich and it was a night to remember! I won't go into the "50 shades of Mama". Needless to say, we clicked really well none the less and had a great time! We caught up a few times and on one occasion Stephen happened to be at home on my couch after I walked in. He said "Where the hell have you been?" This was at 2am in the morning! I replied "Out on a date! I thought we were just friends and there is no ring on my finger!" Very awkward moment because I wasn't expecting it or him to be there!

Stephen obviously wanted to talk, at the time I was working at the State Office for Coles. I remember explaining that clearly it wasn't meant to be if he couldn't be honest with me and was only telling me now that someone else was on the scene. Then I said "it's like turning a page in a book, once you read it, you don't go back!" There was no right or wrong and I did what was right for me! I did love him but it just didn't feel right to me at that time. I said to him, do what you need to do and let us see in 6 years if it's meant to be, it will be!

(We were both enrolled at university but hadn't commenced and I was doing my degree part-time – hence the six years!)

Stephen stood out the front of my house and would turn up to work on most days for about a good 2 months! He sent me the best bunch of roses I have seen and they were beautiful. In fact, I've never received a bunch like that since! He wrote me a card explaining how he felt. I still have that beautiful card and I thought about including it in my book, because it was so sweet (but will keep it to myself). I didn't feel threatened and I knew in time he would move on. He was grieving and I couldn't comfort him because I knew I would be making matters worse.

Throughout the single years, I pulled the card out to read as it made me smile and feel good about myself. Even though it didn't end the way we both would have liked it to, at the end of the day I still love him because we had something special. I'm not in love with him obviously. It's the raw emotion that forges a place in your heart. Some are lucky to have the one and only. For me, I feel luckier because I have been fortunate enough to experience three true loves. All very different and all at different stages of my life! I'd love to get the chance to be friends with Stephen again, I'm sure we'd have a great deal to catch up on!

Duncan and I spent five and a half years together and had some great times. We really enjoyed each other's company. It was through Duncan that I met Rose and her brother!

The first time I met Rose she was heading out to catch up with friends and was heading to a club. I had the brief hello and thought, well she didn't give me the time of day! At the time, I didn't realise that Rose took a while to warm to people, just her personality.

Rose's dad didn't take any time to warm to me! He had the Jack Daniels out and we were singing and chatting (about 6 weeks into my relationship with Duncan). This was after Duncan and I spent most of the day at the pub gambling and drinking so I was quite intoxicated!

Anyway I decided it was a great time to have a spa on the deck surrounded by the beautiful country side (pity it was still day light savings)! With all the Dutch courage and not a care in the world, I stripped down to my bra and knickers! Who would do this?? Luckily there was a black out by the time I got out of the spa but I did bang into a pole. Scored a black eye and Duncan of very slight frame dragged me home to his house! I knocked the poor plants off the porch and woke the next day, asking where my clothes were! Duncan said that they were at Rose's house! I came home in a towel! Lucky Vonnie (his Mum) was really great and she laughed it off!

I'm sure Rose thought I was crazy just after that incident –she would have heard about it! I still rocked up a few weeks later and had a laugh at my expense! That was in the past! Not long after, Duncan and I decided to move in together! So we moved into his factory. Duncan was a great business man, he ran a generator business and was smart with his money! I always enjoyed mine and had the attitude that life is short!

So I lived in a factory where wall and roof trusses were made! We had a bedroom, a little kitchenette, a shower and toilet. I didn't mind, as we worked and were often out so it suited us! The only thing I hated was the stinking mice and rats. They would scratch between the walls. I was in the shower once, and a mouse had run across the rails and back to the recess! The whole factory came to a halt! Duncan thought the hot water system had scolded me! The boys were all amused when I walked out for work that day!

I loved catching up with all Duncan's friends. We would often sing in Reggie's shed. I was always known for being the party chick. Once I performed my famous "roll" to Kung Foo Fighting! It was my signature party trick which I had mastered over many years of doing Judo! Everyone was in hysterics! With that, I felt obliged to do it at most parties or clubs – if given the opportunity! I was making people laugh so in turn that made me happy! (I'd be up singing on the microphone with the band and when my time was up, I'd roll off the stage! I only rolled off stage a couple of times!)

Duncan was kind, generous and caring! He was an extrovert too and had many friends, totally different to Stephen! Duncan would even lend a practical stranger $2000 and wouldn't care if he didn't get it back – when he was drunk! This was the problem! He was often drunk. It suited me during that time because I was still free to work and catch up with friends as I liked.

Just after I commenced work at the head office in 1997, he rang me and asked me to pick him up because his dad fired shots at him! Can you imagine your dad with a gun firing at you? I'd seen his dad, grab a massive wrench and was about to belt him when we ran for the car! When Duncan and I purchased our home in 1998, I was actually working at the time and hadn't seen the house! He said he had made an offer but if it wasn't suitable we could retract it!

After finishing work that day, I headed to his Dad's house and waited for Duncan. His dad said in a very nasty wicked drunken tone with an evil laugh – (all the elements for a horror movie) "You've got yourself a fucking house! If you don't like it I'll kill you!" I thought right, Duncan better get here soon!

On the way to see my new "dream" home, I mentioned the threats to Duncan! He sorted out what he could! His dad would even threaten those from government agencies that would want to collect the surveys! He would order beer by the pallet load. He had one distorted hand from blowing it up when he was in his teens! He was always fanatical about money. In my view, he tortured the souls of Duncan and his brother. So I tended to tolerate Duncan's drinking because he was a great person and I loved him. He was never violent and I knew it was a result of his past!

Before we moved into our home, I was forced to contemplate a major moment in my life with Duncan. I accidently fell pregnant! At the time, my career had just kicked off, I was a project analyst. Duncan and I were not in a position to care for a baby – emotionally! He didn't want the baby or to have kids! I also didn't want a baby at that time! I had been drinking excessively and was worried that it may have caused harm even if I did change my mind. I also wanted to travel and live more of my life, I was only 24! I also didn't view it as a baby because it was a cluster of cells! I also knew, for me, I didn't want to adopt. I also knew that I would disappoint my father having a child out of wedlock. I also thought that the abortion process had been developed for a reason and it creates an opportunity for choice. After assessing what was right for me, the risks and consequences, I had an abortion. I have never regretted that decision nor has it impacted me emotionally. I acknowledged, accepted and moved on. I did learn to be very careful from that time onwards. It was my life and my choice. At the time I was mindful of what others thought so only a handful knew! (Jodie thanks for being there for me on the day, not sure how we lost contact but would love to catch up again and see you!) I'm not afraid of being judged now! No one has the right to tell you what to do in your life, you have to do what is right for you!

Hope this helps others in some form or another. The only reason I included this and the drug rape was that people often find comfort in others misfortune. I don't think it's because people like to hear or see the pain and suffering of others. It's more about how people have come through the other end and it provides hope or guidance for those still stuck in time, dealing with the past. These were negative adult experiences that I hadn't shared with most of my family/friends and the rape only recently. Reason being that I had left them in the past and are now using these as examples! I guess I have now turned these events into a positive in an attempt to help others that may be suffering!

A few months after the abortion, a great friend was murdered in America when he was holidaying with Robyn (another great friend of mine). It was a tragic story and it's not my story to tell it in entirety. However it did affect the whole group. It was never really the same after that, there was a missing link! There was a lot of hurt and anger. It was a shame because this group had so many life time memories, all the boys had grown up together and there was a real brotherhood. It was really a sad time for all. It was the first time at the age of 24, a friend around my age had died. Again, you take stock of your life and consider what you want.

When Duncan proposed I didn't see it coming! It was around Christmas time (that same chaotic year) at Rose's house. He had purchased a ring and it was in a rose velvet box! He said "Mama, will you marry me?" I laughed and after the initial shock, I said "Yes!" (Duncan named me Mama after a few weeks of being together! He said, "I've told my friends about you" and I asked what that was, he replied "I met some funny wog Mama!" But after glares, when out in public, it was shortened to Mama. That's how 'Mama' came about!)

Not long after, I knew his drinking was always going to be a problem and I didn't expect him to change. I also began gambling on the pokies a fair bit! Once, I spent a whole wage packet. I would also head to the casino after catching up with work colleagues on Friday night drinks. This was obviously filling a void of unhappiness. At the time, I was contemplating what I should do and was stuck in transit! I knew it wasn't exactly the life I planned to live, so after 2 'breaks' which were about 12 months apart, we moved on in May 2000! Third strike you're out. Only Duncan wasn't ready to move on and was using every opportunity to rekindle.

Duncan had mentioned suicide. I was concerned about this but I also knew I had to move on. Therefore I arranged counseling and had highlighted to the counselor that I was not interested in getting back together but we needed to address emotional issues for his benefit. I thought I was helping. In actual fact, I made it worse because it gave Duncan a false sense. He thought we were getting back together. I couldn't be entirely honest with him because I didn't want to hurt him anymore. He was already suffering. Damned if you do and damned if you don't! There was no right or wrong, I was trying to find a happy median!

When we brought our property in Narre Warren, I contributed around $15000 and paid the mortgage whilst Duncan took care of his business. I was earning good money as a Project Manager (I was promoted after 2 years) and it worked for us. After about 6 months, Duncan decided to pay the house in full! In light of no mortgage payments, I paid for groceries and bills. I always paid my way! Upon parting, I only requested $25000, quite a significant amount less to what I was entitled to. But for the sake of keeping friends (money was important to him) and mutual friends, I didn't argue for more. I waited over a year to receive my share. Even though I could have fought to get my money earlier, I let it go until he was ready. One, I didn't want to engage a costly lawyer and I didn't really need the money straight away. We brought the house for $92000 in 1998 and sold it in 2001 for $143000. Amazing how prices have skyrocketed over the last 11 years – the house would be worth around $350,000 in today's market!

I had already purchased a ticket to travel to Europe. I did ask Duncan if he wanted to come before we split up but he chose not to. I suspect that he may have been hurt by me taking control of what I wanted to do! Yvette and Lu didn't want to travel to Europe and enjoyed a 2 week cruise instead, with another friend Anita!

I met Lu around the time Duncan and I split. Lu is a very loving caring, giving, thoughtful and funny person! We are like soul sisters too! Just love to have fun and help others, she would do anything for anyone! We have had many a great times together and like Yvette, could tell you many more stories about me than me!

We both participated in a Muddy Buddy event with some of my work colleagues. It was like a fun marathon at a winery. It was when I was right into exercising (baha). We had been out and returned at 3am in the morning on the day of the event. Lu drove, she didn't drink that night. I borrowed a bike from Craig and Linda – gorgeous couple! I lit up a smoke and had a test ride. I hadn't been on a bike since I was 12. I was aware that all the health fanatics were looking at me but I didn't care!

This race was in 2 parts, one completed the run and the other completed the bike ride, then you had to swap. There were obstacles on the 9km bike track and for the 6km run there were wine stops/slippery slide and other hurdles like, walking through a lake. I hadn't even got through a quarter of the bike ride when the next group had started.

I was laughing the whole way, wondering what Lu was up to! Many strangers were offering words of encouragement! I had a ball! When I finally finished on the bike and started my run, I walked the whole way! I clawed up the vines, thinking "I wish there was a bean stalk". I slid down the slippery slide all by myself – all competitors had finished! Instead of walking through the lake, I swam.

There was no wine tasting by this stage because they were setting up for the kids event. The champions came in at 43 minutes and won a trip to participate at an event in America. I had reached the finish line with everyone chanting Mama! It was awesome. Lu and I managed the course in 1 hour and 45 minutes! Not bad for someone who drank until 3am, smoked just before the race and never exercised!

After the race they had prizes to give out and Lu and I won prizes for the most determined team! I also ended up buying a $600 bike! I was drunk after many bottles of wine by then. But the money was going to charity and it was an opportunity to provide for a good cause. It was also a tax deduction for me! I had fun riding the bike with another lady in a lap of honor that I initiated– just spur of the moment stuff for me! (We purchased them via auction as the claimants of the prize were not there to collect them.) I also got up on stage as I often did when I was out and sang with the band! I've never been scared to have fun – I just live a happy life! At the time, I thought I'd tick another thing off my list to do before I hit 30. (Craig, I still have that bike and would love to catch up!)

Anita was Wally's sister but I'll talk about Wally first because I met him first – logical! Wally is another soul brother. We always enjoy each other's company, especially over a beer! He understands my stupid cryptic humour and we have always gotten along. When he first met Donna who is straight to the point, honest, kind, caring, giving and loving (like Wally – no point repeating myself), I would give Wally tips on what to do! Where to take her out! Most the time it was with Duncan and I.

On one occasion, I encouraged Wally to put on a pair of my bathers under his clothes. When we were out and dancing to the band, I cheered him on to strip! We were all drunk and it was funny! No one expects a grown man to strip and see a pair of ladies bathers underneath! Wally and I have always been on the same channel! We are just happy living our life! (Obviously I met Wally through

Duncan!) I have so many great memories and I'm sure there will be many more to come. Again Duncan had given me so much more, I'd met many great friends. If only people could view in total what they have gained when parting ways and appreciate each other, I have no doubt many more would be happy in life! Being bitter and angry only holds us back! I never once blamed Duncan or myself for our relationship coming to an end; it was a life experience with so many memories and friends. Another example of how to keep balanced during a challenging time!

Back to the single days, Anita had recently split with her boyfriend at the time so she joined the singles crew! At that stage, all of us were late 20's and single. When one of us found a boyfriend, we would countdown and say "then there were 3" (meaning left on the shelf). Anita is kind, passionate, loving and caring and she has always been there too! That was the original awesome foursome (– not that we called ourselves that, it just came to me then!)

So mid-June I caught a plane on my own heading to Europe, I had an absolute ball! I visited London, Scotland, Spain, Italy, Greece, Germany, Prague, Belgium and France in 13 weeks. I couldn't get more time off work and I did contemplate quitting to travel more extensively. However I hadn't finished my degree and I still needed to sort out finances with the house.

I spent 2 weeks in Scotland and could have spent a whole lot more time there. Edinburgh was fantastic and I loved the comedy festival. I loved how the bars were open at 7am for those that had worked night shift and for the odd traveler. I found an appreciation for soccer after watching a Celtic game with this "mad" supporter! He was a walking billboard for the team and was so passionate! I thought it was great that he was happy being himself! Crazy in a good way!

I also enjoyed a quaint little Island called the "Isle of Wight". The architecture, cobbled streets and atmosphere were what I expected of Scotland! "Ai" all the people were so friendly too! The castles were grand and so were the highlands! All my life, I've always had an akin with the Scottish and I don't know why! I honestly thought I'd meet someone and live a "happily ever after" but it didn't happen with a Scotsman!

Spain was everything it should have been. The clubs, the food, the siestas, the people, the culture – I could have easily lived there! The street markets were awesome too. Gaudi's artist work and architecture was truly brilliant. I was in awe! I hope I get the opportunity to visit this place with Mick and the family someday.

I also had the pleasure of meeting an Aunty of my dad's - Musette. She lived in an apartment in Madrid and was very superstitious. I didn't realise that she knew so much about me! It must have been my dad's Aunties in Australia who kept her updated. Dad and my uncle David disconnected as a result of managing my grandma's estate and hadn't spoken or seen each other for 20 years! (All over money - how many times do you hear of this happening?) Musette looked exactly like my grandma. She loved music, was very kind, generous and loving. I had never met her and she treated me like a daughter.

Musette never had children and never married. She was very lonely and had no other relatives in Spain. She also feared the streets because of being robbed a number of times. I asked why she hadn't moved to London where another member of the family was or with her sister. Her sister was in Tehran, so that would have been challenging for her given the volatile environment.

Her reply was that her previous partner would seek the rights to her home and she would have nothing. My immediate thought was that she had little in terms of life but was sacrificing it for the sake of a little run-down apartment. After 2 weeks in and around Spain I had to move on, she splashed water down the stairs in the hope I would return one day! I don't think I will see her there if I do manage to get the chance again, because I did hear not long after that she made the move to France.

I travelled through the South of France and loved all the villages and was on my way to Italy. Wow what a great place. I loved Venice, Florence and Rome. The history, the food, the music, the people and the language! It was about 6 weeks into the trip that I wished I could share these moments with someone! I met heaps of friends along the way but it was more about sharing that time when I returned home. If your friends and family are not with you – they could not fully appreciate the experience.

While in Rome, I met Patrick who was from Belgium. It was a holiday romance that should have never happened and a case of be careful of what you think!! I guess I was feeling a little lonely. I did enjoy his company whilst travelling around Italy and we did meet up again in Amsterdam. That was after I had been to Greece, Germany and Prague which were all great too!

I spent a week at the October fest, most as a foreigner in the German tents! There was an Aussie/English tent which was great but I wanted to experience the authentic German experience! Ah Proste! I saw all the National sites that I could and was astounded that you could smoke in the shops and take your pets into restaurants as well! I felt physically sick after visiting Dachau. It was a somber day respecting those that had suffered and died; and appreciating those that survived such a horrific time! It was also great to visit Berlin and the fallen wall which is testament to how society can overcome actions of the past!

When traveling to Prague, I decided to hitch hike through an organized company! Great set up! This guy was in his 40's and couldn't speak a word of English but we managed. He picked me up from the designated spot and he took me back to his apartment! (I thought hello! What the fuck am I going to do here?) My luggage was in the car. Although he didn't seem like the type to render harm I thought I'd give him the benefit of the doubt. Anyway he obviously needed a shower and had to collect things! Next minute he walked in the sitting room with his dressing gown! (I thought I should have run!) Next minute I hear a key being turned in the door and thought, I can handle one but two?

Luckily it was his girlfriend and after he got changed we hit the road! What a ride! He was doing about 200km per hour! I loved it but was clutching the seat at the same time! I wasn't taking a risk by just hitchhiking with anyone– it was a reputable company that connected people for the purpose of transport. Unfortunately there were riots in Prague and come to think about it, there were some in Spain when I was there too! It provided an insight of how violent demonstrations were but I never felt unsafe, I just stayed away from the mayhem!

I loved the beautiful Greek Islands, so different in contrast to other islands! Athens itself was good but very busy!

Oh Amsterdam, what a great place! I don't know if it was the herbal smokes I indulged in or if the streets were all over the place but I always felt lost in this city! It was diverse, vibrant and awesome! People were free to be themselves. I loved how everyone rode bikes through the city and past the canals! (Just for the record – everything is good in moderation!)

I enjoyed talking to Patrick during my travels and he planned to meet me in Amsterdam. So I spent my time exploring sites with him there, in Belgium and Paris! However although he was a nice man, I had no intention of having a long term relationship. I even told him that but he was convinced he would come to Australia! I didn't think he would and was planning on dealing with that when I returned home if it happened.

At that stage, I was briefly living with my sister. My sister was dating Rose's brother. I was meant to be renting his property. However my sister's friends from overseas were using it. After 6 weeks, I moved out, not without fuss mind you! After paying for food, telephone bills and using my company car for trips etc. my sister wanted money for electricity and gas! I said to her "If you can work out the exact cent of how much I owe, I'll give it to you! I can't believe you are my fucking sister!" I wasn't even home most of the time.

My sister was fortunate or maybe unfortunate (still haven't worked that out) to receive an inheritance from Aunty Margaret's estate. She was entitled to this after Uncle Andy (Margaret's husband) who was an alcoholic, died around 1993. It was left to her because they were her godparents and they had no children. My brothers and I never complained and have always made our own way in life! We don't expect handouts but I know if I was in her position, I would have shared. My brothers and I are not the jealous type and never expected to receive a cent.

I was however pissed off at her for even asking for money for the utilities. She was looking after her friends by having them stay at Rose's brother's house and then wanting to charge me! (There have been so many incidents but I will only share a few!) She said mum owed her $5 for a table cloth one day and I asked, why would you expect mum to pay for that? When you drop your washing off and you go eat there all the time. On a trip back from Sydney, in my company car, she wanted to travel all the way home so we didn't have to pay for accommodation. She refused to drive. I pulled up when I had enough, I threw her the keys and said enjoy your sleep. She ended up paying half the motel room. You get the drift, I accepted her for who she is and she wasn't going to change.

However as part of what has recently transpired, I had to address this for me because she was telling others that I have been *different*. She was very negative towards me during that time. She said to my husband "Who is smart now, being in a psyche ward?" She told others how bad my house was and that she was embarrassed. In the past, it hasn't always been about money, she once said when I was at my lowest weight – I better get to the gym because you can't be skinnier than me! Was it all about insecurity, jealousy or competition? Most my friends disliked her for this reason, where as I always protected her and said it's just her! (I guess I expected more from my sister when I needed support, not destructive comments/opinions.)

I couldn't understand why she behaved like this, knowing that she had a great start to life! She invested her money in two units, traveled, studied hospitality and worked but was very covetous when it came to money! She did help mum and dad out and so she should have! I believe the money should have gone to Mum. She cared for Aunty Margaret until she passed away with cancer!

Even though she was financially very stable, she expected Mum and Dad to financially contribute to her wedding (and they did when they were still under financial duress)! Dad even tiled their new house at no cost and had to bring his own lunch. Where were the same morals that the rest of us had obtained? Was it a different experience or event that occurred that changed her? Was it her attitude? Was it her core traits? I have always accepted her for who she is and never complained or made it an issue. I would be damned if I did. People don't like hearing the truth, if they are not willing to accept! I had given her the opportunity so it wasn't as if I was ignoring these challenges.

I can't control how she will react but I do know that it is a lesson for both of us, whichever way it pans out! Hopefully she'll see that I'm highlighting this to provide an example of the different angles of viewing things for a good reason and purpose. I didn't ask to be treated this way; I've always been about respect. Treat others how you'd like to be treated. Was she respecting me? And yet I still feel guilty writing about it. There is no right or wrong, it's about how I felt. I'll guess I'll find out if honesty is the best policy! (Sorry for deviating again, it's easier than back tracking later.)

So after moving and a world wind holiday, I kept in contact with Patrick. He then said he had brought a ticket and was packing up everything to be with me in Australia. I told him not to come for me and if he wanted, just come for a holiday! I thought what have I got myself into? I can't recall how many times I expressed not to come over but he was adamant. I didn't know I had "bitch" in me until he arrived...

The first sign was I accidently jammed his fingers in the window after I picked him up from the airport. The sight of him made me apprehensive and I felt obliged to entertain the notion of being a couple. He treated me like a princess. He would cook for me whilst I went to work. He picked flowers, he'd rub my feet and give me massages. However I was not attracted to him but I couldn't tell him that he was actually repulsing me! One - because I felt guilty that he packed up and left his home for me! I then thought, I didn't ask him to do it or lead him on! I was honest but I couldn't control his ambition. He also couldn't work in Australia and I was supporting him! His father was wealthy but didn't help him out! It got to a point, where I became nasty. He cooked apples and chicken together once, and I said "What the fuck is this?" Yvette was living with me at that stage and she thought I was being harsh. She didn't know how I felt! I guess looking back I was trying to get him to see sense! By me treating him badly, he would lose interest. I was so desperate that I propositioned a friend to spike up a relationship with him to free me! I said "If you're my real friend and want to help me out and you do like him, I think you should make a move! I so think you'd make a great couple!" Their encounter didn't last long.

The funniest though was when Yvette and I had planned a double holiday prior to the bust up and Patrick's friend from Belgium was joining us. It was meant to be a couple double booking but when I got to reception, I said to the lady, Yvette and I have a room booked. She said that's odd, "I have a Patrick". I replied, "No definitely not, you must be mistaken, we're together!" We avoided them like the plague and only saw them when we had to catch the plane home.

Duncan and I started heading out as friends. We always enjoyed each other's company. When I was whining to him about Patrick, he said "I thought that is what you wanted". I replied, "I did but obviously it wasn't with the right person!" I was contemplating getting back with Duncan but didn't know for sure. After assessing what had emerged over the years, where I had come from and what I was prepared to risk both for myself and his sake. I decided it shouldn't be. However it did allow us to remain friends, even though we didn't see each other often. Generally, it was at a party or at his brother's house.

I managed to get rid of Patrick for a few weeks because we headed to Sydney for New Year. I dropped him off at one of his friend's houses that he'd met on his travels! Anyway I was partying with Rose's brother and my sister in Bondi and Coogee. My sister was busy catching up with her traveling buddies so Rose's brother and I headed back into town to King's Cross.

On the way to the cross in a cab, he farted and blamed me. I just rolled with it and said "better out than in!' Well the taxi driver didn't find this funny and stopped the car. He ran to the back of his cab and was dry reaching. He gets back in the cab and starts hurling abuse - "That was inhumane! You call yourself a woman?" Rose's brother and I couldn't stop laughing! I thought what cheek, you smell of body odor and are accusing me of a vial smell my friend produced!

We had a ball and enjoyed the live "transvestite" shows. It is such a diverse and awesome place to visit and again, people are free to be who they are! That's what makes it so exciting. Rose's brother and I are the same, we get along with everyone and just like to live and have fun!

Actually I've always had a brilliant time in Sydney! I love the area by the rocks! The Orient pub is a classic venue! Music always playing and all walks of life interacting having a great time! There is an Irish pub just a couple doors down and some other places that are hip and cool. One night with my sister, Kirrily (a great friend who lived with me for over a year) and I walked out of the Orient down to the water. On one of my urges, I slapped two cops on the ass! They were facing the water and quickly turned round! I said "Cop that! I'm from Melbourne, I'm here for a good time, not a long time! Can you show me the sites around town in the divvy! I'm after a bit of excitement!" Further adding, "It's one of my things to tick off my list before 30." They saw the funny side as they knew I was only joking. Even though I was drunk, I was prepared for that ride or being locked up but ended up with a handful of photos with the lovely policemen instead!

Some people may deem this as crazy and you are entitled to an opinion! I was living life, having harmless fun! I better add I don't want to encourage this behaviour either as it could get out of hand! Everyone is different and it was about timing and the way I executed it! I'm not setting a precedent for it to become a phenomenon! People would often ask me what I'm on; I'd say life and a couple of drinks! I didn't need to use heavy drugs!

Patrick did return! Like fook, this was a boomerang for sure! In the end, after 4 months, I said it was time to go! It was Labour Day and I booked his return flight and dropped him off at the airport. There was no "wish him well as you wave goodbye!" It was a drop and run! Now I do feel bad about what had happened. I could have probably dealt with the situation a lot better, looking back now. I didn't mean to hurt him and I'm sure if I see him again, I could explain where I was coming from and apologise. I hope it didn't adversely affect his life but essentially I had to think of myself. I'm only human!

In effect from May 2000 – March 2003, I lived a single life and loved every minute. I enjoyed going out, catching up with friends and spending my surplus money on having fun! Lu and I would always go out living the single life. Once we even crashed a party in Brighton (an affluent area of Melbourne)! I came striding down the drive-way into the back yard and starting singing "Happy Birthday to ya" (Mama Style) and the party boy said "Thanks but who are you?" We just told him the pub had closed and it looked like a great place to stop! Next minute, Lu's the resident DJ and I'm pouring shots!

Easter trips to Bendigo were a blast! The first year we ended up there unexpectedly. Duncan had headed up to Echuca to water ski with Rose and her friends. Yvette, Lu and I were on our way there, however he must have pissed me off because on the way I said to the girls, let's spend Easter in Bendigo! We managed to get accommodation at a motel that had a bar but the room and facilities were basic. We didn't care we were there for the party and fun!

We'd ended up at the local pub in PJ's on one occasion. Another incident, I asked a random guy to hide under boxes nearby on the street (in the very early hours of the morning), whilst Lu and Yvette were getting food. When they returned, I said "Lets take a picture (with my pretend camera). I then proceeded to say "work with me, work with me now step back!" That was the cue for the guy to jump out! Fook it was funny! CCTV would have been priceless.

Once we had the motel door open and this albino dog came charging in. Lu and Yvette are not fond of dogs and left me to sort it out while they resorted to the bathroom. This dog started humping the bed, it was funny! I didn't want to be the next victim! I managed to find some chips and threw them outside the door to coax the dog out! It stalked us for a good 20 minutes. When we told the people at the bar, they had never seen or knew anyone that had an albino dog! We always attracted something strange!

At the "Sundowner" hotel in Bendigo, we were busting a move and playing pool when a girl (stranger) came up to me and said "were you at Mount Hotham ski resort last year?" I said "yes", she remembered me from one of the bars! She said she recalled that night because I was helping myself to the bar after it had closed and couldn't believe how much I got through– Rose had connections and this girl knew the owner too! The girls always cracked up because I was always bumping into people I knew or who knew me! It even happened when I was in Queensland (Interstate) and Overseas!

Bali was an awesome trip away with Lu and Yvette. Yvette's dad suddenly passed away in 2001 and I thought the first Christmas would be hard so suggested that we head overseas. Lu arrived on Christmas day but Yvette and I arrived two days prior. Well we had that many laughs I could write a whole book about that trip alone.

Christmas Eve, Yvette and I decided to take a dinner cruise. Besides us and two other boys, we were the only Aussies. I couldn't eat the buffet and the music was all Japanese! Seriously it was like we were in Japan (must head there one day and experience the real country). Anyway Yvette and I befriended these two guys and we just drank up on deck. When it was time to depart, I had missed a step and came down about 20 steps as fast as a bullet. How I didn't hurt myself is beyond me! You could almost see a dint in the steel plate around the ship because I hit it that hard! I think Yvette nearly wet her pants and the boys were speechless until I started laughing!

Another time, we headed to Denpasar to do some shopping. Anyway the beamo (taxi) pulls up and our driver says "sorry girls no farking here!" I couldn't help myself and politely said "Why is there no fucking here?" Small things amuse small minds but we laughed the whole time shopping and we had a great time with him on the way back to Kuta!

The Sari club was our favourite place and we spent every night there, bar two out of 16 nights. The only reason why I couldn't make those two nights, I was chained to the porcelain bowl! I had a bad case of Bali Belly! I went through 6 rolls of toilet paper within an hour. The Imodium took a while to kick in and I ended up finishing the packet. It was ridiculous but I was "ore" right by the time Lu and I went white water rafting!

The Sari bar employees were fantastic, they knew us all by name and what we drank. I assume they did for everyone because that's how they roll with things. We'd dance with them and have a chat! I think I even helped them clean up a few times. We just loved the music and atmosphere. It really hit home when terror struck in Bali especially when we were there to celebrate in the New Year of 2002. I cherish those times I spent there with Yvette and Lu because we will never have a holiday like that again! As we won't be the same age, we have different lives now and the place would be different not just from the physical aspect but the sense and feel. However, me being optimistic, I'm sure we could create great new memories with our families, if the opportunity arises in the future.

Yvette and Anita found love again in 2001 so they joined us out until they settled down. Robyn (who grieved for her lost love and didn't really go out for 7 years) came out with us! I think it was the third night out and she met the love of her life! We still remain in contact; she is a great friend who is caring, loving and thoughtful too. Rose started heading out with us in 2002 as a "singles" group. Race days were always a favourite, as our time down at the Berwick Pub, Blitz and Lava Lounge. (The Hallam had changed by then, much to everyone's disappointment and didn't have live entertainment!) Funny we've all been in relationships for a few great years and thankful we've all found some loving!

Choo choo chugging along! Now we're down to the last nine years! I attended Rose's brother's wedding held in a marquee at his in-laws property. The next day I unexpectedly met Mick. It was Labour Day weekend and exactly a month before I hit 30. I was planning on heading to the city that Sunday night with Kirrily! Plans changed because after sleeping in my car, I decided to continue drinking!

I didn't place any expectations on myself about having a boyfriend, children or marriage. I was happy living life and if the opportunity arose then great! So I spent about $7000 on my 30th birthday party – thinking that was my equivalent of getting married! It was a 70's theme and was held at the Berwick Pub, with all food and drink supplied. It was a great night! I performed my musical speech, did my standard party roll trick, had a dance off and we had a fashion parade for the best dressed! I honestly never thought my future husband would be there to celebrate with me!

Kirrily (from Sydney) a gorgeous, spiritual, caring, thoughtful and intelligent friend was living with me. Actually my sister had introduced us! My sister met Kirrily on her travels and encouraged her to live with us in Melbourne! Not long after, my sister treated Kirrily poorly and things were strained. Anyway, Kirrily was happy to head to the local pub instead.

We were heading off with Ponter! This was after Ponter and Dutchman were running around nude doing a "Benny Hill" act! The after wedding drinks were coming to an end! Ponter is a classic clown! An extravert, vibrant, lively, funny and not scared to be himself! When I see him, he gives me an "Ah Mama, great to see ya and plants a kiss on my cheek!" I had often headed out with Rose's brothers friends in a group during my single days because we always had fun, plus it was safe too!

When Kirrily, Ponter and I headed to the middle pub in Pakenham, I was well and truly ready for a great afternoon and evening! We played pool and sang with the one man acoustic guitarist! I had the odd dance move happening and swung the pool cue around like a microphone too! We were in shouts and when I gave Ponter his, I was introduced to "Gazelle" (my Mick) and a couple of others.

Now Mick took a real interest in me straight away but I wasn't interested. I was happy to chat! I said "Kirrily, he is hovering like a helicopter!" Kirrily kept saying he was 40 and so not my type! Mick wasn't my type but then what was my type? I didn't even know! I guess I never pictured being with someone so fair with blue eyes because I'm totally opposite! (He is five years older than me as I later found out!)

By 9pm, Mick was trying to make a move! He asked where I was heading to! I said to visit my sister at the Hallam. Next minute he said there was a taxi for us! I said "See ya! Mama's mix at 9 is still playing (I had selected some songs on the juke box) and I still had 2 bourbons in front of me!"

So he waited and waited until I was ready to move. Mind you he was encouraging Kirrily to talk me around! Anyway he turned out to be a great guy obviously! We talked about everything you could think of! Somehow we were both at the same stage in life! We had similar values and beliefs, attitudes and personalities! The only thing I was apprehensive about was him having children!

I always said I would never get involved with someone who had children because I didn't want to be troubled by the baggage that came with it! I then thought why should I live with such a closed mind and deny myself the opportunity? I also thought, nothing ventured, nothing gained! I didn't really have anything to lose. However I was mindful not to venture into a serious relationship lightly as it could be disruptive or have a significant impact on the children. I obviously had a great deal to learn!

With that, I told him straight up that I treat a new boyfriend like a pregnancy, only tell people about the relationship when it's safe! However because I lived with my sister and friend, I had to put him on 3 months' probation, at which point I'd let him know if it was our way or the highway!

I quickly realised that Mick was very loving, caring, thoughtful, funny, passionate, kind, generous, helpful, respectful and hard working. He treated me like a true princess. He was also great with his children especially under extremely difficult circumstances that his ex-wife would create.

Early on in our relationship, I was able to live the best of both worlds. When he had his children, I would often go out! Actually it wasn't until I had children of my own that I settled down! I cringe to think what I'd be like today if I didn't have any! We did take them places during the day but I thought it was also important for him to spend time with them on his own.

It was funny that Rose and Rose's brother also knew Mick. It was also ironic that Duncan and Mick had known each other from trade school. Actually there were a few that had known me and Mick but we never crossed paths!

I also loved heading to the local football. Mick was a big part of that when we got together. Rose and I would call him the Pakenham walker instead of runner because he was a bit slow off the mark! Rose and I would take our wine, crackers, dips and cheese. We once even featured in the local newspaper for bringing class to the footy field!

Although Mick didn't officially move in to my house until 6 months later, he was there every night. He was keen to get settled and I said "You are not even divorced! What's the rush?"

On our three month anniversary, the probation ceased! We took a short break to Apollo Bay on the coast. It's very picturesque and peaceful! We stayed at Daisy Hill cottages and it was here that I gave Mick a contract of relationship. It was a mock contract specifying that he had to cook dinner once a week, give me massages frequently, occasionally buy me flowers etc. I included things I'd do as well! Needless to say it only lasted about a year but I guess looking back I was setting an expectation. It was about having fun and enjoying each other's company. If things bothered me, I'd say you agreed to that in the contract. I'm sure I'll pull out that contract again in time and have a great laugh too!

For our one year anniversary, we spent the weekend at St Leonard's. We hired a little cottage a short walk down from the pub. We spent the day drinking and punting at the Colindina Pub with friends and I won $2000 betting on the horses. We then headed back to the St Leonard's pub for dinner and enjoyed the band! We also played pool but unfortunately a fight had broken out (not with us) and they closed the pub early! By the time Mick and I left the pub, I was on planet X. I thought mmmm, I'm hot and I haven't walked home nude before, so I started handing Mick my clothes. Another thing to tick off my list of things to do! Mick was in hysterics obviously no-one was around and it was a dark street. It was very liberating until two car lights came up in the distance. At first I didn't care, then I thought fook, what if they were cops and it made the news. So I dived into the bushes! Poor Mick nearly choked with laughter! A night to remember - harmless crazy fun!

While I'm at it, my most embarrassing drunken moment was on a work trip! It was just after returning from having Max. I was in Queensland, Brisbane and was staying opposite the Casino. Anyway after a day's work, I always headed out, no point sitting alone in a hotel room! I was lucky this wasn't a standard hotel for the company.

Wayne, a colleague who I didn't know very well and I were conducting some analysis for a system upgrade. We went out for dinner and had a few drinks. I had a few more and returned to my room around 2am. As it was hot in the room, I only slept in a singlet top and undies.

Not long after I had fallen asleep, I needed to use the bathroom. I took the normal route to the toilet as I would at home, pulled down my pants and was just about to sit, when I realised my room door was shutting! Fook I locked myself out of my room half naked and I was busting for the loo!

What would you do? What did I do? I thought about finding the gym but I knew it would be locked and I wasn't going to make it! All I had was the lift or the stairs. I thought I'd take the stairs but my bladder said no more. In the stair well, I quickly looked around to see if there were cameras. Luck was on my side, so "the waters" ran free. I felt bad but was planning on getting some water to wash it down later after I sorted myself out. I then tried to get back in, the door was self-locking! I'm thinking great work, where to now?

As I proceeded to the next level, I slipped in my own piss and if it wasn't for my thunderous thigh, I would have been knocked out on the next level (that bruise lasted a fortnight). Now I'm half naked and covered in my own piss. Can it get any worse?

Luckily at the next level, the door was jammed so I was able to pull it open. I had to face my fate! I entered the lift and selected reception. As the doors opened, I crouched down to cover my over exposed body as best I could. The attendant was just about to head out for a smoke and got the shock of his life. I said I accidently locked myself out, can I have a key to room 1409.

He basically threw the key into the lift and I quickly returned to my room! I didn't even think about the mirror in the lift as I was concentrating on my predicament. The rear would have been a lot worse than the front! After cleaning up my mess and having a shower, I contacted Mick and couldn't stop laughing! I also called Lu as she was in Las Vegas and gave her a run down! Both couldn't stop laughing and said "Only you!"

It wasn't as if I just plan these events, I just go with the flow. When I explained my situation to my work colleague, censored version, he asked why I didn't knock on his door as he would have helped! Like hell, that would have been worse!! I'd rather engage a stranger than someone I know in circumstances like that. Why? Because they can't re-hash the past and remind you of your mishaps! Again I'm all about fun so don't mind sharing my embarrassing story and hope it provides you with a laugh!

It was quite obvious that Mick and I were right for each other. We had love, trust, happiness and respect - the basic elements for a happy relationship. After he proposed, I seriously started thinking about the future.

We had both discussed children and I was more than ready by this stage of my life. However I did not want to live in the suburbs. I wanted my children to be free to ride their bikes outside without being hit by a car! I wanted them to be able to explore their surroundings in a safe environment. Therefore I purchased 2 acres on the outskirts of Melbourne. Mick was at football and Yvette came with me for the drive. I actually said to Yvette, it feels like I've been here before as I came down the street for the first time. I spoke with Mick and made an offer straight away. I saw the potential in the house as soon as I arrived! Mick wasn't in a position financially to commit not that it mattered, we knew where we stood with each other.

As a result, the pending wedding plans needed to change. I didn't need to have a big wedding, I was happy to elope and take a holiday! However when I mentioned this to my parents, they didn't seem impressed. I could almost feel the disappointment. I could have sold my Berwick property but I wanted to hang on to that and I also didn't want my parents to pay for the wedding. In the end, we did have a great wedding. Mum and dad helped us out as did Mick's mum.

We managed to keep things to a minimum and our whole wedding cost was less than $10,000. We married at the Berwick botanical Gardens in 2005 and celebrated at the function room at the Fountain Gate hotel! Everyone seemed to have a ball! Mick and I prepared our own vows and sung our wedding speeches at the reception. It was very relaxed and we were the last to leave at 3am in the morning! (I might put the wedding video up on my social services site instead of writing about it.)

We honeymooned in New Zealand which was awesome! At the bay of islands we were lucky enough to mix with some fine older locals. We ended up in the mountains, singing and dancing with the friendliest people that took us into their home. We rolled down a mountain in a plastic bubble (zorbing) and loved the hot springs! We also loved the south, especially Queenstown where we jumped off a cannon cliff (109 metre jump) and white water rafted.

When we returned, I thought I'd better get a health check because things were becoming realistic. I had never had a pap smear and I was 32. I never fussed about my health. I was of the attitude that if anything untoward becomes apparent, it's just the way it was meant to be! I hated the thought of intrusive tests.

My test came back showing I had pre-cancerous cells, stage 2-3. I didn't stress and was happy to go with the flow. It hadn't developed into cancer! I also had a mammogram because I had a small lump. That was fibrous tissue, in my terms, a fat deposit! No surprise because I was overweight and it was harmless.

The doctor advised not to fall pregnant and we took precautions. Clearly they weren't effective and I had to make a choice when I found out I was pregnant. Deal with the condition after the pregnancy and be closely monitored. Or have the procedure whilst pregnant and risk a miscarriage.

I decided to deal with my condition after the birth. It just meant I had to have a few "peep shows" that I had to pay for (that's what I called the invasive check of my cervix to make light of the situation) during my pregnancy.

Giving birth has been one of the most rewarding moments in my life! I have been fortunate enough to deliver three healthy, happy and joyful babies. But boy was it frikkin' painful!

Max was posterior (spine to spine-opposite to the normal way). I did have a shot of pethidine and gas. I yelled at the nurses for giving me a placebo but my labour was too advanced for any other medication. I had Max within an hour of arriving at the hospital. Mick had gone to move the car and when he returned, I was naked and full on into it! I remember him asking what music I wanted and I said I don't fucking care! Then I nearly knocked him out with the triangle, as I was changing positions. I was counting down like an auctioneer to humour myself and distract me from the pain. As soon as he was born, I was up and in the shower feeling fine! I didn't get a brief cuddle because Max needed warmth and for me that was more important. It has not affected our bond! The experience was quite euphoric and I couldn't believe how well I was. I was grateful for being all intact – I didn't need to be stitched up! I also understood why people never really tell you what happens in the maternity suite. Although I didn't find it that bad! The mess was cleaned up and your body/mind takes over so you don't think about things in the usual way! Oh and the bad cells had disappeared either through the natural delivery or as a result of hormones according to my awesome gynecologist/obstetrician.

Harley was also a quick labour but he decided to appear with his arm raised, head plus fist made for a wicked experience. What you don't want to happen while giving birth, I copped. I sounded like a primal beast. I freaked at the thought of the nurse wiping my butt – I was about to deliver a shit head! After a very intense time, Harley arrived however I was not intact. Just after giving birth the doctor asked if he could insert his fingers in my rectum to check if it had been compromised. Then the student doctor had a turn. I thought "no go ahead", I don't want shit flying when I have recovered from the birth! It then happened again so they could fix the problem, third time lucky? (You have to see the funny side!)

Dignity was a thing of the past! Surprise, I was all stitched up! No-one told me how many but I didn't need to know as long as it worked. Harley was placed on me straight away and shat all over me too! I couldn't walk and it did take me a good day to get back on my feet. I didn't pass stools for a good 2 weeks due to fear! The thought of having to return for a re-stitch was a risk I wasn't prepared to take!

With each birth, you think it's going to be easier. For me it got worse. I shouldn't have set an expectation because all pregnancies are different. I labored all day with Lexi and the hospital would not admit me. Even though my waters had to be broken with the previous two! Eventually they admitted me and when they couldn't get a proper read and realised she was distressed, they broke my waters! I had Lexi in an hour of the staff breaking my waters. However during the birth, I heard a snap! I thought I broke my baby. I actually broke my coccyx. Lexi was posterior as well. Both with Harley and Lexi I didn't have any drugs and gas was minimal. The gas didn't work for me, it just regulated my breathing! I could barely walk for days after doing my coccyx. I had a combination of drugs to choose from and gee did I need them (endone, tramadol and panadeine forte).

Now I have always been healthy regardless of my weight. My blood pressure never fluctuated during my pregnancies and it was always in range! My vitamin D count was extremely low compared to normal standards and has been all my life –I guess that's why I have panda eyes (dark shadow under my eyes). Even when I took tablets this did not improve, it didn't affect my children nor has it affected me. I have never broken a bone in my body! You would think after all the drunken episodes over the years there would have been at least one! I have had a slight fracture but not fully broken any bone (besides my birth injury)!

I did have gestational diabetes with Harley but never required treatment. I was also told that if I fell pregnant again that I was almost 99.9% certain I would get it again. That didn't happen either!

I did hemorrhage after I miscarried in between Max and Harley. That was a horrific experience. Not emotionally because I thought, I'd rather a healthy baby and it obviously wasn't meant to be. Physically I was ruined, I lost so much blood and was left alone, in pain until I was on the verge of passing out! I didn't move an inch. As my body was contracting, I could feel the release of blood. (My sister returned to get my husband as we drove my car that day to shop for her wedding dress!)

Blood had managed to make its way up to my pillow and to the bottom of my feet. I had about 3 or 4 doctors, pulling out clots and the like once they finally attended to me. (I had waited at least 2 hours at that stage.) When they cleaned me up and were inserting a catheter, the privacy sign fell down. Here I was at the centre of emergency with legs spread for all to view, the nurse did shut them pretty quick but I still thought what next! I ended up having an emergency curette. I was borderline for a transfusion but I didn't want one. It did take me a good 8 weeks to recover from that.

After that episode, the pre-cancerous cells came back so I had laser treatment. After what I've experienced, I no longer fear those types of tests. One, I have a great gynecologist and two, I've experienced most of the invasive tests. Certainly made up for my share of not having any up to the age of 32! Generally I'm quite healthy, yes I could be healthier but can't we all! I rather live than be a health fanatic! Whatever rocks your boat...

I do have a shonky bowel. On the odd occasion when I eat something not right, I manage to make myself and others laugh!! When I need to go, I must go! Often with little warning! Therefore I have a number of shit stories too! What's funny about shit stories is once you tell one others fess up and you spend the whole night talking about shit! Well that's how it is for me when these topics arise!

My sister and Mick were encouraging me to walk one night when I said I didn't feel well. They kept badgering me, so in the end, I decided to take that walk! It was about half way through on a public footpath, next to a main road, where my stomach decided to cramp up! I was doing the "hot coal" jig (like walking on coals), knowing full well I wasn't going to make it anywhere, other than my pants!

I didn't want to throw caution to the wind and let rip in front of my man! Even though he was telling me to drop my pants! However it was a better option than walking a good kilometre with soiled pants (we had to take a short cut home)! I therefore crouched like a dog in the lower part of the grass, hoping no one would pass! Thank goodness no one did! Anyway, I collected what green roughage I could find to attend to business while my sister and Mick were laughing! I squished walked half bent over so the acid wasn't burning my ass for the rest of the walk home!

As previously mentioned I can't handle the smell or sight of unpleasant things and ended up throwing up too! All for a short walk but it also proved that Mick was not afraid of my shit! I won't give you the top ten of my vial shit stories because that was probably enough!

Now as much as I was full of shit, I couldn't believe how much shit Mick received from his ex-wife. It was ridiculous and for a good 5 years especially after we married it did affect our relationship on many levels. However it wasn't until I changed how I reacted that I actually gained control.

Just to give you some background, Mick's ex-wife never put her children first. It was all about her and how to use the kids to her advantage. If Mick didn't comply with her, she would use the kids as pawns. She would tell Mick he couldn't see them.

She would drop the kids at strangers' houses and head off into town or work. The kids would often mention how they felt uncomfortable at some of the places that they were forced to stay at. They also came home to an empty house and had to fend for themselves.

The kids had an enormous amount of time off at school and had no basic knowledge. Isaiah could not read or write at grade 3. When the kids visited on the fortnight, I also noticed unusual provocative behaviour and was concerned what they were exposed too. Isaiah had mentioned living with drug dealers but Mick was powerless to do anything. Isaiah and Ebony (Mick's oldest daughter) had been physically abused by her ex-partner. When Mick confronted his ex-wife, there was always an excuse. She never accepted any responsibility.

She often made up illnesses for the kids. One minute Ebony had a lactose problem. (When we said she couldn't have cheese, ice cream and milkshakes – suddenly Ebony was fine!) She once told Mick that Isaiah had cancer! I said to Mick wait until you speak to the doctor before you believe her! And sure enough, there was nothing untoward. It came down to stress!

Part of the stress was caused by instability. Mick's ex-wife would hook up with men, move in and then move on in a short timeframe. This happened numerous times over the years! The children had been to 4 different schools in one year and she was basically living out of the car! She had been to court for deception – cashing fraudulent cheques and had obtained money from a church that she never repaid. She had exhausted all avenues and even her mother had wiped her at that stage.

Fortunately it forced her to concede that the kids would be better off in our care. We made it clear that it would have to be at least until the end of school years. One month after they were in our care, Ebony became a lady. Her mother didn't even want to know about it and instructed us to just place some pads in her bag. I was appalled! I couldn't believe that she would neglect her daughter at such a crucial time of her life. I was livid, I couldn't understand how a mother could do that to her child. (Before I continue, you don't need to have children to substantiate your view on such matters. It is common sense that prevails and knowing what is best for children.)

Mick and I had a lot of work to do. Hygiene was a problem, education, routine and controlling their diet as well. When it came to meals, Ebony had a tendency to over eat. I was mindful that it was a result of her emotional pain and the environment she grew up in.

However as a mother, I didn't want her to suffer and experience issues with self-esteem, confidence and bullying. Ebony struggled with this. I assumed she thought I was being too controlling even though we provided many explanations. Over the two and half years prior to her returning to her mum's we did make some huge positive advances. There were many heated discussions. I never assumed the role of mother and never expected them to call me anything other than Annette.

I had Max at that stage and was still working full-time. Mick was at home full-time as he could not work due to a shoulder injury. I was annoyed for the fact that, I'd been working close to 20 years and I could not enjoy the luxury of being home with my son. I was sacrificing my time and the financial future of my children. Therefore I became angry and bitter. I did realise that this was a negative emotion that I couldn't hold on to, as it would have destroyed me and my relationship with Mick. Furthermore, it would have given Mick's ex-wife the satisfaction of splitting us up.

Two weeks before I had Harley, she dropped the kids off after having them for the weekend. She proceeded to say 'I don't want to cause trouble but Ebony needs glasses!" I asked Ebony, "Ebony why haven't you mentioned that you were having problems?" Mick's ex-wife butted in with, "I'm her mother and you have no right to question!" Well that was a red flag to the bull! Normally I would not have said anything in front of the kids. Mick and I were always mindful not to expose them to issues that they didn't need to be involved in. However being pregnant and at my peak with her behaviour, I was ready to slaughter! I gave her a summary of what kind of a mother she was and told her never to set foot on my property. I slammed the door in her face. She called the next day, I thought for fucks sake, what didn't you understand? I said "Other than your brain which is obviously suffering some mental condition, you should consider donating your organs because they are a wasted resource!" I then chose not to answer any more calls. All drops offs and pick-ups were arranged at public places. If I was annoyed by things, I'd vent and release the anger, frustration or bitterness. She could not get to me because I didn't allow it.

Surprisingly she lost control because I wasn't buying into her games. I just believed in karma too.

Although she still bothers me from time to time, especially when she manipulates her children, I let it go. It's not my problem. Isaiah has been torn between two places only because he doesn't want to say no to his mum. She had recently been encouraging him to move back for high school. She advised that she would be at home and not working because she is currently on Workcover. Isaiah has his sport, friends, tutoring and has come a long way. He has been living with us full-time for over the last 5 years and is happy to remain at home with us - for the meantime at least! (I keep the peace and she can drop off/pick up Isaiah from home not that it happens very often.)

Children, especially in their teens know how to play one off on the other when they have options. Ultimately it is their choice at that age but all risks and consequences need to be explained. It also needs to be with boundaries as it affects the other siblings too. I know Max and Harley miss their brother when Isaiah has gone for a weekend or a week. You need to be mindful of emotionally impacting their lives if their brother was to continually move back and forth! I'm hoping it doesn't come to that but at least we are prepared if the situation does surface! Always thinking ahead!

Back on the work track, I was a Project manager for the last 11 years of my 20 year career for the same company. I worked on multi-million dollar projects. I implemented a number of payroll systems across 700 stores. I worked on procedures, disaster recovery plans, waste management, change management and cash management, management of expenses, business to business and human resources. I spent a great deal in operations and information technology. I loved the diversity of my role because I had the opportunity to manage projects from conception, design, testing and implementation. Although I completed my degree in Business Management – majoring in accounting, I never wanted to be an accountant. However the knowledge came in handy. I loved my work and made some great friends.

When Coles was brought out by Wesfarmers, changes were eminent. As with any take-over, management is always reviewed. I could not appreciate how many international employees were employed over people who had great skills and knowledge. I understood it was part of the strategy to change the culture but not hire an entire English town to service an Australian business. It was Senior Management that had the control but most were all wiped out in the process.

About 6 months before I left, I sent the CEO of Coles (Ian McLeod) an email advising that Coles had not established its true identity in the market. At the time, they were planning on returning to basics whilst providing quality and service for a reasonable price. I came up with a song to the tune of "Video killed the radio star" and recommended that we needed consistency with our marketing campaign. I wasn't expecting a reply but I did get one! Everyone was amused that I had taken such action. I had nothing to lose. I was showing an interest in the company. I assume others wouldn't have the courage. I just saw it as an opportunity to give my view for what it was worth. (Jan recently brought this up. I hadn't thought anything about it so obviously people do marvel at some of the things I do!)

I was well and truly ready to move on! I wanted to be at home with my children. I couldn't put a price on those precious years and was prepared to make the necessary sacrifices to our lifestyle, if we needed to. I was on a salary of $133,000 a year which included a car. I didn't even think twice. I'd planned to have my second child Harley, extend the house and then write a book.

I decided to buy an on-site van for future holidays so we could still take a break. In fact we spend a good 3 months at the van and we would sell our house before our van; if we became that financially strapped. Those are happy memories that again, I don't put a price on.

I didn't set any timeframes on any plans because I don't like being ruled by time. I don't wear a watch either for that matter. Lucky I didn't set one on the house because I would have been disappointed. After the Black Saturday fires, it took me 18 months to get the permit sorted to actually dig a hole in the ground due to all the changes and to get to that point it cost me $5,000.

I coordinated the building as a builder-owner and did not encounter any major issues. In fact, to-date there has only been one! I've run out of money to finish the outside decking and verandah roof to get the building approved. We are now waiting to see what will happen with the council! Surely they won't kick a family of 6 out on the street when we live in a fully functional house! I'm not worried about it, just play the game and ride the wave!

When Mick was returning to the workforce, he found it hard to find a role in his trade. He ended up working for an abattoir in Poowong. This company took full advantage of their employees; they were over worked and underpaid. In fact Mick worked on average 65 hours a week and only received a flat rate of $22. No overtime, no cold-work allowance etc. Fairwork still haven't managed to investigate this properly and we are in continued discussions. Even though I prepared a 30-page report in seven days back in April! They have taken 8 months to confirm that they can't validate details when they only have to look at the operations of the business and the proof we have provided. (This government agency is meant to protect employees but has failed to deliver.)

Due to the significant drop in our disposable income I had to sell my Berwick home. When I purchased my house in Berwick (2002) and only looking at it for the first time, I said to the agent "The maximum price I'd pay for this house is $162,000. Do what you have to do and call me if they accept". I wasn't interested in dealing with negotiations, that's what I was indirectly paying for. I knew the median price for houses in the area at the time was around $180,000 and the owners were asking for $170,000. It was a fair deal. I told the agent I wasn't in a hurry and I had others in mind. He called me back that afternoon. At the time, I could have afforded a bigger and better place but I didn't want to financially commit to more. My friends and family couldn't believe how quickly I made that decision. That's how I roll with things.

I knew a bit about building from listening to my dad talk about the problems on jobs that he encountered. I also applied common sense and logic. For example; checking to see if the doors opened and closed easily, as this indicates that the house foundations are secure and stable! I'd checked for moisture near windows/frames. I poked my head in the manhole to see what the exposed wiring looked like and if it had insulation. Turned on taps; checked the drainage and pressure. I looked at the plaster closely to determine if it was susceptible to cracking. I walked the house to see if there were differences in the floor. All basic logical stuff. Even when you rely on special services, no one takes ownership or responsibility so I didn't waste any extra money. It was a sound investment and the surplus funds were required to finish most of our home.

My redundancy package was therefore used to make up the shortfall in wages and provide for a growing family. All children participated in sports which isn't cheap. My Children are termites, literally eating me out of the house! So it didn't last long and I said to Mick that if he didn't find another job by February 2012, I would have to return to work. It wasn't feasible for both of us to work plus I didn't want the children in full-time care. I had more earning potential so it made sense.

At the end of 2011, it was a bit rough financially. Especially when Mick's company didn't pay him correctly over Christmas! Jack and Diane spotted us $1000 so that got us through. I wasn't planning big presents for the kids and cashed in on the loyalty vouchers. However Jane and Elle who are great friends from kinder had been shopping unbeknownst to me.

They rocked up at our house, with 6 large bags full of presents for my children. I was shocked, humbled and amazed at such a generous, kind-hearted act. I am a proud person but focused on the positive. It wasn't just for the presents but for the fact that they thought so much of our children. They had taken the time to shop, wrap and label each one and placed them all in separate garbage bags. It still touches my heart when I think about it – it truly made mine and Mick's Christmas that year! I couldn't thank them enough and said I will be fixing up my dues as soon as I'm in that position.

Jane said there was no expectation and I know that because she is the first to help out when she sees anyone in need and like me doesn't expect anything in return. Both Jane and Elle are very caring, kind, generous, loving, funny and thoughtful. Hopefully I won't be waiting too long to return that great positive karma ten-fold! All my friendships that I have made through Max's kinder are great and I feel lucky to have met such a great group of people.

I was starting to stress about money only because I have always had it. I also didn't want to find myself in the same position as my parents. I always paid my bills and mortgage on time. Mick would say, "Ah but we are rich in love!" I'd turn around and reply "I'll just ring the bank manager and explain that we are rich in love. And find out if it is possible, as a gesture of goodwill, if they could add another month to the loan!" Mick never had any idea about finances so never understood, why at times I was fanatical. He always relied on me having a reserve somewhere!

I'm not a massive shopper. I'd rather be doing other things. When I go shopping it is because I need something and I'm usually in and out fairly quickly. I find it a chore and so don't enjoy it. I have on the odd occasion when I'm catching up with a friend and we do lunch.

Last time I was out with Yvette, I said to a stranger who was picking up some bananas "oh they are my bananas!" Others in the area looked to see what was happening. The guy looked at me and didn't know what to say. I proceeded to say, "I'm only joking just wanted to see your reaction." I then started laughing so did everyone else. Harmless fun!

While I'm on shopping, I had brought a stereo from Harvey Norman when I moved in 2000. However the stereo wasn't loud enough when I set it up at home. Yvette came with me to return it. The service manager advised that they could not sell it as new because the box was opened and they deducted $50 from my return. I had packed everything to perfection as I understood how retailers work. But I was really annoyed! I asked Yvette to retrieve a CD from the car.

Poor Yvette, I stood in the store pumping music testing all the stereos that were in my price range. Loud music then a break, insert the CD again, loud music! I did this at least 10 times at which point the Manager proceeded to tell me off. People were just looking! I didn't care I was getting $50 worth of entertainment and making sure I used my credit for the replacement wisely. I explained to the manager why I was doing it. I told him I wouldn't stop until I'm satisfied that I had found a suitable replacement. He couldn't say anything. Yvette couldn't stop laughing! I think she had a leakage that day too! She still laughs about it today. I never brought anything from that store for a good 10 years after that! So I guess I've been "out there" all my life!

In summary, I've always been about having a great time, enjoying great company, great food, great music and appreciating great places! Currently the most important and fulfilling moments are those spent with my children and husband. As well as friends and family of course but you don't live with them every day!

For the last six months, we have been living a fulfilling life. We spent time at the van and beach. We've always had food on the table and enjoyed the simple pleasures in life. We haven't been out much. Mick was successful in obtaining a job in his trade in February, funny enough. In June, I said to Mick after he worked 9 weeks away, "Oh we are finally starting to get some traction on our financial situation." Not that we are totally out of the woods but we didn't suffer and are extremely happy!

So there you have it Doc, the good, the bad, the ugly and triumphant! Me in a nutshell! I'm tipping I'd make a great case study too after all that! If it leads to that! I could have put so much more in but I might as well let others share some of me too, if fame finds me! If not, it doesn't matter, my kids will hopefully learn from my experiences good or bad! Or I might save the rest of me, for another book! Before we change directions, just in jest, I always said I have so many stretch marks because they resemble the Kokoda trail of my life! But upon reflection, I think it's a pretty damn accurate analogy for me! Choo choo choo...

4. Full Moon/Full Circle

Back to my realisation phase, whilst I was in the realms of sub-conscious, my mind was clearly functioning on a different mental plane. I was considering many dimensions simultaneously. My mind was totally open and there were some very bizarre connections that I made in that frame of mind.

I articulated what was happening and the impacts when I was functioning in the sub-conscious. The following models illustrate this at a high level:

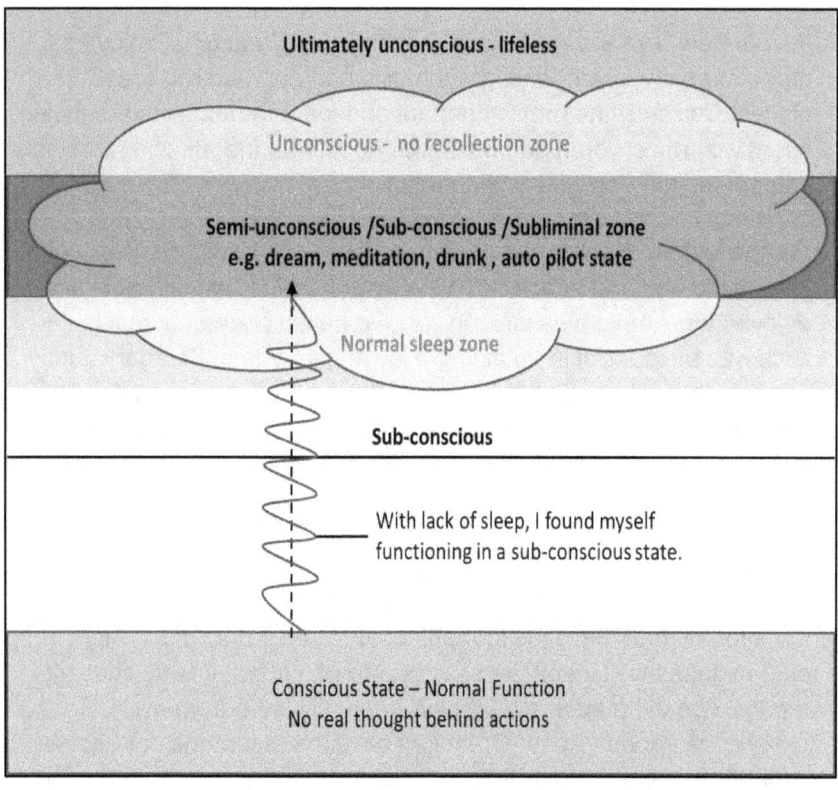

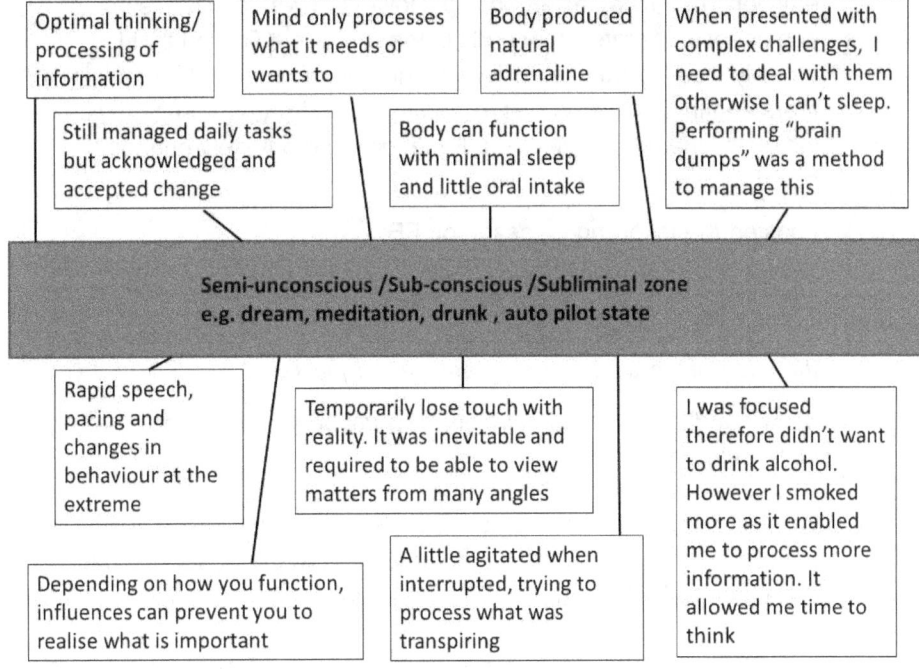

I did have control in the first phase to a degree. Once I completed what I needed to and after some much needed rest, I returned to my normal self. Consequently I did change, but my core traits remained the same. I had a greater perspective and outlook. I had an acute sense of interpreting body language and understanding language at a greater depth. My senses worked in unison. If someone told me something that was emotionally raw, I would get goose bumps all over. If I heard or read an evil story, it made my skin crawl. I now experience extreme physical sensations as a result of my realisation. Again, if I had slept and continued my normal day-to-day routine, I guess I would be living without real purpose, i.e. just existing. I would not have had the opportunity to self-explore. I would still be burdened by expectations, fears and inhibitions to some degree.

For me, my emotions were in check because I've considered myself balanced because of my mindset. As always I dealt with my emotions as they arose. However upon receiving great praise, I did become off balance for "my normal self" and had to deal with those emotions that I was experiencing. However I was doing this in my sub-conscious state. Very early in the process, I figured that I actually was my true self when I binged on the booze. I had minimal fears and inhibitions. Whilst exploring in my dreamlike state, I was indirectly sharing my views on Facebook and privately engaging others.

I posted the following message on FB:

June 23:

It's ironic that I drank to be myself, not sure if the world is ready for the ride but we will have a great time! Mama xx

(Now I drink to solve my problems, I must be like everyone else! Only joking!)

On the 21/6/2012, I had come full circle with what I was exploring on my self-discovery. During that cycle I explored the positive aspects that came to fruition on the 19/6 and negative matters on the 21/6.

I did believe some events would take place, as previously highlighted, the Olympics being one. However I quantified this during that phase when I was researching. It wasn't as if I had a thought and just accepted that I was right. When I was exploring politics, history, religions and other theories regarding the 21/12/2012, I had identified some interesting connections and interpreted these differently.

I had read and viewed a couple of documentaries regarding Richard Clarke who served as a national security member for counter-terrorism, during the September 11 investigations. There were a number of inconsistencies that he highlighted with the investigation pertaining to the 9/11 terrorist attacks. He believed that not all plausible matters had been thoroughly investigated. (Obviously I don't draw any conclusions on the validity of any claims. I was digesting an enormous amount for what I was researching and the connections I was making!)

Wesley Clarke, a politician in America was also trying to provide insight and a different perspective to the management of public affairs. In essence, he was highlighting that there were a number of discrepancies with the American government and was trying to create awareness, for example; the war being based on false claims. I won't go into the detail because it would be a book in itself. Principally it was a matter of you can't always believe what you see, read and hear.

I came across a documentary that highlighted an interview held with Osama Bin Laden captured by a CNN reporter. This interview was 10 years prior to the US Government actually capturing him. The US government had every possible resource to hunt the terrorist down and it took 10 years for the US government to find him when a reporter found him earlier. During those years, a war against terror evolved. Why? The documentary had creditability from that perspective and linked back to Richard and Wesley Clarke's theories.

Following that research, I discovered a few articles regarding the earth. One in particular was about the Earth's magnetic force. Apparently scientists had discovered that it had been compromised. From what I could gather, the alleged damage has been caused by the environment and could explain the changes in climate. The magnetic force is responsible for the earth's balance. If it is compromised, then logically the earth is susceptible to shifting.

We have always assumed that the earth rotates on an axis and it is a given. However it is highly plausible that if the magnetic force is compromised that the earth could be significantly impacted. We were not around to witness or experience the ice-age and obviously there was a trigger for monumental change. I also questioned why NASA would cease all space discoveries after spending billions of dollars to explore. Why would they change their direction unexpectedly? Was it because of the magnetic force and they had to divert their area of studies? Was this linked to the theories around 21/12/2012 – impending doom?

In addition, I also came across reports from 3 different sources which contained footage of massive storage facilities in a couple of American states that housed portable coffins. These disposable coffins could contain up to 4 bodies and were made of plastic. I thought this was very unusual. Why would the government be spending a significant amount on such a project? What were their intentions? What did they know that the rest of the public did not? Were these coffins produced in the event of any future terror attacks or were they potentially required for any ill effects caused by nature? Were they required for war? Could it be a combination of all three? I was not concerned nor did I stress, I was curious and intrigued. Again I was in a dreamlike state when conducting my analysis and was very open to many possibilities.

With respect to the Olympics, I had explored the predictions of Nostradamus and Rockefeller. Apparently Rockefeller had made some earlier predictions that had come to fruition. He also highlighted impending doom at the Olympics. I further discovered that Rockefeller was an American industrialist and philanthropist who was the founder of an oil company that dominated the oil industry and revolutionized the petroleum industry.

He created foundations to explore and develop research in the medical, education and scientific fields. He was very influential on all accounts especially political. I then considered that given his influence, access to funds and his depth of knowledge along with contacts, it could have been possible that the previous predications were executed or staged for an ulterior motive. (I'm not suggesting that it was the case but it was what I considered in my different mental state. I don't want to discredit any great work of significant influential people.)

There was also coverage of the terror attacks at the German Olympics in 1972 during that time. My psyche model was based on the eye and many theories relating to terror at the Olympics were symbolic of this too. The mascots had one eye and the pyramid lights were symbolic of it as well. For some reason, all that I had explored was connected, hence why I believed that the terror attacks were inevitable. Ultimately, my aim was to assist and ensure there were resources available if the event took place. I could not control or avoid such matters. I guess that's why I sent the notes to the President. In essence I thought I was doing my bit to help others in the event of a catastrophe. It was my choice, I didn't harm anyone. I assume they would have deemed it a crazy notion from a crazy person. I had nothing to lose!

On the flip side, I also was evaluating my friend's responses to my obscure predications. I did this in my phase and post, I understood what, why and how they would react and behave according to who I was and their traits. It was very interesting. I obviously shared my thoughts privately with a select few who found my comments quite confronting. At the end of the day, they could not understand without all the pieces being presented and appreciating my mental state during that time.

I also believed that there would be some significant damage to the world through nature's force. I had mentioned early on in my phase that Rose was hit by a tsunami. I don't know if that lead me to believe that there could be a repeat of such natural disasters post 21/12/2012. Again I made connections based on religious beliefs, details of the earth's magnetic force and the events that had occurred in history.

In addition, I had made personal connections. When I completed the positive phase on the 19/6/12, we experienced a significant earth tremor. This was unusual for our area and I perceived it as a sign of things to come. I had been in Bali 9 months before the bombings. I had been at Marysville 8 weeks prior to the Black Saturday fires. The Kooweerup Floods (close to home) occurred on the 21/6/2012 the day I had completed my first cycle of my realisation. I guess I was interpreting the impacts of events and connecting them on my self-discovery for whatever reasons that I can't exactly quantify.

Obviously when I posted the following on Facebook, those who I had engaged privately about impending doom were very concerned for my welfare.

June 25:

Now I know why I've lived my life by the seat of my pants and it's coz I've been able to expect the unexpected. Didn't realise the impact of that until last night. Like a lightning bolt! Must live for the moment, my ride has started! My reality!

I had posted this after a dream or vision. (It's difficult to describe because I don't know if I was asleep or awake in the sub-conscious at the time.) I had visualized that the earth was in total darkness and that there had been a massive explosion. Which would have related to my research, clearly it was triggered by my mind processing this information. Upon reflection and back in the land of consciousness, I interpreted this as my book evolving unexpectedly (from keeping in the dark to exposing myself) and the impact that it would have on me and others. The "ride" was referring to my journey and enjoying each day by living in the moment, which was my new reality.

Veronica, another great friend who I met at our mother's group is caring, generous, thoughtful, funny, happy and kind. She doesn't judge and accepts matters at face value. She visited toward the end of the first phase. I shared some of my theories and my predications with her. I think I freaked her out a little but she didn't say anything. She had spoken to Jan and mentioned I was a bit all over the place. From what Jan tells me, she explained to Veronica that I was going through a phase and I would work it out. Love my friends!

During this time, my kids became "free range". They ate when they wanted to. I let them do anything they pleased (obviously nothing dangerous). I did shower and bath them but at different times to the standard routine. The kids accepted what was happening around them and were helping around the house. I didn't ask or tell them to do anything. They didn't fight with each other like they tended to do. Mick obviously didn't know what to make of the changes and relaxed household boundaries. To a degree he accepted to accommodate what I was endeavouring even though he had no appreciation for why I had changed.

All the expectations I had lived up to as a child, I was rebelling against. I suspect my mind was processing this in the physical sense whilst from a mental perspective, I was mindful of not impeding my children by the boundaries I was creating. In retrospect, I guess I was resetting the boundaries to restore a happy balance. In essence, adapting and managing change, change in the physical and mental sense!

Another one of my findings during the realisation was confirming that the best opportunity that we can provide our children with, was a positive experience. They needed to do what they wanted to a degree so they could learn and grow from their experience. If we were over protective and created too many boundaries, this could ultimately hinder their progress. I understood that if they did experience a negative event as a result of exploring, it was my role to highlight the positive. For example; my children were always focused on winning and would get upset if they didn't succeed. They would fight amongst each other when they lost. I would tell them it was about enjoying the activity and if you win, it's a bonus. I heard Max explain this to a child's friend recently and thought my goodness, he listened and understood. I have also realised that he is still competitive but is not obsessed with winning. Obviously I wouldn't expose them to any dangerous situations, for example pouring boiling water into a mug or crossing the street, if they are not capable.

I've always taught my children there is no such thing as "can't", you can do what you need/want to and if you fail, try again. If you are physically unable to complete a task, then find a substitute/alternative. Mum always said where there is a will, there is a way and she was right! I'm grateful that I did have such a positive role model and am able to teach my children the same!

Tracey is a great friend who I met through Diane. She is very loving, funny, thoughtful, caring and kind. Tracey has been suffering from depression and has had an enormous amount to deal with recently. She was struggling in her life and I was trying to provide her some guidance. However when I posted details about my reality on the 25/6 she was very concerned as I had informed her of my predications. I believe she contacted the Crisis Assessment Team (CAT) to express her concerns in order to help me, as did a couple of others.

Mick had been speaking to friends/family and he wasn't sure what to do. He knew I was going through a stage but his concerns were intensified by the influence of friends and family and with good reason.

On Wednesday 27/6/2012, I had planned to have a break. I had slept well the previous night and I was slowly returning back to the conscious state. I recognized where I had been mentally. It was a gradual process to return to my normal (conscious) state because the body was adjusting to the decline in natural adrenaline. I also had to digest what I had explored.

I called Elle and I filled her in on what transpired. Obviously she was concerned about what I was saying/doing. She said that she would pop round. On her way, she bumped into Bel another friend I became reconnected with through kinder. (Bel was previously a friend of Rose's and I knew her from way back.) Anyway, Bel and Elle visited and I was filling them in on my wild mental trip. Obviously they had no idea what I had been doing. Mick had also arrived home too, obviously someone had called him. Then my sister dropped in. Nothing like a friendly/family intervention!

I explained that I was fine and I just needed rest. I did what I wanted to do. They weren't satisfied and insisted that I head to the doctors. I said I would give them peace of mind and attend at the end of the week. I explained if I had been up studying law no one would have had a problem with what I was researching. I wasn't talking as fast as I had been. I also mentioned that people believe in god and they weren't deemed crazy. Just because I had mentioned a few wild predictions/thoughts, terror attacks and natural disasters it doesn't mean that I'm unwell.

My sister ended up taking the little ones to her house. The phone rang and I told Mick to tell my Dad not to come. Mick didn't say who was on the phone but I knew. I didn't need to be told by my Dad and it was better for me that he kept his distance.

Elle and Bel were upset for a number of reasons. They cared and were worried that I would act negatively in respect to the intervention. I reassured them and said it will create awareness. At the time, I was talking about the Olympics. (Keeping in mind, I hadn't completely returned to my normal conscious state. I also didn't have time to understand what I had processed.) After an interesting couple of hours, my friends left.

Once everyone had gone, it gave me the opportunity to explain to Mick what had been happening. Mick was very confused because he couldn't understand why and how the situation arose. He also had a number of people contacting him and he wasn't sure of himself or me. It is difficult to appreciate if you have not experienced this situation first hand. It is even harder when everyone else is telling you otherwise. Without all the facts, it did complicate things. Mick and I understood that friends and family became involved because they cared and loved us. I was never angry at them for taking action because they were acting out of love.

I knew I was inadvertently hurting people but it was inevitable and uncontrollable. I didn't ask them for help. I did engage some for various reasons but as previously highlighted I couldn't control their reaction or my behaviour to a degree. I had a different focus which created situations outside of my control. When I was in a different state of mind, I had no inhibitions, fears and was emotionally disconnected.

Thursday 28/6/2012, Michael and Fleur from the CAT visited me at home. I knew I was fine and declined to attend their office hence they conducted a home visit. I basically gave them a brief overview of what had transpired. I had shown them the pool effect theory and the sub-conscious model. I explained that I had applied myself in that manner before however the content was very different and I hadn't delved that far into the sub-conscious.

I validated my actions with my analogy of studying e.g. law and people believing in god not being deemed mentally ill. They did not inform me who had contacted their office but wanted to confirm some questions. I could tell by the questions who had called. They asked whether I had engaged in excessive spending. I advised that I paid for bills, groceries and brought my son an iPod (for his birthday). They made reference to music/songs. I said I normally sing or quote songs when I was drunk and I was in a dream-like state. Even if I wasn't, what was the crime? They queried my memory at which point I rolled out with my tax file number, credit card number and license number. I briefly explained the notes to the president and my intent. I wasn't harming anyone. I even said that it would make for a good story/book.

I asked why they were labeled the "Crisis Assessment Team" as this would be confronting for someone that was mentally challenged. Michael agreed and mentioned it should possibly be community. I responded that "community or care" would be more suitable and conducive to assisting a patient in need. I was indirectly highlighting my depth to language and positive affirmation.

They were satisfied that I was well and sane. They obviously didn't understand my theories or my actions but accepted that I was different. Michael did mention that I was quite articulate and intelligent. However he suggested I attend the office to speak with a doctor. I asked him for what purpose or how would it benefit me? Michael advised that it would give himself peace of mind so I politely declined the offer. I didn't want to waste my time and knew I was fine.

My Facebook posting for that day:

Welcome back Cotter! To give everyone peace of mind I've clinically been stamped sane, makes for a good book! Positive experience overall and am feeling the love! It's ok to be myself – thank goodness couldn't think of who else I could be! Hope you're having a great day!

I found it interesting that some friends and family did not want to accept my word when I told them I was fine. My dad in particular was very dubious and kept questioning me. I guess he assumed that I was like his mother or was scared and just wanted to help. I could appreciate that but what frustrated me was that when my brother was suffering from a drug addiction he failed to help or was in denial.

My brother for whatever reason was addicted to ice/meth and goodness knows what else. He is a great man but was quite lost at that stage of his life. He would do anything for anyone. He is kind, generous and caring. He can be quite aggressive too when fueled depending on his mood. I assume he never addressed what happened during our childhood and drugs may have been a release. I tried to seek assistance in order to help him. But it was difficult because he had no fixed place of address at the time and I didn't know where he was. My dad didn't believe or wanted to believe his son had a problem.

The last time my brother had made contact was when we celebrated his birthday and he was on another planet. I was pregnant with Max and we ended up in a fight because I would not tolerate his poor behaviour. My dad was upset with me because I could have avoided the situation. My dad claimed he was just tired even though my brother made no sense at all and his eyes were rolling back into his head. He could barely walk and yet he had jumped into his car and drove off. I was furious, more so with my dad!

To cut a long story short, my brother managed to break the addiction and admitted that he was addicted to some heavy drugs. He was on the road to recovery when he visited me in hospital when I had Harley. I was thrilled and congratulated him on such an amazing effort. It would have been very difficult for my brother to overcome a drug addiction, especially without family support. I was delighted that he found a way to help himself. Not many can achieve that independently! My brother did pay a price for his addiction, he rarely sees his girls because after he split with his ex-wife, they moved interstate.

Upon reflection, my Dad didn't deeply know either of us because we kept things from him. We both knew he was a proud man and didn't want to hurt him. My dad's lack of trust in us complicated matters. In order to avoid such situations, like my recent phase, it was better to share less with him. (The little you know the better theory – another one of my Mum's great sayings!) I accepted that he would always worry and I couldn't control his reaction or behaviours. Therefore by managing the expectation for me, the overall outcome was more positive. This also helped free the frustration of accommodating his fears and concerns.

On Friday 29/6/2012 I arranged to pick up some clothes and nappies from a good friend Angel, an ex-colleague. Angel is very kind, loving, thoughtful, generous and religious. I never swear in front of her and I respect her religious beliefs. Not that we ever spoke about religion. Angel hasn't seen me drunk or heard most of my crazy stories because our friendship originated through work. I was very professional at work and I did tend to live two lives. (Rather than having lived a double life, I prefer to view it as adapting to different environments. Time and place for everything!)

Angel wasn't home but I had a brief chat with her husband, they were in the midst of moving house. Angel had mentioned that she had included me as a reference for a job she had applied for and I assured her that I would provide a glowing summary of her great skills and assets. Angel is very diligent, extremely hard working and very passionate about her work. She is very friendly and accommodating too. After collecting the items, I couldn't thank Angel enough and called her to express how grateful I was.

Angel had no idea what had transpired during the first phase and I didn't mention it to her. I assume she hadn't noticed any change in me. We rarely caught up in person because we both have busy lifestyles. However we do catch up over the phone every couple of months and she is a great friend.

Choo choo choo let's change tracks! After a few full on weeks, I couldn't wait to get to the caravan for the July school holidays. The weather wasn't too bad considering it was the middle of winter. The kids had a ball playing at the park and spending some time at the beach. We also played mini golf and when the weather was bad, we headed to the play centre. Mick travelled from the caravan to work and we all had a great time.

I also caught up with Veronica and her husband Ferg. Ferg is a great Irish man who is very funny, caring, kind and generous. He loves a joke and is quick witted. He actually built my extension and has a great work ethic too. It is always great catching up with them. After spending time at the beach, we had a laugh about what transpired. I filled Ferg in on some of my theories. (Veronica was obviously aware of them when I freaked her out prior to my break.) Anyway I figured my experience made for an interesting conversation with others at the very least.

During the two week break, I did continue with my research but not as aggressively. In order to appreciate Rose's plight at a greater depth, I found a web site for Mum's with cancer and came across a raw, inspiring, courageous, honest and emotionally charged blog called Punk Rock Mommy – by Andrea Collins-Smith.

Andrea had just finished her psychology degree when she was diagnosed with Inflammatory Breast Cancer. She had 6 children (her youngest was about 12 months old) and a beautiful husband Kelly who was a tattoo artist. I read 210 blogs across two nights, it was better than reading any book. I was in awe of such a magnificent lady and marveled at how well she handled her plight and fight with cancer. Even though it was a gut wrenching story, it was very uplifting. It made you appreciate your life. I was also able to truly appreciate where Rose had been in terms of her cancer and what was ahead. Punk Rock Mommy was able to capture the essence of managing her life, her concerns, her fears and her love for her family including what would eventuate once she had caught the plane. She never gave up hope and faced adversity head on. It felt like I knew her personally after reading her thoughts and I did feel privileged. I decided that as a tribute to her and others including Rose, that I would get a tattoo by the great Kelly, when the opportunity arises. I have always said I would never get one because I don't like needles. Never say never! I figure it's a small gesture and would signify a monumental time in my life. Unfortunately Punk Rock Mommy has caught the plane but has left an amazing legacy. As I'm sure others have too, I just didn't have the time to read all of them.

I did come across reports of the US government building a secret hideout for the elite in the event of a catastrophe. There were also a couple of pictures of this but in my normal frame of mind I considered that these could have been falsified. However it could have been quite plausible. I just accepted it at face value and was not concerned about anything untoward. You can't always believe what you read, see and hear so I was not misguided in that respect. I guess I found it interesting and was intrigued by what I explored and the connections I made.

I further researched details pertaining to 21/12/2012 and was reassessing what I had previously found during the sub-conscious stage. I was trying to confirm whether my thoughts/beliefs were skewed or if they had changed. Although I strongly believed some of my predications during the first phase, it was not a concern for me in my normal state. I just continued living each day doing what I wanted to do, gradually returning back to my normal self.

Mick wasn't his normal self. He was complaining of being tired after a full night's sleep and was irritable. I explained that ever since we met, he would sleep like a bear but sounded like a steam engine. He suffers from sleep apnoea but had never attended to it. He was also complaining of a sore leg and foot. I ended up calling the doctor to make an appointment on his behalf. As usual, men are very reluctant to fend for themselves when it comes to their health.

The doctor provided him with a referral for a sleep specialist and was also concerned about Mick's high blood pressure. When Mick mentioned his pain the doctor recommended an ultra sound in the event he had a clot. Mick returned to the car and he was anxious. His leg was rattling (he does this when he is nervous), his face was red and stress was written all over his face. I explained that there was no point stressing over the weekend and encouraged him to go to hospital.

Mick said he would after Max had the opportunity to undertake his project. Max had made some bird beaks that looked like pyramids that he wanted to sell at the shops. He said he wanted to buy tic tacs. I said to Max that I'd buy them for him. His reply was "but sometimes you need money for other things." I thought fair enough. I asked how he was going to sell his product. His reply was "People just go out and shop, I'll set up a stall". My original reaction was he couldn't do that! My second thought was why should I deny him that opportunity? After considering his request from his angle, I encouraged him. Initially Mick was apprehensive and said he couldn't for the same reasons as me. I said just explain the situation if anyone asks.

While I was shopping, Mick was sitting with Max who had started to sing, "bird beaks, bird beaks really cheap cheap chip chip". People started to pay attention, his nature and character was infectious. People were curious. Max had the opportunity to meet new people. He wasn't disappointed that he didn't make a sale. He had fun and got to achieve his goal for the day. He was happy with himself and was thinking of ways to improve for next time (not that there has been one since). Mick enjoyed it more because his expectations were originally negative and was only concerned about how people would react. Mick actually found it fun. I guess I was more open to other ideas as a result of my findings and adopting my theories, i.e. managing the change.

Following Max's expedition, I dropped Mick off at the hospital around 6pm on 13/7/2012. I dropped into Elle's on the way home thinking that I would be able to pick Mick up in a couple of hours. We left Elle's house around 9pm. Mick had not been seen to at that stage. After having a blood test and receiving a blood thinning agent, Mick was ready to be released at 3am in the morning. However I wasn't going to drag all the kids out of bed during that cold night. I told him to catch a taxi. Unfortunately Mick had tried a number of taxis but most declined to take the 30 minute trip into the sticks (bush), except for Fazel!

Fazel was a lovely Muslim who was in his early 20's. On the way home, Mick had a great chat with him about the regimes that ruled his country. He told Mick that his family had to flee for their lives. They had to leave a 150 hectare orchard and their belongings to save themselves. His parents had made it to London and he managed to find his way to Australia. He hasn't seen them since. Fazel provided Mick with an insight to his country. They spoke about the Taliban and about the Muslim religion. Mick loves history and has always been interested in understanding more about cultures/countries. He thoroughly enjoyed the ride home and enjoyed relaying the story to me.

Mick found his trip amusing because I had mentioned in an earlier conversation my thoughts/comparisons I made in respect to religions. At that stage, even though Mick didn't know how much research I was performing at night, I would subtly mention the odd thing and we would discuss them. Therefore when Fazel started highlighting similar matters, Mick thought it was very coincidental. I did have the pleasure of meeting Fazel when I went to pay the fare and he was very friendly. I thanked him and said if we ever need a taxi, we'd be calling on him again!

While Mick was at the hospital in the early hours, I was talking to our best man Grant. Grant is awesome, he is very kind, caring, generous, thoughtful and understanding. (Grant's wife Robyn is pretty much the same and we all have a great time when we catch up.) Grant has always been there for Mick (and me) and loves him like a brother. Grant and I have always got along too. We mentally challenge each other at times but it's all in good fun! I was reluctant to fill him in on my recent journey but obviously Mick had been speaking to him earlier. I expected that he would reject my predictions because he doesn't believe in any psychic matters. I'm not sure if he was entertaining my thoughts or if he was intrigued but we spent a good couple of hours on the phone. He couldn't understand why I was endeavouring down that path and I couldn't really justify it to anyone. Mainly because no one would understand until I had finished my book and secondly, it was a work in progress. I had started to work during the night again and was slowly making my way back into the sub-conscious. I was compelled to explore more because of what I was able to articulate and I wanted to test my physical and mental boundaries.

Mick had to return to the hospital on the Saturday for an ultrasound. He was very relieved that all appeared to be fine. He was expecting bad news but it was good and his stress disappeared. He wasn't concerned about his sleep apnoea because he has lived with it for years. (Hopefully he will get that seen to soon because he hasn't had the opportunity since my episode).

By the Sunday, I was actively into the sub-conscious zone. I was transcribing a great deal of what I was covering. My parents had called to say they were going visit. I said to Mick this is what my dad will do:

- Dad will say hello and sit on the arm chair in front of the TV.
- He will talk about another friend's daughter or son successfully achieving their goals. (For example: Dale who was in advertising and was very successful in his career. Then it was Sophie who was an architect who invested in property). On that particular day, it was Matthew who was building a resort in the Philippines.
- He will recommend something for us to achieve.
- He will say he is happy but appears unhappy
- His face/complexion will be tinged with a colour of grey

Sure enough, my Dad did exactly what I had perceived, looked how I described and behaved as I predicted. He even recommended that I develop an APP. Mick was captivated by the whole scenario. He couldn't believe that I had articulated what eventuated.

When my Dad was watching the TV, he noticed a person with the same family surname as his, on the credits of a cartoon. This led to another conversation. He explained that there was an uncle in London who was a doctor. My dad's uncle had provided generous support for the uncensored edition of the blue book on the Armenian genocide. There was also another relative that my dad mentioned who resided in California. I found this very bizarre because it indirectly connected to my research. I then proceeded to explore my mum's ancestry. My mum sat with me beside the computer and was very interested where as my dad seemed disinterested and continued sitting on the chair. My mum's heritage was just as intriguing as my dad's but I didn't have time to delve deeper. Consequently over the next few days, I was compelled to research more on my heritage and a great deal more on other matters.

I ended up deeper into my sub-conscious. My mind was processing that much information that I couldn't stop. I was pumped with adrenaline. I had performed many "brain dumps". I captured audio, footage and pictures leading up to my peak. My theories and connections became extreme. My tone and behaviour became erratic and my imagination ran wild.

The night before I lost control, I was grilling Mick about my theories. I wanted to know if he had been listening and if he was ready to be my coach. It was very confronting for him where as I was just rolling with things. I went shopping at 11.30pm. I purchased packaged food which I don't normally buy a great deal of. Mick called it astronaut food when he inspected the cupboard. I even bought beef jerky. (I guess I was practicing what to buy in the event of a catastrophe). I took pictures whilst on my shopping expedition. I also bumped into a friend from the footy club and said I was doing a social experiment. At that stage, my mind had clearly flipped back to natural disasters. I compared my basket of goods to those I bought Rose in terms of value and price when I returned home. I took hundreds of pictures at different angles of the house. I even recall lying on my back on the floor and happily snapping away. I assume I behaved this way because I had recently explored these matters and my mind was acting out instead of processing. I knew what I was doing but I had no control. It was very surreal and bizarre!

In essence, I had come full circle. I understood my psyche and had developed models and theories to assist others. I explored psychology from my own perspective. I had tested, changed and implemented those theories for myself. I had also stretched my physical and mental boundaries to the extreme. I was able to view the world from many aspects. However upon reaching the extreme, I was about to endure the ride of a life time. The crazy capers that a full moon brings was about to unfold for me….

I trust you are ready for my extreme ride into the psyche world! The train has just picked up some momentum; we will be travelling full steam ahead……….

5. The day & the night – Dancing on the ceiling!

Wholly fucking Mama!! Mama fucker!! Fook me!! Oh Me, Oh My!! Um............. I've really pushed myself past the limit, like the cliff man on the "Price is Right" but instead of going down, I was on a high! As I previously mentioned, I was articulating coming full circle with what I was researching, testing and implementing at home. On the morning of the 18/7, I was buzzing around like a bee! I rang Mick to ask him to come home but he said he couldn't because of work. I told him "The kids will be fine but I can't be held responsible for anything that happens today."

Basically my brain was processing too much information. I was awake in a drunk like state but I had full recollection of all the sequence of events, this included who I called, what I did, most of what I said and the tone (yes I was the mouth from the north, south, east & west), how I felt, why I was behaving in that manner, where I was on all accounts, the names of my captors – only stirring John and Mal. (I was lucky I had two good looking nice policemen who I entertained at home before being dragged out of my house.) Everything was about change, some of the topics I covered were cancer, divorce, the world, carbon tax, childhood, adolescence etc. – I was about to be the rebel of all time.

Sound exciting? Man was it ever! I just wanted to have fun! I knew that I had slipped back into the sub-conscious and felt like running. For those that know me, I couldn't run to save my life! For the physical aspect, the best way to explain it was; I was doing and caring too much. I couldn't turn off my mind. My body had been gradually producing natural adrenaline to allow me to keep going and it must have sent a surge on that day that created a short circuit.

I believe this caused the receptors in my brain to react and behave differently (like when you consume copious amounts of alcohol and do crazy things). I came to my conclusion after I had my rest of course, all lights may have been on but they weren't connected properly!

As highlighted in the first phase, for every action, there is an equal and opposite reaction, this was no different, basic logic. I assume what heavy drugs do to a person; I did naturally and had articulated that all throughout the first phase and in part leading up to Mama's big day out!

From a mental perspective, despite speculation, I was sleeping but nowhere near enough. I haven't worked out the math at this stage and nor do I need to but the 4 days leading up to that day, I probably had 10 hours sleep.

My behaviour changed as I progressed into sub-conscious but I still knew what I was doing and why. My mind was linking short term memory of recent events/situations with behaviour's not normally present for the everyday real me. What I was seeing was a reverse angle (mirror image) or perspective to information being processed. More of this will be revealed as you progress on my train but it gives you a small insight to what was happening in my active mind and what appeared different to me on that fun filled day.

When I got out of bed I picked up Lexi (she had been sleeping with me) and went to the kitchen and placed her in the high chair. I made her wheat bix with fruit and Isaiah fed her. Isaiah had already made his lunch and was ready to go, so he caught the bus to school.

For some reason Max didn't want to catch the bus. I made the boys toast with nutella, the usual! The whole time my mind was processing information at a rapid rate, pretty much my whole life, what I recently studied, my family, my friends, the government, religion – the last two being things I wasn't interested in but were obviously tucked away in my vault – it was frikkin' crazy! My "temple" (I assume that because it sounds good and forms part of the brain) went BOOM! BANG! And later BOOM! The BOOM was during the day and the night being the BANG, for good reason too.

I changed Harley's and Lexi's nappy. I rang Angel and told her I knew why she didn't get the job she recently applied for and I had an important job. I said she needed to get to my house straight away. I was aggressive in my tone and knew she would call the police. (Just before I continue, the company didn't ring me, but I'm assuming

Angel may have thought that, she may have wondered what had happened, why I was behaving like that, what should she do? Angel did the right thing, she called the police. Although she may have been feeling guilty, confused etc. - Angel would have to confirm, this is the equal and opposite reaction of how people effectively think in connection to others- more on that later).

Many queried who called the police and although Angel didn't say, I sent her my address and told her it was the white house - at 8.23am (before you jump to conclusions I don't have a number on my house hence the description).

I also called Jan and said she needed to get to my house as soon as possible. Jan knew the urgency from my tone and my intent was that she was there for the kids.

Therefore I inadvertently planned this in my moment of craziness, bizarre! Looking back, I guess I had control of most things but behaved abnormally depending on who I came into contact with, the reverse of how I would normally treat or react to people or situations. I assume part of the reason for calling Jan and Angel was that I had recently been in contact with them.

I also answered two calls that morning, one from the Child Support Agency and the other from the Fairwork Ombudsman, just thought I'd add that so the academics can validate my side with government records – you have my permission not that the privacy act holds any value!

I put my kids in the car, Max wanted to travel in the front seat and of course Harley did too, I strapped both of them in the front. I'm tipping I won't get mother of the year this year, I wasn't expecting to, so no big loss! But hey it was fine when we were growing up, rolling around on a mattress in the back of the van choking on cigarette smoke!

I do smoke but never in the car or the house and no, in normal circumstances I would not let two kids ride in the front – bad mum! No one saw them so I didn't have to fess up but I'm expecting people to judge me! It's your choice, I'm not beating myself up on past actions plus I was in dire need of sleep and in a state of hypo-mama madness. No one was in danger!

Once the kids were in the car, I then planned the start of my rebel with a cause and effect. I left the wet dirty nappies on the floor, opened all doors in my house, heaters were running, TVs blaring, tipped up the washing basket, there was an opened packet of coloured popcorn so I spread that across the floor. I was the junk yard dog of Hairy Mole (my nickname for the town I live in). You couldn't see the kitchen bench. I was rebelling against myself too, that is, what I expected my children not to do, I was doing. Again in effect, I was acting out what I was processing.

On my way to school, I actually passed the police and waved, for some reason I took the alternate route (the old way I use to take to get to the highway). I had a chuckle to myself because I knew they were heading to my place. I rang Sally who is very loving, caring, thoughtful, kind and generous, would do anything for anyone. Even clean infested sores and care for the nastiest, most wicked and abusive man I have ever come across, her father-in-law Bob. Anyway I said she needed to be at my house on Saturday and she must be there, I wasn't going to take no for an answer. Again, I was quite aggressive in my tone and her reply was "I don't know if you know but I'm actually very sick". I responded with "you have cancer get away from Bob, he is sucking the life out of you". I was trying to help and care for Sally in an odd way!

I called Sally for her birthday (after I was released) and sung my usual "Happy Birthday" and apologised for that day. She asked if I remembered telling her she had cancer. I said I did but I didn't mean that she physically had cancer but Bob was making her sick. I guess I was using cancer as a metaphor for all things. No surprise because obviously this was an indirect trigger for my obscure journey.

Sally had always been a great friend and still is, thank goodness. She has never judged me and even when I filled her in on my bizarre predictions in the first phase, she said you have to do what you've got to do! I have so much respect and love for her. We don't have to catch up all the time and we pick up where we left off! I'm one lucky person to have such an amazing friend, she is phenomenal. I'm sure all her family and other friends think the same.

Obviously it would have been confronting for Sally to hear what I was saying on that day and true to her-self, she never judged me and accepted my apology. I'm sure she would have been thinking, what was that all about? What is happening with Mama? Is this why I'm so sick? Again I don't know what Sally was thinking because I'm not her and I didn't mean to express what I was thinking in that way, I was just rolling with what I was processing in my head.

The next person I rang was my ex-fiancé, who is also Sally's brother in-law. I left Duncan a message telling him that although things didn't work out between us, I still had a special place in my heart for him. (Any love, past or present always forges a place in your heart and there is nothing to be ashamed or guilty of!) I also said that I needed a generator and I wanted to know the fuel consumption required to run the average household. Not sure if this related to my earlier predictions about pending doom or an alternative to using electricity due to the rising costs of utilities. My tone with Duncan was more emotional, I believe this was because I didn't show much (if any) emotion when we parted ways.

When I rang him and apologised for my behaviour and let him know I was all good, he said he couldn't understand most of my message. I wondered if he had but I basically told him the same thing. I said that I heard he had gone off the rails and it would be a shame to let life slip, when he has an opportunity for so much more. We joked about one flying over the Cuckoo's nest. He asked if anyone had been raped in the place and I told him it was funny he mentioned that because I was just about to tell him something a patient said. (I'll keep you in suspense for the moment and share that a bit later). I also said he was welcome over anytime if he needed a chat or wanted to catch up. Obviously Mick knows and is not perturbed, no secrets in our relationship. We have a very strong foundation based on love, happiness, trust etc. and the negative traits are not part of who we are, that's the way we've always been. Like any couple we may have our moments but we always bounce back just as quick as it started, we'd rather be happy than sad and miserable.

I later heard that when Dutchman (a mutual friend) told Duncan the news, he assumed it was pay-back until he heard I was in hospital. He wanted to visit me which I thought was nice but Wally and Donna suggested it wouldn't be wise. If he had come in drunk, I don't think the staff would have let him out and I would have felt really bad because that place would have done him over!

Back to the day and on track, I arrived at the school and took Max into the office. I was dressed in my long sleeve red top, black pants and thongs. I proudly became a feral (I can judge myself, that's in part what my book's about!) I immediately drew attention by apologising for Max being late, placing $6 on the counter and asking them to order him something for lunch. They asked Max if he was fine and he said he was. I said we have got to change and they had no clue what I was on about and why would they? I was in a world of my own. I asked them if they had an iPhone and requested them to take a picture of another iPhone and then I showed them mine. I told them they couldn't get the same picture and only my phone could take a reflective shot. Of course they knew something was wrong but they were happy to go along with my charade. Jay the principal was fantastic, even though I know he knew things weren't right he didn't challenge and took it at face value. The others weren't sure what to do, I assume they were all perplexed by my behaviour – I'd say their faces were one of bewilderment.

Upon reflection, it dawned on me that my eyesight was working in reverse, the mirror image that I was referring to earlier, no wonder I couldn't get my point across, they weren't seeing what I was! I'm sure I would have been the talk of the school – that hasn't bothered me!

I have since been to school for the book parade and enjoyed that morning. The school has one of the best learning curriculums and it stems from a great leader and a vibrant enthusiastic team. I had a quick chat to Caitlyn, Bel and said hello to a few others. I didn't feel awkward and I wasn't embarrassed by attending. After the parade, Jay made a special effort to pat me on the back and say "great to see you back", simple but meant so much! No explanation required and I kindly said thank you! Such a great school, hope it can cater for high school in the future!

Before I left the school on that day, I received a phone call from the police. They asked me what's going on, I said that they are there for a reason and a purpose and to take a good look around - I'll be there soon. I put Harley in his booster seat on the way back and proceeded home. I did drive safely and I didn't reverse all the way home so something was working right on that front – for those that are wondering!

I pulled into the drive way and thought well I've locked the police in; they aren't going anywhere because I have a party planned and a heap to communicate. I entered the house with Harley and he went off to play in his room. Jan hadn't arrived at this stage. John and Mal asked me what's going on and again I said you're here for a reason and a purpose and we are going to have a party. They were both Blues supporters and made mention of that because a scarf was hanging off the hook near the door. I said Fevola's coming to my party too. (Fevola –a footballer, has always reminded me of my brother, only my brother wasn't famous!) I said before I begin, I'll just grab Lexi out of the car. I don't think they realised my baby was still in there so Mal went to get her. I think Jan arrived around that time. Anyway I was rambling on and decided to grab a permanent marker and start explaining what I was trying to communicate on my walls, "graffiti" style! (Most people assumed I did this before the police arrived. I didn't, John and Mal can validate that. Mick later told me that he asked the police to distract me from the green walls. I laughed and said "Really? I had no intention writing on my green walls because I knew I didn't have enough paint". We had a heap of white paint left over from the extension).

I was bouncing from one spot to another, I was almost like a human pinball, start with writing something and then head to another space and wrote something else. Basically here are some of the items I ended up with on my walls in no particular order (including an explanation of my thoughts):

On the day and post my episode, I was referring to change, which the triangle represents in shorthand.

Beehive
Behave

I was explaining how these words were created. I said that a bee would not sting unless you misbehaved. I also made reference to paedophiles having their own protected cell.

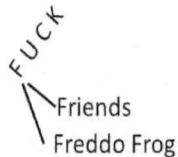

I said we were all fucked. I then wrote FUCK and John said that isn't nice. I said give me time to explain, if you look at each single letter it represents something different. I asked Mal for the first word that he thought of for the letter F, his reply was Freddo frog at which point, I said it was interesting. John said Friends and I told him I liked the way he thought.

I was highlighting that there would be destruction at the Colosseum. I was also referring to the pillars of society and how it needed to change.

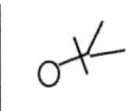

I said we all had to be at the right angle when the world started moving. After my episode, I realised it was in reference to providing people with the opportunity to view and understand many angles to many matters.

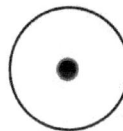

I was referring to the core of challenges, people's perceptions and how we are blind sighted.

I was highlighting that the safest place to be when the earth started moving was near trees, as they were rooted into the ground. I also advised that people needed to change to minimise the impacts to the environment.

World   Destruct   I was talking about destruction in the world, predominantly with the earth moving. I asked John and Mal if they knew how contemplate was derived. They didn't understand what I meant but I said, earth plates move (plate) continents move (conte) – contemplate over a period of time (tem- latin) and it results in earthquakes /tsunami's. In essence, the word means think and I was trying to highlight that we need to think about the consequences of our actions and the environment.

WHEN   N3HW   I had started to write in a mirror image as well without any thought. I did this to perfection when transcribing the mirror image. I have struggled to do this now, it takes me a lot longer to complete and is no where near perfect.

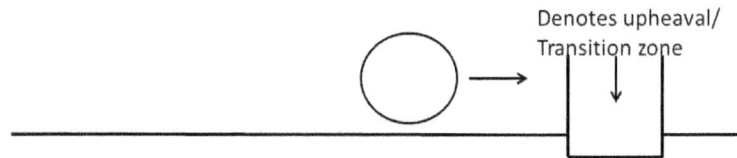

I drew the world on a timeline and said that there will be a moment in time that the world would be forced to adjust due to nature's force and there will be a new world. Upon reflection, I was referring to change; current world, transition and brave new world. It also represented my three states of mind at the height of my episode current outlook, transition and improved perspective/outlook.

155

(The remnants of my graffiti still scar my walls but I have chosen to leave as is, for a while, in the event any academic professionals want to validate the physical evidence.)

In that time, I was also showing them my phone, my computer and some research. Of course this was all pointless as I was on a different mental channel – Mama's cosmos! I grabbed a full bottle of bourbon from the bench which was sitting next to an empty bottle. I went out to the deck and told them that our spirit (human spirit) now comes from a bottle; people just can't enjoy themselves without a drink. I think John, Mal and Jan thought I was going to drink it and I guess there was also a perception that I may have been drunk because of the empty bottle. I had no intention of drinking it but I was giving my take on what I was interpreting from the label. Mal seemed intrigued but I'm not sure if he was just entertaining my thoughts. (I hadn't had a drink since the 16/6. I use to label myself a weekend binge drinker because I loved unwinding with a drink at the end of the week.)

Now I'm laughing as I type because I still have visions of this and if ever a movie comes out, it would make for a good scene. After I had Lexi, I had a real bad case of mastitis and the doctor was going to send me to hospital at which point I declined and roughed it out at home. I blistered up badly and was left with a scar. I called it my "after birth natural tattoo" because at that stage I said I would never get one. Anyway in my height of madness, this 'tatt' resembled the mankind symbol similar to a star in a pentagon. Out of nowhere I flashed my right tit (bosom, breast whatever you want to call it) to Mal & John and said I'm doing this for mankind. Like they had just seen something out of a horror movie or were startled by bright lights, they raised their arms across their eyes in a flash (pardon the pun). Their reactions and facial expressions were priceless, no amount of money could buy that reaction! Jan quickly said "There is no need to do that Annette." So with that I took off my bra and threw it at them (take that!). He he he fancy throwing your bra at two nice policemen! Jan said she suspected they thought that I would take off all my clothes but I stopped there at that stage!

Not long after I saw the ambulance arrive and this angered me. I thought there was no way I'd be leaving my home in an ambulance. If anything I'd rather go in the back of a divvy-van (police vehicle) and tick off that on my list to do before I hit 40. I have had many ambulances attend my house over the previous 12 months because my son suffered from chronic asthma. I always have the utmost respect for the care and service they provide. However because I was behaving in an opposite manner, as soon as they walked in I said I didn't like them, they are evil, they're bad, basically told them to get out of my house. Hopefully I'll get a chance to apologise for my behaviour on that day. As previously mentioned, I was in a very different state of mind. Jan did make mention that my body language changed dramatically when I saw the ambulance and they were nice (sorry guys, if you are reading this).

Now John and Mal did ask me if I would go to the hospital and I told them I'm not leaving my house. I was not going willfully because in my mind I had important items to communicate plus I had not done anything illegal. It's not a crime to write on your walls. Yes it is crazy and I knew I needed help but I needed to process what was on my mind so I could fall asleep. I didn't think that there was anything wrong with me helping myself. I just wanted to do it my way! (Frank Sinatra is another favourite of mine and he was arrogant – so why couldn't I be?)

With that they tried to drag me by the arms. I planted my big fat ass on the floor and grabbed the side of the brick wall. I was kicking and yelling at them. They couldn't control me and I broke from their grip. I then moved to the hallway where I sat on the floor and said can't you see what I'm talking about? They were trying to lift me up again. I said I was zapping their energy. Had I planned this? It was after I had written beehive on the wall (referring to zap)? And I did write behave and I wasn't? I wasn't actually zapping their energy but I was so strong because of the adrenaline pumping through my veins.

They eventually dragged me out of my house kicking and screaming. I did try to grab the laundry door to no avail. At one stage, I think I yelled out or thought "a dingo's got my baby". I believe this was because the final inquest into the Chamberlain case had concluded just before my incident. As John and Mal dragged me from the front door, I was still yelling out obscenities. I think I used every explicit word that you could possibly imagine. I was Mad Dog Mama – one reckoning force. Out the front door across wooden planks and some broken glass from the toilet window (from when I locked the keys in the house). I was lucky I didn't cut up rough! I remember holding on to the sides of the divvy-van. As they pushed me in, I was kicking and growling in a beast/primal like fashion. Oh Mama Bear!

Strangely though, in my mind I was having fun, I was actually enjoying it! Thinking wow I gave those policemen a run for their money? Who would have thought a 39 year old woman could physically challenge two strapping fit policemen? Geez, I flashed and threw my bra at them? If only someone had caught that footage, who is going to believe this? Jan also told me when they had given her an update (after I was locked in the van) that they were both huffing/puffing and seemed physically challenged from the scuffle.

In the back of the divvy-van I was talking out loud, winking at the camera, re-living my past. I found it strange that I didn't have to put on a seat belt. When I told John I wasn't wearing one, he was surprised and said "Why not?" I replied "I was enjoying the free ride". Wonder who should have copped a fine in that circumstance? I pretty much laid back with my arms to the sides, back wedged against the backside of the van with my feet on either side of the window. Hopefully you're not having visuals because it wasn't a pretty look. Etiquette has never been one of my fortes. For those that have not had the pleasure of travelling in the back of a police van, it's basically all plastic and there are no padded seats, just a pure white hard fiberglass shell. I guess it makes for easy cleaning at the end of the day!

I assumed we arrived at Casey Hospital in Berwick around 10.30am. I didn't have access to a clock and I never wear a watch because I dislike being ruled by time. I didn't get a chance to grab my phone in the mayhem, normally I would refer to that if I needed to know. Mal and John were contemplating how I would react. They were circling the car and trying to determine the best approach to unleash the beast. I guess they perceived me to be a violent mad woman but I was only reacting to being forced out of my home– equal and opposite reaction. I had accepted what happened and in an odd way was riding the wave/going with the flow for my unexpected inadvertent plan.

They left me in there for a good 10 minutes and kept asking me if I was alright. I happily said I was fine but I wouldn't mind a drink of water – if that wasn't too much trouble. Mal and John deliberated a bit more and asked me how I would behave. I replied, "I'm all good, happy to go with the flow". They said, "Are you going to behave when we let you out?" I said "Of course, I'm all good." With apprehension, they opened the door, and I proceeded out slowly so I wouldn't scare them. I wanted to ROAR RAAAAAAAAAAAAAAAH but I knew it wasn't appropriate. I thought this because I felt like a lion trapped in a cage and it would have been funny. I did ask if the camera in the back of the divvy worked because I wouldn't mind a copy! I think John and Mal just laughed.

I entered the hospital and was given a room to the side in ER. Hmmm interesting, normally you just get allocated one of many beds across a wall divided by curtains. I decided to call it my cell for the day; special treatment for special person? I continued talking about my findings, thoughts, analysis and observations. John asked me where my thong was and I told him that it fell off when they were pushing me in to the divvy - it was in the drive way.

One in three people get cancer, one in three couples divorce and suicides – there is a connection between these statistics. I elaborated on the suicides and said there had been 6 on the tracks in the last 6 months from Beaconsfield toward Pakenham. John and Mal looked in amazement and asked how I knew this? I said I've read the newspapers!! (I didn't insult them but I thought der!) Oh yeah, that makes sense was the look they gave. I told them to write down my tax file number 178 778 369 because we are all prisoners of society. I have no drama sharing this number because it holds no value to me. I also gave them my credit card number (I didn't provide the expiry) and told them to write that down because I knew in normal circumstances people have no recollection of most things so

I was trying to highlight that I was different when the time was right and that my memory was intact.

I asked for a piece of paper and pen so I could keep writing but they refused because they thought I was going to write on the wall. I said I wouldn't ask for a piece of paper if my intention was to write on the wall. Obviously they didn't trust me because they perceived I would because of what I had done at my home. My request for paper.....denied.....so I kept talking and talking like the donkey from Shrek! John did ask why I kept talking. I told him that there was nothing else to do so might as well educate everyone (reason).

I was trying to keep awake because I wasn't sure where I was heading (purpose). Some of my observations were: I was asking why people were wearing visitor badges in a hospital. People wouldn't be there if they didn't need to be. I was questioning why people were doing so much paper work when technology had come so far. If they changed, the under resourced system could better care for patients, rather than put pen to paper.

They asked whether I wanted food or a drink. I wasn't interested in food, I was too busy talking. I requested bottled water; I didn't want anyone to spike my drink. I was told I had to buy one but forgot to grab my purse in the turmoil (sarcasm-love it!). I did eventually get that bottle of water.

John kept re-assuring me that I was a good mother and that my children were beautiful kids. I said I know. I think he was concerned that I thought I wasn't. John also told me that I nearly kicked poor Mal in the knacker bag (testicle) - adds a new meaning to cop that! Poor Mal, I think it was one challenging day for him!

Not long after I arrived, they advised that my parents had turned up at the hospital and I told them I didn't want to see them. They would have been too emotionally charged and would spoil my day. I was thinking of myself – for once it was all about me!

When Mick turned up, I said "Hey hun, what are you doing here? Mick replied "I was at Werribee when I got a call from the police" (I thought, well there is no more shit in Werribee cause I'm causing a flow of it down here! Werribee was renowned for this because a major sewage plant is located in the area. I'm happy to confirm it is a very diverse and pleasant place; hopefully it will continue to thrive in the future). I said "Well can you please tell these two good looking nice policeman what I'm on about so we can go home because time is of essence". Mick replied "I can't do that". My response was, "Well, you can get out of my cell. If you're not on my team, go home and look after the kids." With that I kissed him good bye. Mick just rolled with it. John was baffled and asked if Mick was okay, I assume he thought Mick would be upset. Mick replied "She knows what she wants and calls it how it is!"

I would talk about something, then turn it into a song and then talk about another subject; it was like performing in a cycle. John and Mal marveled at how I could fluently do this but I guess it was the drunken state of mind I was in. Or maybe it was a hidden talent that had just surfaced! There were two other younger policemen and I asked what they were in for. Obviously they were babysitting another nutter who didn't venture out from their cell. I was stirring them up too. A plasterer was repairing the wall and I got the odd glance from him because of what I was saying. I perceived the ER to be very quiet that day, I'm not sure if it was because I blocked out the noise with my verbal spray or if people were listening to me.

Mal was writing some side notes on some of the things I was talking about and seemed interested in what I had to say. John kept saying "You guys have a connection". I told them that Mal was exactly like my husband but an introvert. At one stage, I asked Mal who was walking back from the vending machine when his birthday was and said check the back of the chip packet. I think the expiry date (month and day) was the same as his birthday. He appeared to have freaked himself out; I still wonder whether I did or if he was playing with me! Not sure why I asked him that!

At one stage, John said we should just go to the pub (he was joking of course), how long is it before a doctor gets here? I told him one won't be coming for a while. I did give him a reason but don't need to discuss that in this book. I was mentally challenging them the whole day, telling them to do what is right for you and not to worry about me. Empower yourself to think for yourself. I apologised for mentally infiltrating their minds and stimulating mine. I was playing mind games and had an acute skill of reading body language and a greater depth to language. I also acquired a very open mind as a result of my self-discovery.

Just before the doctor came they were physically and mentally exhausted. I know this because Mal was down on one knee in the "thinker" like position in my cell and John asked if he could sit on the couch. They even said so themselves and all they had to do was "babysit me" until the hospital decided what they were going to do with me.

It would have been around about 5pm before I consulted with a Psychiatrist and student doctor. I was sitting on the bed with my back to the wall and legs crossed. I told the doctor that I was prepared to answer his questions if he answered mine. I asked him his place of birth because he looked Middle Eastern – similar to my Dad. I guess my Dad always tried to exert control of me and my life and still was at 39. I saw the doctor being no different. I challenged him on a few things and told him that his body language was not conducive to being open to my questions. One-way communication, I expected this because they are trained professional academics with experience and what patient would know better. I could see out of my peripheral vision that John and Mal were turning their heads left to right like a tennis match. I suspect they were thinking what the hell is going on here? Why is Annette challenging the doctor? What is the doctor going to do?

I said I was more than happy to speak with the student doctor because she was more receptive and seemed open to my views. I'm sure she would have found the consult interesting. The doctor left and the student stayed. I knew I wasn't doing myself any favours but I was just rolling with it. The Psyche Doctor returned and deemed me too hard to handle so they decided they were going to transfer me to Monash in Clayton.

This time I was happy to ride in the ambulance. In true form of being a rebel and testing the system, I told them I wasn't going to put on my seat belt. One of the ambulance crew said they couldn't move unless I did put on my belt for safety reasons. I said I wouldn't unless the police gave me a fine. Mal didn't want to give me a fine, not sure if it was because I hadn't broken the law or if I was deemed mad or he just felt sorry for me. My intention was to leave another marker. I wanted to know the time and have a record for where I was because if you are of unsound mind, people can stretch the truth. We compromised and Mal wrote down the time 17.30pm in his little black book stating he will issue me (I provided the contact details) with a fine. This is also how I knew that the doctor saw me around 5pm. Another example of something eventuating for a reason and for a purpose - I might have been deemed mentally ill but I wasn't stupid. In my opinion I was far from it. I wonder how the medical profession would analyse/interpret that! Maybe it is outside their realm or reality of their trained mind?

The poor ambulance drivers copped more of my verbal diarrhea. I was talking about Tsunami's and what you would do in the event; for example: move people to the country, turn off power/gas, shut down sewerage, ground modes of transport, and provide prompt clear communication for all. Control rodents by sending out cats and using pest control regardless of the cost to minimise disease. (I mentioned this at home and the hospital as well). I questioned why there were two seat belts, was one for death and other for living. Of course it was one for child and one for adult but in essence, I was referring to the fact that we are all a dying race but we just don't know when it's going to happen and how – not that we need to know! Everyone I directly or indirectly engaged or encountered during my discovery or crazy phase couldn't appreciate (not even my husband) what I was doing and why. Although I was in a different state of mind, I was creating awareness the whole time. People were going to remember me for a cause and an effect in the not too distant future. Also the experience would be beneficial for my book!

I was talking about a plethora of things that morning and day. Some of it I won't bring up at this stage because it isn't the right time or it is not appropriate but I do recall everything even though I didn't have full control over my behaviour.

I rocked up to the back door (fire escape) of the Acute Management Area (AMA – funny how, this abbreviation is the same as the Australian Medical Association) at Monash Medical Clinic at approximately 6pm. I questioned why we were coming through the back door. Didn't I deserve the courtesy of walking through the front? I wasn't being loud; I was quite calm albeit I was still talking a bit. I don't believe talking is a crime or issue for today, or was it? I wasn't violent either and patiently stood there. I didn't even contemplate running because with one thong and feeling very sheepish by this stage, I wasn't going to get far. It would have been more trouble than what it was worth anyway.

Upon entering AMA, I was instructed by the nurse Friedda to sit on a chair. (Funny because Mal had mentioned Freddo earlier that day!) I replied, "If you want to help me, I need sleep and I need it now." They then gave me a room to the left of the door I had entered. The window in the room was high but I could see a church with stained glass windows. This was to the left of the bed and opposite to the room door. I had a couple of hours sleep. Michelle another nurse checked on me (I'm assuming around 9pm) and asked if I wanted something to eat. I said yes and expected the food to be delivered to my room. That's what normally happens in hospitals right? Not in AMA and I didn't know this so I just went back to sleep. I wasn't really hungry anyway.

Now the nurses kept pestering me to take medication, I called them drugs. I knew I was there due to sleep deprivation and I kept refusing to take anything without a diagnosis. Mind you, I had never set foot in a psyche ward and I was unaware of my rights at that stage. Had they said they were sleeping tablets I would have consumed them. Can someone of total unsound mind articulate this?

I was still in that drunken state of mind. I was becoming annoyed and harassed by the medical staff, so I thought I'd play a practical joke, obviously not appreciating the other side of how it would be viewed. I was in my clothes for approximately 40 hours and had not had a shower. The smell was unbearable for me alone and I would have given any skunk a match on the scent sweepstakes! So I stripped and placed a hand towel around my neck; the towel was meant to serve as a distraction. (Not sure why there was a hand towel because there was no shower or tap in the room). If I had been wearing boots, that would have been funnier – Puss in boots! I waited at the door patiently pissing myself laughing and imagining what the reaction would be.

Gragan was the lucky man - BAAHAA! His eyes popped out of his head, his hands immediately went to his head – Shock Factor Plus! He walked to the centre of the room and returned to check if what he saw was right. At this stage the door was slightly ajar. Fuck I haven't looked in the mirror for some time but it would have been an ugly sight! I was dying of laughter on the inside but held my composure. I was smiling like a Persian cat from the movie Cats and Dogs! Gragan then circled the room and took one more look before he left. The reaction and facial expressions is one that has been etched in my memory (and like the incident with the police) has brought me many a laugh and chuckle. I should have put my clothes on in the time that he left so they would have thought he was crazy! However I'd thrown them across the room and they did stink so I thought let's see what happens. Boy, I did not expect what was about to happen next!

Next minute there were a couple of security guards, nurses Gragan and Simi and there may have been one more, I thought oh shit! Anyway they asked why I was naked. I told them that I was removed from my home and by default, the system has made this my home for the night and I would be naked at home. I also said "What's the fucking problem? It is a hospital and you cut up naked bodies on a silver platter all the time". They advised that didn't happen in that part of the hospital I was in. "Who cares….that's not my problem!" was my reply. I didn't ask them to enter my room or look! Obviously I was feeling threatened and annoyed so one could perceive that I raised my voice or maybe I was talking loud because no one was listening to me. I told them the other patient (JC) was asleep and he hadn't woken. They advised it was not acceptable and I would be moved to seclusion. I thought fuck that!

I immediately dived for the base of the bed and hung on for dear life like a koala bear clutching a tree. I wasn't going to move willingly and so was resisting. Again I had an enormous amount of adrenaline and it did take a bit for them to peel me from the base. I'm not sure if I pulled the sheets over me as I dived to latch on to the bed or if the staff did but they were over my head for a short period of time. I didn't panic and asked them to remove them so I wouldn't suffocate. The security guard had his knee in my back as he was trying to pull my arms and another person was trying to release my legs. I can only imagine what they saw – assholes! Hahaha well they saw my big ass! Jokes on me!

I held on that tight that my shoulder was about to pop. Simi also made comment that they were going to hurt or injure me. With that I released my grip but the fucking security guard (and I remember his face) twisted my arm so forcefully behind my back that my shoulder nearly popped in the opposite direction. He also pinned my knee down and I was dragged to seclusion. I was a dead weight; the tops of my feet were rubbing across the floor while my soles were facing up! I wasn't going to make it easy – I'd already been abused! What else could they do to me?

The security guards threw me on a mattress on the floor. It looked disheveled and I don't think it was clean but what creditability does a mental patient have? Anyway the security guards pinned me down as I was doing a violent version of the 1980 caterpillar dance move as they sedated me. I never once was violent; I did not punch, bite or kick. I was calling them a "pack of fucking cunts"! Who wouldn't be angry after being abused in such a way? I was only reacting to how I was being treated. I did not have any support person/s with me. It appeared that I had no rights. They didn't even ring my husband to advise that they were going to sedate me. In actual fact, they told him not to visit for a week. They didn't know how much I weighed! They didn't even check if I had consumed any drugs or alcohol. I did not have a blood test at any time leading up to this. Could this sedation drug have had an adverse effect if I did? This was wrong on all accounts and I had every right to behave in this manner, what "normal" person wouldn't?

Now how on earth would this treatment help a person? Wouldn't this make their situation worse? I'm lucky because I am strong and have always thought of others that were worse off than me. I also kept thinking it was more material for my book! Therefore I was not angry for how I had been treated and I was not remorseful for my behaviour. I knew my book would provide great satisfaction and that was enough for me. I would also be able to tell my side of the story and help others by doing so!

After reading my rights, patients are normally moved to seclusion if they are at harm to themselves or others. Like fucking hell, how much damage did or could I have done to their eyes? I only grabbed the bed because I felt threatened and didn't want to be moved. Yes I appreciate I did do something crazy and didn't consider their side but I've done crazier things drunk leading up to this point. I assume I was sedated between 11pm -1am on Wed/Thurs 18-19/7/2012.

Mick first visited me on Wednesday 25/7/2012 and I explained what had happened. I also explained what I had been doing over the last month; he was totally unaware of my research for the book. He could tell I was back to my normal self and was appalled by my so-called treatment. He wanted to take me home but he couldn't because of the order I was placed on. Before he left, I took some photos of the injuries – this was 8 days after I was placed in seclusion. It was funny because I had just finished pulling up my pants when a nurse knocked and opened the door – they never waited for a welcome reply; they just invaded your room. She must have thought something was going on. So before I half-moon you and for the sake of political correctness, photos on the next page may offend some!

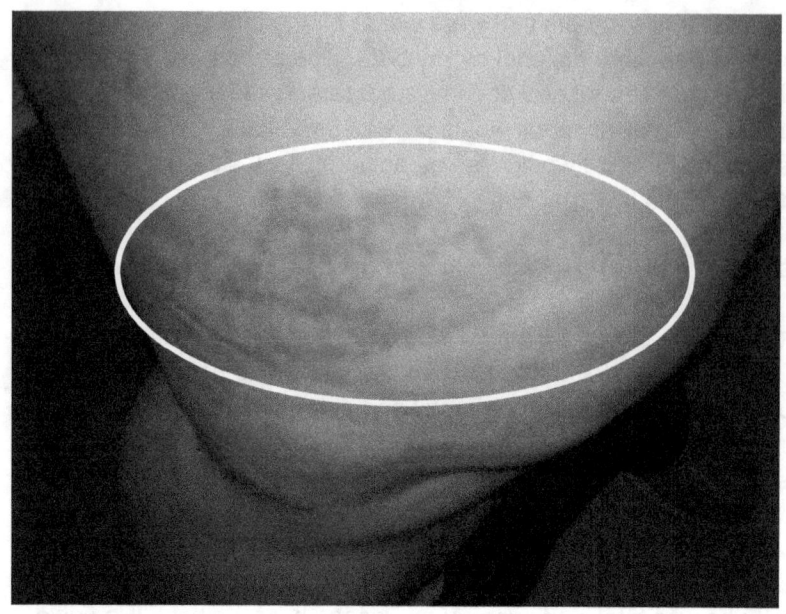

Above: bruise on my thigh above my knee and below one of the stab wounds on my butt cheek as a result of resisting treatment!

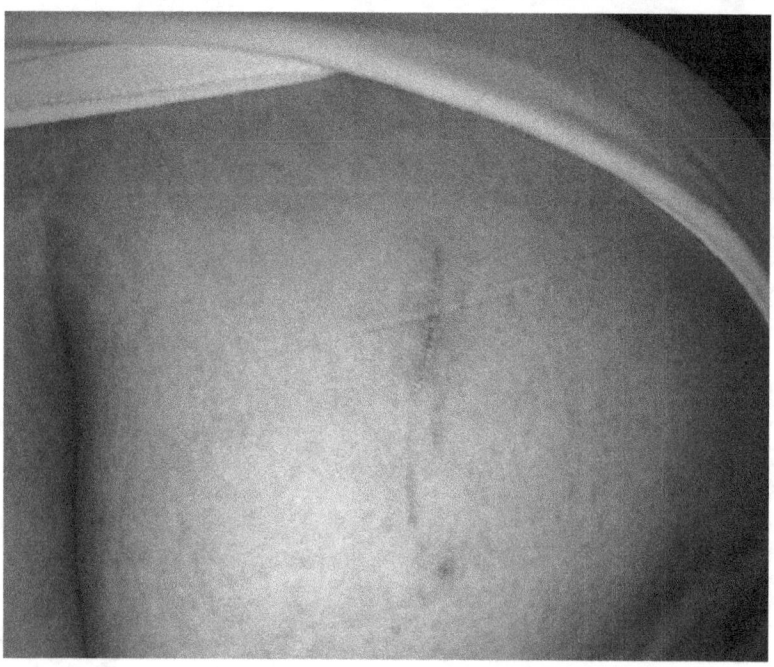

Below: my forearm injury from holding onto the bed, bruising on the bone when individuals were pulling me from the frame.

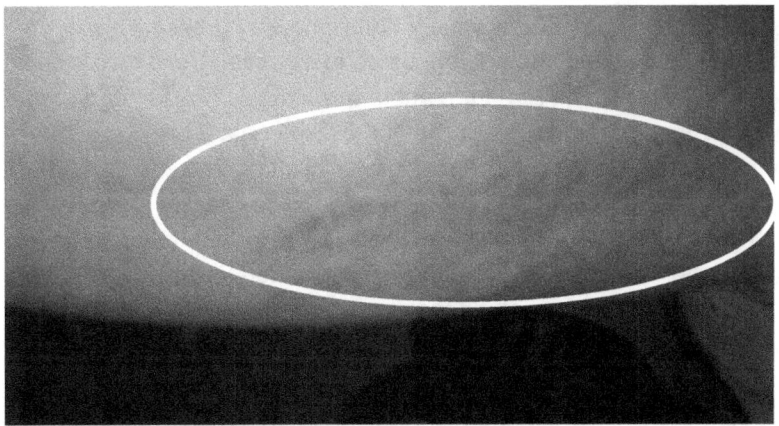

Back to the den, knocked out and nowhere to go! I drifted in and out of consciousness. The clock and date behind a glass window was incorrect so I managed to keep track of time by food being placed in my cell and using the lighting as an indicator. I refused to eat or drink as I was not prepared to use a cardboard cowboy hat to relieve myself (I'm seriously not joking). I did see a straightjacket and thought thank fuck they didn't use that!

I had the displeasure of meeting Doctor Julian Hughes (I didn't know his name at the time) around 10am on Thursday 19/7/2012 in the presence of a nurse and two security guards. What the fuck would he have been scared of? I was a slab of doped up meat on a mattress, in a cell. Oh and the cell wasn't padded either so it would be quite messy if someone did start banging their head across the wall – logical, not! I had blurred vision at that stage and I was hurling abuse. I called him a fucking cunt and told him that I was going to fight this. (I meant mentally of course- I couldn't even lift my head.) I said a few other things but can't recall the content, obviously it wasn't important. I do remember a nice Islander looking security guard who later waved and smiled when I was moved to the ward. I also remember the guard with the goatee. I was unaware that Dr. Hughes could have revoked an order placed on me. At the time, I didn't know I had no rights and the doctors were at liberty to treat me as they saw fit! FUCKED!!! Such an unjust system!

I also remember two other nurses, Martin who was dressed in black who I never saw again, he must have been a casual. Penny was the other; she was wearing a red top and a black skirt. I asked her if I could use the phone and dialed the number to contact Mick, this was around 7pm Thursday night. (Nothing wrong with my memory but my physical state was shot!) All I could manage to say was "What are you doing to me?" Mick's reply was "getting you help". I told him "to fuck off, this is not help" and hung up. I also asked Penny for a gown, because I felt dirty and if that was clean, that was the next best thing!

Every time I heard the door being unlocked, I woke up. I know I had my blood pressure taken and temperature once whilst in seclusion. I don't recall staff taking a blood test after being sedated, they could have. I was very vague given my lead up to being sedated. As I knew sleep deprivation caused my "moment in the sun" madness, I discarded any drugs that were given to me. When I was in seclusion, I popped them in my pillow case. I also did this when I returned to the AMA area as I had nowhere to store them. Friday morning they left the cell door open, I never once moved from the mattress.

I was released back into AMA early Friday afternoon. After three days I finally had an opportunity to have a shower. I ended up getting my period and thought I hope I left a mess for the fuckers to clean up! Demeaning, disgraceful, inhumane, appalling and sickening treatment! Would you trust anyone in a hospital after those events? Who is going to believe you? That's why I had to take the photos! I was just a walking zombie after having little sleep leading up to being sedated. I was emotionally sterile, I didn't cry or get upset. I did vent at the time but was back to my normal self in no time!

I apologised to all the nurses and they were all surprised that I remembered. Why, because patients don't normally remember. I had not seen Gragan until 15 days later (he must have been suffering from shock or maybe it was the unsightly map of Tassie, sorry it was too funny for me not to share!) and I apologised to him for my behaviour. He also apologised for being so forceful and said that they were the procedures they had to follow. He also made mention that I accidently knocked him in the face during the clash. Hopefully he completed an incident report which will further validate what transpired on that night! Wonder what has been captured in the medical report for the day and night that my mind was dancing on the ceiling?

The first of many positive experiences was meeting Justin (JC). I had the pleasure of meeting JC on arrival who was venting and the nurses were telling him to settle down. I told them to let him go and get whatever was on his mind off his chest – better out than in. JC was still in AMA on the Friday night and remembered me. His mum had been in earlier and gave him $40. JC was ordering pizza for dinner that night and insisted on buying me a pizza too. Even though I wasn't hungry I didn't want to reject his offer, I had one piece and gave the rest to Madrid who had just arrived. I thought this was such a kind act from a total stranger. I was totally surprised by his generosity.

At that time, I also didn't realise how much love I was about to receive from the most unexpected place I found myself in! It was a bitter-sweet experience but overall positive, more on that soon! As I mentioned before, you take the good with the bad and make it good again! I get knocked down and I get up again, you're never going to keep me down! (Hope you're singing it!)

As I remember a great deal, I assume some people maybe judging me at this stage, and that's fine, everyone is entitled to an opinion. I'm not embarrassed and I know it will help others, to what extent I'm not sure – nothing ventured, nothing gained.

But if you are deemed mentally ill and you do crazy things – are you helping by judging? How can you comment if you have not experienced it for yourself? Are you ignoring a wider problem? Is it easier to judge because you don't want to face your own demons? Does it make you feel better or normal? Is it because people are not living up to your expectations or society's expectations?

Every person who suffers depression or is on anti-depressants could end up in a psyche ward deemed mentally ill! Anyone who excessively abuses drugs or alcohol could too! Anyone who has had a traumatic experience could as well! In fact, anyone at any time who is emotionally challenged or lacks sleep could! It is a wider problem than we think, just thought I'd throw that in the mix while it comes to mind!

Choo choo choo…..Surfing is fun and riding a wave is great! But dancing on top of the train could leave you with no brain! Please keep safe!

6. P-Block Mates

I had the pleasure and privilege of meeting some great friends at P-Block. For this chapter, I have provided an insight of my mates who I got to know really well. I have also highlighted some of the issues that were evident and different observations. I don't claim to be a doctor but given that I was misdiagnosed and I had some valuable knowledge, I thought it would be beneficial. My mind was totally intact the entire time and therefore provides a voice for those suffering behind closed doors.

Some of my findings could potentially be explored further to improve current treatment that may assist my mates or others.

Nanna G (Lynette) was the first person I met in the ward. She was very cheerful, endearing, loving and caring! We got on like a house on fire!

Nanna G had fallen into a life of crime early in her life because her local GP had her on valium (up to 6 a day at her peak), for depression (which originated from childhood).

During her life, she had been challenged but she was a fighter who was very strong willed. First thing she handed me was a handful of smokes, I was ever so grateful because I had no money nor could I get any!

Nanna G had been admitted a week or two before me and gave me the run down! Giving me the heads up on the nurses and the doctors and what goes on. For example; we were singing one night in the courtyard having fun and she made comment on how we'd all get extra meds (medication not tampons) and sure enough she was right!

I couldn't believe how drugs were handed out like candy! Nanna G and I always cared for the others because we could see how the system had been failing the vulnerable patients.

We always shared a laugh and conversed on what was happening around P-Block. We knew how to work the system! She actually gave me the name Queen Bee (from the TV show Prisoner). We laughed when I asked "who is vinegar tits?" (You would have had to watch the show to understand that!)

Nanna G was always giving me little tokens from the paper during my stay. I was able to fully appreciate the true meaning of "It's the thought that counts" (no funds required). Two special ones were:

Think Feel Speak

The second one, an Irish Saying (which I so needed to do but how could I effectively change 39 years of me in 3 weeks?);

"Shut your mouth, you have no conscience"
"Don ash vale, Nob e consh"

For me, it was a matter of, I should have kept my mouth shut, not because I didn't have integrity but I was not given credibility. I was never going to get it in there! (I'll expand on that later!)

I also helped Nanna G out a number of times. Prior to my arrival she was suffering from a bad tooth, it took the staff a week before a little Asian doctor visited her and he extracted the tooth on her bed. She said she was bruised on her chest and gave us a laugh when she was describing the dentist performing this mastery.

However on two occasions, Nanna G had an attack. It appeared to be stemming from the tooth as she said she was in excruciating pain and it was affecting her physically.

The first major attack I witnessed was on Tuesday 24/7/2012 at 9.50am. She had just left the nurses' station and I knew she didn't appear well. In fact, I thought she was going to pass out. I was sitting in the lounge at the time.

I immediately checked on her and found her collapsed at the bowl of the toilet. I went to get a nurse. When the nurse arrived she instructed her to get into the chair. I was thinking, the poor woman is weak and you could tell she wasn't physically able. So another nurse assisted and dragged her up from under the arms into the chair. I'm pretty sure if it wasn't a mental ward you would have received more compassion and care. The tone alone was enough for me to bite back but I just kept saying to myself, "more material for my book". I moved the bed so they could bring the chair through and I was told to go away. I respected that because it was their duty of care.

Their duty of care for an abscess was appalling! The night before she basically had to beg to see a doctor who advised her gum was infected. The doctor was called after I stepped in and asked the nurse what she would do if she was in the same position? I told her the treatment was inhumane and their dismissiveness about this issue just highlighted how sickening the so called care was for patients in P Block!

The other incident occurred in the lounge on 31/7/2012 and I went to get Nanna G's nurse. I was told that she had to wait because her nurse was on a break! Seriously a nurse is there to assist when required!!

If Nanna G wasn't in the lounge, I would have pulled the suicide card and watched how quickly they ran. In the end, it was too overwhelming for Nanna G so Russell (a nurse) and I ended up pushing her in the chair down the corridor to her room.

Gary (another nurse) then arrived at the room but they wouldn't pick her up and place her on the bed due to safety reasons. Like fucking hell! Why not have the equipment available if it's that much of an issue? (She was only about 50kgs if that!) Hypothetically are people left to die in chairs these days? Or was it because it's a psyche ward and only your brain has a problem and nothing else matters? So Bubbles and I were going to do it because of how distressed she was, in the end, they did. Funny how they let patients drag a chair, duty of care if it suits? Lack of resources? Or ineffective use of resources?

I haven't had the chance to touch base with Nanna G but will be in the not too distant future. I have full confidence that her life will be rich and rewarding.

Marky Mark always brought an instant smile to my face. He is very animated and is full of expression. He brightened up the day and the ward with his antics, all good of course.

He is a practical joker as well. He'd answer the phone as Jesus or would ring the radio stations and say he was Lucifer and request to speak to Jesus. He loves to sing and bust a move too.

When I first met Mark, the only thing that was important to him was buying a new mobile phone so for the first week or so he carried around a JB-HI-FI catalogue. I assumed he had a bit on his mind and this was a small distraction to get through each day, through the fog of drugs. The doctors may have their own take on the matter but it's my view from a different perspective.

Mark could not handle confrontation and if anyone mentioned alcohol, you could tell it hit a nerve. Mark's father and grandfather were alcoholics. His dad died falling down stairs as a result. I assume he grew up in a very volatile environment hence his attitude towards the booze.

Mark is very smart but essentially wants to live a happy life however his past and obviously present are preventing him from doing so. He has a lot to offer and deserves more! I'm hoping I can provide Mark with the opportunity to land back on his feet. I ring him each week to see how he is doing and thoroughly enjoy our conversations.

Like a few others in P-Block, Mark was always after a Mama hug! Most of the time I got away with the no contact rule. In return, I felt and received so much love in such a depressing environment.

Mark rang last night (8/10/2012) and he sounded a little deflated. His Nan passed away and had mentioned that if he wasn't locked up he would have had the opportunity to visit his Nan while she was alive. I reassured him that things happen and he couldn't change what had occurred.

Mark couldn't remember how he ended up in P-Block other than a few men holding him down while being sedated. He did mention he wasn't sleeping well or very little leading up to this event. Obviously he has had many episodes before. Is the treatment effective if people keep relapsing? Are the chemicals making it worse given that there is no conclusive test developed to-date? (I'll extend on this later!)

Aleck the Great was a gorgeous young man. He had a cheeky grin with the cutest of dimples that you could barely see through his beard. He reminded me of a playful cub. Most of the time in P-Block he was happy go lucky.

Like all patients, these drugs sent people up and down like yo-yo's. Aleck was into hard core music which I now have an appreciation for (it's not my kind of music because it is too dark). But I assume it is a form of release for Aleck.

Aleck has many talents too including art, music and literature-poetry. He has published his own book and is very intellectual, not that he gives himself any credit. I believe this stems from childhood and his constant passion to please his great mum. From what I could gather from our conversations, he was always trying to please her and required re-assurance. I kept telling him to do what is right for him and there was no right or wrong, it's all about his journey.

Here is something Aleck shared with me:

Imposture: The state of feeling to want unfairness is not defined by the laws of logic. The "fear" of what they possess – shows their mistrust in themselves.

In other words, it is illogical to want to harm others and is unfair. Our fear is derived from mistrusting ourselves. Imposture alludes to your inner-self. Aleck's expose comes from a deeper mind/ perspective!

Aleck and I were on the same channel mentally only I was positive/positive and he was negative/positive.

From what I observed, he wanted to be loved and express himself rather than live up to expectations. I have no doubt he will be living a great life.

Aleck had been involved in drugs. He compromised his eyesight by pouring bleach in them under the influence (not sure how long ago). It is extreme but under these circumstances, your behaviours are not controlled and can be dangerous.

Just as a side note, in my view, when we consider the deaths or incidents on the street, someone "in control" getting angry and violently attacking another person would appear mentally unstable (sober or not)! You only have to watch the news to appreciate what I meant by this being a wider problem. At least there is a reason and purpose (or excuse) for those deemed mentally ill! Interesting?? Are we more ignorant than we want to admit?

Bubbles had a heart of gold and reminded me of Tracey. She was suffering depression and had a short stint in P-Block. While Bubbles was emotionally tormented she still provided lots of fun and laughs. She was straight to the point, honest and great company – just like Nanna G. We were like the 3 amigos.

We'd stir the boys up and decide whether we'd pass on smokes or dish out the hot chocolate we'd use to stash because it would always run out. (At one point, we had to wait 3 days for a refill of hot chocolate. Breaking news in the block when that's all you had that was nice and enjoyably free – Nestle' commercial brand should be on the shelves). I always handed out smokes even if I had borrowed them. I couldn't handle people taking them out of the bin.

Bubbles actually remembered me from one of my Coles implementations. I thought this was interesting; small world and was amazed that she remembered me. We both had young children and I could tell she wasn't coping thinking about them and herself.

From what I saw, the drugs were making it worse. (Bubbles, if you are reading this, that lactating problem is a side effect for one of the drugs, not surprised you haven't been told!) Poor Bubbles had to keep getting extra tests and she was off balance!

Bubbles use to cover for me as well on the odd occasion when nurses bailed me up to take the meds. (Hope you get in contact with me Bubbles, would love to catch up!) I didn't get Bubbles details because you basically wanted to run for the door and escape once you got the free pass!

Flynn was a champion; he was probably 6 feet tall and quite well built. He was always singing. Flynn was a happy gentle giant and I never saw him get violent or nasty. He did suffer the yo-yo effect and on those days he was normally passed out or a walking zombie.

He was diagnosed with Schizophrenia. He had been hearing voices since he was a child. What I find intriguing is, it is acceptable in society to talk, see and hear spirits (psychic) but when it is deemed extreme you are classified as mentally ill.

I don't know if Flynn has tried to harm himself but I do believe his condition could be better managed with a combination of therapies. Especially if the research I'm suggesting opens more avenues of treatment.

Flynn also loved a Mama hug! He would sing all of my Bon Jovi favourites and other songs like Stand By Me, Flame Trees, You're the voice etc.

One night he knocked on my door at midnight for a smoke, which I happily gave him but told him not to come back. Then at 3am in the morning, he came back again and I had to be stern and said "Piss off Flynn, I'm trying to sleep". I wasn't angry (as the drugs sometimes kept patients up at night because they had to sleep during the day) and he was very apologetic in the morning.

When I asked what the nurses were up to that night, they asked why? I said "I had a fairly strong visitor at 3am in the morning" (I wasn't going to dob my mate in!) They said I should have pressed the buzzer, as if I was crazy.

My reply was "well what if I was being raped and couldn't get to the buzzer?" Nurses reply, there was none – no comment. I guess the standard political response when you can't give an answer.

The nurses lock a door at the back of the block so you can't pass through to the ladies side but obviously they were on a break or unproductive round, when Flynn passed the nurse's station.

Some girls and ladies did feel intimidated. I'm definitely not advocating it to be segregated but ensure that policies protect all and not driven by the dollar.

Flynn's aspiration was to design and construct his own guitar. I believe he will be able to achieve this and I hope I can support him. He is a great man. I was actually touched by a poem he had written for Nanna G and me. I felt this way because he thought of us and he waited 3 days before sharing it, on the day he went to 'Parks' (an integrated place to transition patients back into society).

Here it is:

Annette
I'm a song writer and I just want to jam it,
I won't get a ciggy of Lynette
So do I walk away and utter "damn it"
Lynette
I'll take you through this step by step
I know nothing of smoking etiquette
For I won't get a smoke off Annette
I won't be forever in your debt
Asking of you for one cigarette
Bear with me while I
For a smoke I fish with my net
Lynette
For a smoke I fish with my net
I know nothing of the etiquette

So I'll take you through step by step
I won't get a smoke off Annette
She might have a monetary debt
Annette
She too has her smokes too collect
Like myself a recipient of neglect
So before I take off and I jet
Is it too much to ask for a cigarette

Rusty – was a very young 20 year old. He was very intelligent and considered himself a method man. He previously had been heavily using marijuana. He had a traumatic past and with the excessive substance abuse, he was unstable at times. He was very kind, appreciative, opinionated (it's a good trait) and passionate. His art work was fantastic too, truly amazing.

He also suffered from the ill effects of the medication. Again I know I'm not the doctor but I was in the system with a clear head. I could see for myself, what went on. No-one listened! I didn't see one psychologist whilst I was there. It was obvious that there was not enough time for these professionals to actually take the time to get to know their patients and address the real core issues. They did not offer or provide proper guidance. Using basic logic, if you only provide a band-aid fix, it is only a matter of time before a person relapses. With appropriate strategies and medication, there could be a more successful outcome.

Rusty actually broke his wrist in AMA and they would not plaster it for safety reasons. They also didn't provide a bandage for the same reason. He had to request a family member to bring in a glove instead, to compress the injury. I found this comical given that you're in a hospital. If you had a broken wrist and you planned to use it to hurt someone, wouldn't you avoid hurting yourself first? Plus you didn't need a cast, some of the men could have torn down buildings with their bare hands! And if it was to prevent harm, one hand is probably going to disable you from causing injury to yourself. (I'm only going on Rusty's word but from what I experienced, that held more value than the doctors.)

Rusty also taught himself to play the guitar through a "You Tube" clip. He tried to teach me but my fingers aren't that co-ordinated. (I'll just stick to the drums!)

I have no doubt that Rusty will succeed in any avenue he chooses. I hope he doesn't relapse into a life of drugs to mask his problems and neglect his unbelievably rich talent. If he was provided with the correct guidance, he could be living on the right path without the complications. (For Rusty, less medication and more mentally stimulating activities come to mind – which are something that the hospitals don't currently offer!)

Lyn was a young 61 year old who was born in Germany. She reminded me of my mum who was the same age and origin. Lyn was on an emotional roller coaster ride. She recently had a hip replacement and was learning how to get around again. (I thought of Emma (another great mum figure in my life) when she mentioned this because I couldn't call her to wish her the best for her hip replacement!)

I assumed Lyn suffered from a deep depression and always felt that she had no options. She always gave me praise about how happy I was and that I was a good person. She wished she could be like me, live in the country and have a good life.

She felt institutionalised and had stated that she had lost full control of her life. She hated the thought of people having access to her house. She worried about not being able to pay the bills and didn't seem to have any assistance at home (from what she was telling me).

Lyn didn't like swearing so I contained myself around her as I am always respectful. By the time I left she said, "All I want to do is swear!" I thought this was great progress because she was dealing with some emotions.

Lyn constantly talked of her grandchild who she couldn't see but called as often as she could. When my family came in to visit me for the first time in 19 days, Lyn asked to hold Lexi. I knew Lexi didn't want to leave my arms but gave Lyn the opportunity. Lexi didn't cry but Lyn had a brief cuddle. It was a small gesture to make her feel good and smile; amongst the fog of confusion, pain, lack of control and suffering as a result of bad experiences and the medication.

I hope the hospital provides Lyn with more emotional support at the very least. If she was receiving some, it clearly wasn't assisting her and needs to be reviewed!

Liam was 35 and appeared to have lived a very hard life, he looked 10 years older. He had been homeless since the age of ten. I immediately thought of Isaiah and pictured him on the streets, I was horrified.

Liam told me how he slept in the Salvation Army bins from that early age. He also expressed that although it provided warmth and shelter, it was very dangerous as people torched them. He didn't really go into his childhood but you could tell that he grew up in a very unstable environment.

He was very private but did open up occasionally. He mentioned that he did hold a job for a brief time as a night shift employee at Coles. He often wondered what his life would have been like, had he continued down that path.

Liam seemed happy living on the street as long as he had enough money to buy cigarettes and bourbon. He was dressed in rags and stored any extra food at meal times. He always carried his black shopping bag with him. However, as he mentioned his previous work history, I did notice a glimmer of hope.

I asked Mick to bring in a bag of clothes for Liam. He couldn't thank me enough and was excited with the brand new bag as well. He said he tried all the clothes and most fitted. I wondered why he chose to wear his old clothes. It then dawned on me that he was saving them for when he was released.

One night (29/7 just before midnight) when Bubbles, Nanna G and I went out for a smoke, the nurses didn't let us out and locked the door. Poor Liam was left out in the cold – of course we didn't know at the time. They found him at 2am when they realised he was missing. (Just goes to show how good these nurses rounds and checks were!) He just quietly blended in and often spent his days laying on a bench or the ground in the court yard. I never once saw him in the lounge.

Liam's main concern at P-Block was the fact that people were trying to take control of his life. They wanted to gain access to his benefits and dictate how to live.

He did need assistance and stabilisation but he also needed to be heard. If you have been on the streets for the last 25 years and someone was now trying to help you in a manner that was foreign to your way of living, that help could actually do more harm.

The hospital's solution was to provide drugs and find a half-way house. All Liam was interested in was finding his trolley and heading back to the streets as the type of help was not what he was after. I'm sure with greater support Liam could have the opportunity to create a better life for himself.

I often came across homeless people when I worked in the city. If anything, Liam indirectly taught me to be more aware of others. Instead of throwing coins in a bowl, I'd be taking the time to have a chat with them when others crossed my path. I guess prior to my realisation, I feared these people. I had nothing to be scared of. These people are neglected and misunderstood in society.

Ingrid was 23 and was born in Germany. She had no family or friends in Australia. Her boyfriend was abusive. Ingrid had been working as a nurse. Her breakdown was a result of her experience and drugs.

When I first spoke to Ingrid, she reminded me of a young version of my mum. She was afraid, timid, lost and confused. She use to shake like a leaf but I've since realised that it may have been a side effect of the drugs.

Ingrid was very fond of her cats. In fact, I thought it was odd that most patients had talked about their loving cats. I found that this was weird probably because I don't like cats. Anyway she made mention that her neighbour and ex-boyfriend had managed to look after them and was grateful.

I assumed like most, Ingrid was depressed. Who wouldn't be in a foreign country, alone and desperate?

I'm tipping she left with an insight of how disgraceful people are treated from a profession she was a part of. She herself as a nurse could not believe the lack of compassion that patients were subject to, especially in an environment that was meant to be of total care. All patients were considered the same and effectively treated the same. How could this be conducive to assisting people that require help when everyone is different?

Ingrid left before I did and at the time I wondered what support they offered, especially knowing that she was vulnerable in society. I've called her since and she seems to be doing well. Her dad visited from Germany and spending time with him helped her immensely. She was all the better for being in hospital not that the treatment was great but the experience was positive overall. She keeps in contact with a few from the block. I was very pleased to hear that she was well on her way to recovery.

Vera was a gorgeous lady who was also a nurse. She was caring, loving and thoughtful. She did seem to worry a bit too. She was fanatical about giving me my receipts and change when I asked if she could get me smokes and some tennis balls on one of her trips out.

She had previously suffered breast cancer and was very petite. One of my legs would have weighed more than her! I was shocked that she had read "Punk Rock Mummy's Blog" as it wasn't easy to come across (if you weren't looking for the exact name of the blog). I thought gee that's odd, I only just read that!

We named Vera – VV because she was on that much valium that we hardly saw her, sometimes for 3 days at a time. She stressed about her home life and had a lot going on. I assume she was losing control of her life from what she told us.

VV was riding an emotional wave in hospital but managed to find her way out the door. From her last day, I got the impression that she was happy but uncertain. I could tell she lacked confidence and was still struggling. I hope she was able to find the support that she needed.

On most occasions, the hospital was content on releasing people once they had adjusted to medication. There was no management of any issues that caused these problems.

Lois was a gorgeous Ethiopian lady. She was happy, funny and vibrant. I think she was the same age as me. She had four children and her youngest was the same age as Lexi. She suffered from post-natal depression.

Her husband Paul was a great man. He was from England and worked for "Plan". He brought the children in most days and spent the whole day with his wife when he could.

Her little son Hayden was restless in the room. It was a bit distressing for me at times because it reminded me of Lexi. I understood that Lois needed to be close to her young but at the same time, the place was not suitable for children.

I didn't want my children to come in until they had to. I thought it was important for them to remain in their routine rather than visit as it would unsettle them more when they had to leave. Furthermore it was not a place for children, as it was unpredictable. There was no right or wrong, it depended on what felt right at the time.

As there were a number of patients with children, you would think the hospital had the facilities to at least cater for mothers adequately. I couldn't even spend time with my children in the foyer or café, because the doctor had not signed a leave form, which was completed 6 days prior. Absolutely ridiculous, considering I didn't put anyone in danger or displayed behaviours of self-harm! Criminals had more freedom than I did!

Micky was a very caring and nice man in his 60's. He didn't have any family or friends. I couldn't believe he was so lonely because he was so kind and gentle.

He also rode the wave of drugs and suffered from depression. I was appalled that his treatment included Electroconvulsive Therapy (ECT) - shock treatment. In my terms, this treatment fries your brain and you lose memory. This treatment is so primitive considering that there is no official test or indicator to confirm a condition. Research in this area has not developed and is years away. Would you allow someone to fry your brain? At what point do the doctors know when to stop? When you are literally brain dead?

Most patients can't protect themselves by rejecting this treatment because of the orders placed on them and most have no idea of their rights. Even when you do have rights, the hospital ignores them! I will expand on this in great detail when I share my experience.

Micky has also been on a kidney transplant list and has been receiving dialysis for the last 7 years as a result of the medication. I felt for him so much that I said I would visit him at home. He didn't think he was worthy of my company and kept saying he felt sorry for me! He had accepted his fate but couldn't understand why the hospital was detaining me, preventing me from returning to my family!

Micky knew the ECT was causing him more harm than good, most people know what is right for them. No one can tell you how to feel unless they miraculously jumped into your body.

Hopefully as a result of this book and further research, I will be able to help Micky and any others caught in the same plight. I was even shocked to hear that they perform this treatment on adolescents (not sure about children). Disgraceful!

Jimmy Bear was a funny 40 year old guy. He was about 6"6 and just took things in his stride. He spoke about Dr. Hughes and how much he hated him. I knew exactly where he was coming from not that I hated him, I just detested him! (He had no bearing on me psychologically because I knew what I was doing and I couldn't hate him as there was no emotion attached.)

Jimmy always commented on how nice I was and loved the way I worked the system. I guess most were afraid to challenge where I wasn't concerned because I was playing the game and was actually enjoying it!

I don't know much about Jimmy's condition, because his memory appeared to be intact and he didn't speak fast or display any other signs of a mental displacement. It was obviously of a serious nature for the time he spent at P-Block. He did mention his eldest daughter committed suicide at the age of 23. I assumed that was the reason and he suffered from depression.

In actual fact, he had slit his stomach open and was trying to clean up the mess when his mum walked in the room. I thought "Oh My Goodness". He was quite jovial and openly talked about it to me. I found out it was because his girlfriend had left him. Wow I thought Jimmy must have been in a pretty unsound state of mind. I hope Jimmy keeps his promise and never tries that again.

Erin was 27 years old and a delight to speak to. She was funny, direct, intelligent and genuine. She was way beyond her years, probably because of her experiences in life. She had two children but her mother had custody of them.

Thank goodness Erin was there for my last week as all of my other mates had left. I found it great that her ex-husband Jason and fiancé Axil came in most days to support her. They all enjoyed each other's company. It was great that Erin and her ex could still maintain a friendship especially when children are involved.

Erin suffered from agoraphobia (extreme anxiety in public places) and was on a very high dosage of Seroquel. This medication had major side effects at the level she was on. Particularly her heart, she had put on a lot of weight. She showed me a picture of when she was 47kgs only 8 years earlier, I was shocked.

The doctors were concerned for her health but from what she was telling me, the main issue was that they needed to reduce the level because of the cost. She was afraid that this would create more panic attacks and that she would have no control over her situation.

It didn't make sense to me, because why put someone in this position in the first place? Create a high dependency on a drug? Compromise their health? Then reduce one drug and provide another for more side effects? Were there techniques to identify the core issue and help them manage the fear whilst taking medication? From my research there are aspects of managing the condition but not addressing or managing the core psychological issue.

Meghan was gorgeous, happy and considerate of others. She was also very polite and friendly. We often had a great laugh and I'd fill her in on my plans or what I got up to in the ward.

Aleck had a crush on her and Meghan enjoyed his company too. Meghan didn't appear to have any issues but there were some major events in her life that did impact her. After a few weeks, her doctors did provide her with a diagnosis that she was happy with and could manage.

Like every other patient, Meghan was lethargic, constipated and experienced bouts of vomiting, whilst adjusting to the medication. You would have thought that they noticed that out of all patients, one was super healthy? Me! Obviously they were blind sighted or too busy to notice!

Rocky was generally a happy Muslim who actively practised. He was short and of slight to medium build. He enjoyed his gym sessions as well. He was caring, compassionate and had a great nature; he also appeared to be loving. He always called me Mama and wanted the occasional hug too.

Rocky was very tormented though. He was deeply depressed and had obviously been on the wrong side of the law. I'm not sure why but he had spent some time in prison. With one inadvertent comment of the word "gay" in reference to a song, Rocky flipped out. Chairs flying, fists of rage and an innocent comment clearly hit a deep dark nerve.

It became apparent that Rocky may have been gang raped in prison. In the courtyard, he had mentioned he always carried a pencil in his sock to protect himself and knew where to stab if required. I didn't feel threatened by this but thought that obviously his experience in prison has added to his emotional and mental state of mind. Rocky was basically a walking time bomb and very vulnerable. If his treatment only consisted of medication he could have been a threat to himself and potentially society. But is the government responsible for his experience in prison? Has it made his matters worse and could this potentially escalate to something more sinister? He needed to release that anger, burden or whatever demon that lingered inside.

Rocky was released within 2 weeks only to return 4 days later. Prior to him leaving, we always had a good chat and I encouraged him to see the good things in life, trying to keep him positive. When he returned all he could say was he was a bad person and couldn't even talk or look at me. It was a classic example of how the system failed him. It wasn't even 4 days and he was back worse than when he arrived the first time. I felt really sad that day.

Madrid was a 20 year old gentle giant, actually Totem, standing about 6'8' who originated from the Cook Islands. He was very spiritual, funny and enjoyed his music. He took great pride in his daughter that he couldn't see and often showed me pictures of her. He loved his family and his four brothers.

He was a man of respect and expected others to be the same. From what he told me, he had been in trouble with the law because of an issue with his sister's Muslim boyfriend who treated her poorly. Obviously Madrid took matters into his own hands and I know the other person would have come off second best.

He was the protective type because when I joked about feeling safe about Rocky keeping a pencil in his sock, Madrid slept in the spare room next to me. I heard the nurses tell him off in the morning because he should have been on the other side of the block. Where were the staff during the night?

Madrid was always eager to obtain leave but to no avail. He would dress appropriately and ask for my opinion. I'd give him tips like lower his breathing and control his speech/tone. One Saturday 28/7 he was under the impression he would be seeing a doctor to gain leave. He waited until 2pm before he took matters into his own hands and escaped from P-Block. He was caught not long after and paid the price, more drugs and had to wait longer before he could get leave.

Each time he had an appointment you could tell it didn't go well. On one occasion he was walking the block with 2 billiard balls in his hand. I said to my husband Mick, did you see what Madrid was loaded with? Mick did the gulp thing!

The great thing about Madrid was you knew where you stood or where not to sit! Poor Liam was heading to one of the benches in the courtyard one day when Madrid in a deep tone said "don't sit behind me brother!" Liam didn't take any chances.

Madrid and Erin had a great laugh at my expense. Someone had mentioned "chard" and I thought they were talking about chardonnay. So I said "Do you guys drink chardonnay?" They laughed; clearly I wasn't very street wise. Apparently it is a drug or a way of consuming one!

Madrid played the guitar for my kids and placed Harley on the bed. I think Mick was getting something from the car. Harley's facial expression was like "What the? How big is this man?" Mick was a bit uncomfortable because he had seen Madrid's mood change at different stages. However he was never aggressive in hospital and I never felt threatened. I guess Mick was apprehensive and was a little threatened as there could have been a potential outburst!

I truly believe once Madrid is able to clear his past and find his way, he'll enjoy a happy fulfilling life! He has a big heart!

Cristana was 38 years old although she could have easily passed for a 21 year old. Cristana was very thoughtful and kind. She was also very artistic and loved music.

She was very highly strung when she arrived in P-Block and very opinionated. Sometimes she inadvertently got the others off side. She was also considerate, for example: she wouldn't be fazed by the fact that Sonia - a kleptomaniac was stealing her things.

Her challenges stemmed from her over bearing European mother. She was the eldest of four children – so we had a fair bit in common. She had recently split up with her fiancé and there must have been a lot going on in her life.

Cristana advised that she was suffering from Bipolar. There were a few in the ward that suffered from this condition. She did appear to be erratic but she was never at harm to anyone. She knew a lot about the system and wasn't shy to let the nurses know where she stood. She made me laugh!

She did advise that she was at a ward in St Vincent before being transferred to Monash. She was only at P-Block for just on a week before she was released. I found it interesting that her step father was a prominent psychiatrist (no longer practising) and was unable to help her.

She had a great nature and left me the nicest note:

Thank-you for all your advice and you are or shall I say have a special heart Mama. Good luck and enjoy life and never let anyone take away your dreams! Cheers Cristana xx

I was touched by her kind words because I didn't do anything out of the ordinary other than listen and talk. I'm glad she found comfort in the sea of confusion and uncertainty. I guess it's another example of how much love I received from total strangers, it was weird and rewarding all the same! I know with her determination she will ride the wave and hopefully get on top of things, if she hasn't already!

Callum was in his late twenties. He was full of energy, thoughtful and was spiritual. He enjoyed singing too and was a bright spark. He often used his tarot cards to perform readings for other patients. He did one for me but I won't disclose details in this book. I might save it for the next one. However it was very interesting to say the least.

Callum had obviously suffered in his life. I didn't get to know him very well because he was sent to AMA after an aggressive moment and never to be seen again. He was saddened and hurt by the recent news of his fiancé who had miscarried triplets.

I did find some of his notes around the place and I hope to get in contact with him post this publication to return those. I hope he knows that people do care and this is a small tribute to him. I'm hopeful he did receive the right help and is enjoying his life.

Craig was in his forties and had obviously suffered a breakdown. He loved his sport and we enjoyed a game or two of footy. He won fifty cents off me and gave me a few tips, like first team to 100 normally win. He was a proud dad and thoroughly enjoyed talking about his boys.

On one occasion, he actually asked what time I was finishing. He thought I was a nurse. I said I was a patient and filled him in on my story. He couldn't believe it and probably assumed I was another mental patient with grandiose ideas! It was a fair call. But hopefully this story offers Craig with some confidence and hope that he can restore his life. I'm hoping my book provides guidance, creates awareness about a failing system and changes society's view on mental illness.

Aiden was a humble and quiet guy. I didn't get to know him that well but I listened to what he had to say. He thought he was well and wanted to be free of the hospital. I believe his quest was hindered because he constantly spoke about a secret society. This was very bizarre and freaked me out a little bit because of my research. Although I didn't think there was a secret society, I had come across similar details during my course of studies. It was another odd coincidence. Much to his delight, Aiden was discharged before I left. I hope he has been able to land back on his feet!

Some of the other patients included:
Nick, Tony, Inuska, Lisa, Mumbling Lisa, Sophie, Chelsea, Justin (JC), Geinne, Trevor, Geoff, Zoron, Anna, Souka, Stravoula, Margret, Leonie, Samantha, Joseph, Samantha, Paul and Joseph with dreadlocks and Steve

It was appalling to see how these patients were treated. They had no voice; they did not know their rights and were disrespected. Some knew that their treatment caused more harm but had no support to contest it or lacked the knowledge. Others trusted that the doctors had their best interests in mind and rightfully so!

Some nurses were great but the majority were there just to perform their day-to-day tasks without much consideration for the individual. It was no surprise that most patients had been in and out of the hospital many times before and sadly, over many years!

Chugga chugga chugga, next time you find yourself judging others, take time to assess and ask yourself why? Sometimes we can learn more from those that are different than the people we willingly accept.

7. P-Block

First thing I saw as I left the Acute Management Area, a door to the psyche ward, was an old style black phone box, like you see in prison movies. My first impression of the ward was 'this is going to be interesting!' I expected that after my time in AMA and solitary confinement. The nurse who escorted me around P-Block first showed me the nurses' station and highlighted the plethora of pamphlets. I never received any advice or explanation of my rights but I'm tipping this was a substitute and all I deserved! Maybe she thought that I was another drugged up zombie with no interest in my rights (WRONG) or she had no time or she was not adhering to policy and procedures; just another example at how many angles one person can view something.

Next was the ladies lounge, the plaque securely fixed to the glass window stood out like sheep balls (they are bigger than dogs and I do live in the country!), like that's really contrary of the times when discrimination should be a thing of the past. This lounge had a table, a lockable cupboard with nothing in it, one damaged TV – you had to use a pencil or the like to change the channel, a 3-seater couch, 3 single arm chairs and a broken recliner. The recliner was removed in the last week I was there, maybe deemed unsafe? They couldn't care less about the TV even though there was a potential to be electrocuted if a metal object was inserted. Most patients preferred this lounge because it was cosy and had more natural light. It was opposite to the glass bubbled nurses' station and even though you were constantly being monitored on how you moved, what you said, your interactions, what your facial expressions were, your language etc. patients still gravitated to that room.

We proceeded down the block to room 8 and I was shown my room, very basic. I was fortunate enough to get my own room and shared an adjoining bathroom. I was a bit disappointed because I was calling it my tax payer funded holiday and the place would have been lucky to get a 2-star rating. (That just reminded me, apparently a patient had asked for a bible and they got the reply "this is no hotel motel" answer – how disrespectful of the staff!) Obviously for safety reasons there were no handles or no taps, there was a chair and desk, pigeon hole shelves, lockable side drawers (which had to be opened by a nurse) and a bed. I assumed the curtain rail was magnetically held because a couple of times I saw patients putting them back up after they had fallen down when opening and closing them. Now I know this will be controversial but the desk legs and bed could have been strategically used with a sheet or clothing for that matter, if anyone wanted to harm themselves. Therefore I found it odd that they went to the extreme in terms of appliances. The staff did do their regular checks which normally ranged from 30 minutes to a couple of hours, depending on what was happening around the ward. Other than sleeping and the odd retreat to write during the day to make it look like I was suffering the ill effects of the *so-called* medicine, I spent little time in my room. To kill time, I did enjoy my 20 minute showers twice a day without any interruptions, a luxury for me. (Since having children, it's a thing of the past).

There was a small gym no bigger than the average dining room, approximately five metres by three with a multi station gym set, one treadmill, a stepper, a rower, two exercise bikes, a boxing bag, hand weights, a fit ball and a mini trampoline. This was open for 30 minutes at around 10am daily (also the time most doctor appointments were held) and 15 minutes in the afternoon, sometimes the afternoon sessions didn't take place. The room smelt damp and you only needed a few good men sweating it out before my sense of smell and dry-reach mechanism kicked in. Therefore I only spent on average a good 10 minutes in there, when I had the opportunity. If 30 odd patients wanted to utilise the gym, it would make for a very interesting exercise program! One nurse was always supervising; majority females and most were quite slender. If any violence was to eventuate and there were some mighty men, I would hate to think who would have come out best by the time security or others were able to assist. Thankfully I did not observe any events in the gym.

There was a games room that was locked 80% of the time. It had a billiard table, a tennis table, a round table with a couple of chairs and another exercise bike. This was the only room that had a touch of colour, a green mural wall. The games room cupboard was locked. It contained the broken cue, bats and ping pong balls. I found it odd that the billiard balls were left out on the table for the first two weeks given that they could be potentially harmful. A couple in a sock would knock anyone out! Made absolute no sense to me!

The dining room contained:
- one whiteboard
- two vending machines (one drink and one food)
- another black box phone
- two inpatient phones for inward calls
- a bench with plastic pockets above (which sometimes had puzzles or colouring-in activities and no pencils mind you unless you brought your own). These sheets provided no more stimulation than watching grass grow or paint dry!
- a book shelf that contained no books and about 4 empty game boxes and one puzzle.

There was also a small tea-room, two court yards, one paved and the other synthetic/paved. There was a second lounge that was very dark. This lounge had three double seater couches, three gym mats, a table and a couple of single chairs. It also contained a dvd/video recorder with four films – 3 Sci-Fi movies e.g. Doomsday and the movie Step Mom. Given that some of the patients spoke of unusual things, I thought this was an odd choice of movies to provide inpatients. They also held group discussions in that back lounge.

There was one laundry that contained one washing machine and one dryer for 30-odd patients. I found it bizarre that you could use the laundry unsupervised and toxic washing powder was unaccounted for. I assume if a patient was desperate, they could consume the powder to cause themself harm.

General Day consisted of the following:

Time	Activities
7:10 am	Breakfast
8:00 am	Medication
10:00-10:30 am	Gym
12:00 pm	Lunch
12:30 pm	Medication
15:30-15:45 pm	Gym
17:00 pm	Dinner
18:00 pm	Medication
22:00 pm	Medication

The Occupational Therapy employees are responsible for activities. However for the first 15 days they were not present. Therefore no activities took place in that time. When they returned from their leave, I had the opportunity to paint my toe nails, file my finger nails and make jewellery. I encouraged the guys to participate and some did make jewellery but really, how do those types of activities cater for anyone? It helps bide time and is a distraction but it would have been more beneficial to have a psychologist conduct these activities and talk to the patients. I'm also sure that this approach would be more conducive to the needs of the patients and provide a better insight for medical staff (less threatening or confrontational).

There were one or two discussion groups held weekly. I only attended one with Mick in the last week. It was about relationships oddly enough. Mick had a great time expressing himself. The time allocated to these discussions wouldn't have provided much benefit as it was not at the depth required to assist patients. It did highlight though that patients were happy to talk and discuss their issues if someone took the time to listen.

On Saturday's the nurses catered a barbeque, which was good. Madrid could cook the perfect meat on that hot plate! What I did find amusing was, patients couldn't use a toaster at breakfast but they could use a barbeque! You can do more damage with a gas bottle, than a plastic fork in the toaster! Illogical and little common sense but what would I know? The barbeque was always supervised by at least one nurse but their attention could easily be diverted. We did get to use metal cutlery at dinner times which I also found comical because they never checked whether all items were returned to the tray.

There was also a public toilet facility opposite the lounge. P-Block at its best, no music, no activities and no fun, other than what you made of it!

Most nurses turned a blind eye to smoking. Some tried to assert control and although some patients would put their smokes out when told to, my jovial comment was "what are you going to do? Kick me out?" and just kept puffing away! Call me Puff Mama! It wasn't illegal to smoke and I was there against my will. I wasn't taking any shit, certainly in a place that treated you like shit!
Smokes were like gold or a form of currency in P-Block. I loved the idea because although it was forbidden, I was still being a rebel. Oddly enough, I did manage to find a legal place to smoke which was in the back court yard attached to a planter box (near the gym). There was a sign stipulating 'no smoking beyond this point'. This contradicts rule number one: Smoking is not permitted under any circumstance. That's how much time I had, observations are me! (Let them be, let them be, they are not free, so let them smoke in the court yard, for a tiny bit of peace! – Mama re-mix of the Beatles classic!)

From a personal perspective, I emotionally disconnected from my family. It is a technique that helps me manage myself in difficult situations. I couldn't spend precious time with loved ones and it was outside of my control. I also knew that if I was emotional it would have been misinterpreted in hospital. I would have been deemed depressed and given extra medication.

Within the first 6 hours of entering the ward, I had met at least 15 patients. Just after lunch, I had a crew singing (Nanna G, Callum, Aleck, Flynn, Mark, Rusty and Valium Vick – but she had to go back to bed!). The first line I belted out in true Mama fashion was "I don't know why I came here tonight, I got a feeling that something 'aint right, I'm so scared in case I fall of my chair, I'm going around in circles and I'm not sure where, clowns to the left of me, jokers to the right, here I am stuck in the middle with you!" Flynn sung another couple of my favourites by Bon Jovi – "It's my life!" and "Live when I'm alive and sleep when I'm dead" (appropriate for me given what had occurred). Basically everyone contributed a song. (In between me, having a crack of all the songs I normally churn out -Mama's mega mix juke box style!)

My singing time was cut short by Yvette and Marie (sisters) who paid me an unexpected visit mid-afternoon on 21/7/12. They brought me some magazines, fruit and lollies but I would have preferred the smokes instead. (Just kidding, I was grateful and didn't want to cause them any inconvenience by asking them to go and get some.) I gave them an over excited update on what had transpired. You could tell by their expressions, actions and conversation that they didn't know what to believe. You do expect to be in the best care in hospital or that is the belief.

I was also conscious of lurking nurses who observe and listen to everything so they can update your file, if they feel it's necessary. I assume my sisters would have been thinking…How could this be true? Is Mama mental/mad/crazy? Gee she needs more help than we realise? Is she lying? She never lies! Maybe they just didn't know what to think. They stayed for about an hour, which was great. Quality not quantity is what I'm about. I was keen to get back to the crew, enjoy my time and find out more.

Before they left, I showed them my room and the physical evidence. I was laughing on the inside when I mooned my sisters in the hospital. (Two words…Gob smacked!!) I hoped that my injuries allowed them to validate my side of the story. It was only natural for them to perceive things as they wanted to. I did have an extraordinary crazy moment so they had every right to come to their own conclusions. But should they? Why? I guess this is in our nature! Was it because they care? In essence, does it really matter – if they are true to you, then it shouldn't matter. I know what happened, why was I trying to prove myself?

Most of my life I haven't bothered entertaining what other people perceive me as. That's why I have enjoyed my life. Now, it was like I had to justify myself because I knew potentially what they were thinking. I know (and myself included sometimes), we do judge and this can be very harmful!!! If you don't call it judging, it's drawing your own conclusions on a matter or matters!

I believe I was justifying myself because I can now acutely read body language and comprehend terminology at a greater depth. Consequently, it has enabled me to ascertain a greater perspective on how others think. I can't read their mind, I'm just more perceptive! So I guess I was trying to provide them peace of mind. (Strangely I was doing everything I said I wouldn't do, i.e. what I posted on Facebook - 19/6.) Coming full circle, simple but complex!

After Yvette and Marie departed, I was disappointed to hear that the crew had been told off for singing in the courtyard. I thought to myself, "I am woman hear me roar, I'll be singing a hell of a lot more!" Well at least for the next few days while I was stuck in transit!

Sunday 22/7/2012 at 9am – Day 2 in the ward and 5 days after being admitted, I wrote the following on the whiteboard in the dining room:

PRISIONER OF SOCIETY

What is normal for you; is not normal for all!
Yet we are confined to a ward and are all given drugs
to mask mental problems
How is that normal?
When it is illegal on the streets!!
You tell me?
Will you take Provigil?
New magic pill that provides more energy and makes you smarter

> Drugs for what your mind can do but we can do naturally!
> Using logic but doing extreme things so labelled i<u>ll</u>ogical
> and given p<u>ill</u>s for being i<u>ll</u>?

In basic terms, I was referring to being mistreated for one moment in time. This was the first time being admitted to a Psyche ward and they did not know me, so how could they judge? From what I saw in that short time, drugs were the answer to mask problems rather than dealing with the core issue. The purpose of the message was primarily to have a crack at the doctors and medical staff! It may have been beyond their comprehension; maybe they just didn't care or they didn't have the time!

My first doctor's appointment was on Monday 23/7/2012 around 10am. It was fascinating, to say the least! My nurse Kelsey (who was young, friendly and very nice) collected me from the yard. We proceeded to the entry of P-Block and she unlocked the door. I thought to myself it is unusual for doctors to be hiding behind locked doors. I guess they may have been attacked before. If they were, why weren't security guards present?

As I entered the room, I immediately recognised (the pipe cleaner – reminds me of shovelling out shit) Dr Julian Hughes, my nemesis. He was the one who visited me in the Lion's Den and declared minimum 14 days as an inpatient. I cheerfully said hello and shook his hand. I also shook Afea's hand, the Psychiatrist Registrar who I later realised was as ignorant and arrogant as the pipe cleaner. For me, she was the colostrum bag – full of shit! They both looked or seemed a bit bamboozled by my polite hand shake. Maybe no other patient had done this before? (Well that's my take on the matter and it's my book/story so there is no right or wrong!)

I proceeded to pull my chair forward. I knew that this would get them thinking. Dr. Hughes quickly advised, "You can't do that!" and I asked "why?" He said it was for safety reasons. I didn't say anything but thought; well excuse me, whose safety? Especially after being so poorly treated and abused in their care! Would you consult a doctor you didn't trust? Or who didn't trust you? I pushed my chair back a little but not all the way. Through my actions, I was highlighting that I was different, I was testing boundaries (not that he could appreciate it then) and I meant business!

The crux of the consult is outlined below:

He proceeded to ask the standard questions:	My reply was:
How are you or how do you feel?	I'm very well thank you
How have you been sleeping?	Good
Do you have suicidal thoughts?	No
Are you having racing thoughts?	No
Do you know why you are here?	Yes, due to sleep deprivation

He also asked "what do you think lead you here?" I replied "I'm being an anarchist, if you know what that means!" Probably something I could have toned down but I was being myself. I was responding in a constructive way considering the events that occurred prior to and in hospital. I assume most would have still held on to their anger and given him a serve if faced in a similar situation. (If patients were able to remember that is!)

He did say I appeared a bit better and making progress; non-committal of course because he didn't know me. He asked me how I felt (on that wild day) and I told him I felt like running. (No surprise, as I was full of adrenaline!) Another question he asked was "how long do you think you need to be in hospital and should you be here?" My response, knowing that he had already made up his mind in the Lion's Den was "Keep me here for as long as you think I need to be here!" Reverse psychology in its finest form; from a person deemed mentally ill! Why else would I be there? At that stage, they had not given me a diagnosis but were still dealing out the drugs and assuming I was happily consuming them!

For all my consults, I always held my composure, was polite and friendly. I was direct but assertive.

Both doctors were forward facing, with arms crossed. Dr. Hughes did all the talking; he was quite pompous and condescending in tone. Perceptibly he knows best! I perceived this as him being a dictator, who was not listening. Superficially, it did appear to be a two-way street, we were conversing. But he was not actively listening and as a result his perception of why I was there was skewed. What he wanted to see or hear was totally different to mine. Justifiably so however, I already knew him before he knew me, without him realising – as previously explained! (Just to throw in another tune from the Great Tom Jones – If he only knew, what I knew – to make me, make him happy! Hahaha – Gee I crack myself up!)

I normally speak quickly if I'm passionate or excited and I was conscious of their time (reason/purpose). Apparently speaking a little faster than most is another symptom of some mental illnesses. (I wonder how many people are assessing themselves after reading this?) Therefore me being me, not that I realised at that point, I wasn't doing any favours for myself. He hadn't given me a diagnosis so I had nothing to gauge it on.

He concluded by making reference to the time by stating twice "we will have to leave it there", even though I wasn't finished. (I did hear him but wasn't I the patient? Is 15 minutes all I deserve? Is he trying to help? Or was I just another dollar in his pocket?) After the consult, Kelsey said "That was interesting!" She didn't need to say why, I already knew!

I decided to write down my "Prisoner of Society" message and when another patient had finished, it gave me the opportunity to have the final word for that consult. I slipped into the door way and said "Here is something else for you to think about!" Big wheel keep on turning, proud Mama keep on stirring, rolling, rolling, rolling in the Psyche ward – gave myself a pat on the back and went out for a smoke! No fear, inhibitions, expectations or emotions, I was cruising! This is an example of how I secretly made my own fun, especially messing with the main head of the Psyche ward at the Monash Medical Centre.

On the reverse side of the whiteboard, after my first consultation, I wrote the following for patients:

> What may be right for you; may not be right for someone else!
> There is no right or wrong.
> Empower yourself/inner-self to do what is right for you!
> Drugs may assist to clear darkness
> However if you don't address the true essence of "one"-self
> You end up in the same spot, one vicious cycle.
>
> Child – Innocence – Inner-Self
> Lost by boundaries created by society,
> Best thing we can do for ourselves and children (future)
> Give, teach, and show them a positive experience.
> We are all here for a purpose but it is your own journey!

The reason for communicating this on the board is that many patients were traumatised by events or experiences most of which predominantly stemmed from childhood. Although many weren't given an opportunity, its purpose was to highlight that they are here for a reason and can make it a journey, rather than just existing. (I probably should have put it in simple terms but just expressed how it came to mind!) I flipped the boards around several times over the few days and encouraged patients to read. I highlighted the prisoner of society message to nurses. This also gave me something to do! Some patients were suffering post-natal depression hence another reason for referring to a child. It was also part of my earlier findings.

It was great to see other patients use the board to inspire patients too! JC provided the following quotes:

> If you treat people like you want to be treated, then the world wouldn't be at war with anyone!
> Every end, ends up with a silver lining!

Most patients had also been in and out of these institutions over many years. (I will still refer to them as hospitals but from what I saw and experienced it was just that! Hopefully that will change in the future). I was trying to provide patients with some guidance in taking control of their lives because not one staff member had the time to properly care for these vulnerable, lost, confused and depressed patients. It was quite obvious to me, that the drugs were providing a Band-Aid fix and once a person was stable enough they were released. However when they became immune to them, they ended up relapsing and back in a Psyche ward, a total failing system!

I found it funny that I was told off by Sandraya who was one of the nurses. She told me to stop helping people. I said "I'm only talking and if you deem that to be helping, that's your problem. I can't control how you perceive things!" She didn't comment and never said anything in respect to helping after that. Nor did anyone else for that matter! Was it now a crime being social? I assume my response was deemed as being agitated and worked against me!

Sandraya was heavily pregnant and I thought what on earth is she doing working in the Psyche ward. It would only take one chair or a shove from an out of control patient to render her baby some harm. I knew I wouldn't put myself at risk! I was also surprised that the hospital didn't have a duty of care to their staff in this situation! I'd seen enough in 21 days to be able to draw that conclusion. Logic or dollars?

Some patients produced amazing pieces of work (literature, music and art), all worthy of their own exhibition. If only someone, family, friends or society gave these people some direction without clouding them with chemicals or trying to chemically engineer who they were, I have no doubt that they would be better off. In my whole time in the hospital I never once saw a psychologist. How are patients able to find stability in their lives when they are not talking about the core issues? They should also be shown how to manage their problems more effectively. Don't get me wrong, some did need stabilisation but others could have been managed without drugs or a combination of both. Training or retraining a person's mindset would have a huge benefit in managing mental health yet the hospital failed to do this! It was quite obvious that drugs were the only avenue of treatment.

From my observations, every patient was on at least one or two of the same tablets. Sodium Valproate/Epilium is predominantly used to treat epilepsy – (brain seizures) and nearly every patient was issued these drugs. At one point, they were administering 3 at a time for me, two or three times a day. They also tried to feed me Valium and some other drugs which I refused to consume, unbeknownst to them. I know for a fact, I would have been violently ill and comatose if I had consumed them. How is it possible that many patients with varying illnesses are issued with the exact same pills?

I've worked in retail and supplier relationships can be quite lucrative. Is there a supplier incentive for prescribing these drugs? If it's not a financial benefit, it may be a funded holiday under the disguise of "medical" research or similar. It definitely warrants further investigation, the medical profession would only need to complete an audit for that time to validate my observations. You don't need to be a doctor, basic logic highlights potential discrepancies. When money is involved there can be a conflict of interest. I'd like to think that a patient's best interest is always the priority and there is a duty of care. However, from my experience, unfortunately this was never the case.

Now as you know, I'm a person that loves music and likes to sing! Due to the lack of atmosphere and music, I'd thought I'd get patients to contribute songs that we could sing. I didn't realise at the time that this was also deemed a symptom/condition for some mental illnesses! Like fucking hell – I thought "music saves your moral soul" and the medical profession was killing it! Obviously that went against me in my first week on my now "Contiki, the Mole, Big Brother, the Voice, Australia's Got Talent and Survivor tax payer funded holiday". It was literally insane that I couldn't be myself! Anyhow, here is the song list and the contributors:

Satisfaction – Rolling stones – (Aiden)
Sweet Home Alabama – Lynard Skynard – (Trev)
We are the world – USA – (Marky Mark)
You can't stop the music – Village People – (Mama)
The Gambler – Kenny Rogers – (Mama)
One Love – Bob Marley – (Mama)

Rock the Boat – Pirate Ship – (Peter)
You are the chosen one – Skyhooks – (I think it was Justin - JC)
She has deathly wrongs – The Earthly Souls – (Aleck)
Imagine all the people – John Lennon – (Rusty)

After more than a week since being admitted, I still had not been given a diagnosis. I assumed they had already categorised me and because I didn't ask, it was never mentioned.

Donna and Wally dropped in for a surprise visit and I was thrilled. They had travelled over an hour and half (one way) to come and visit me. They also brought me some treats, smokes and sweets, I was very grateful. As the other patients were eating dinner, we had the lounge to ourselves for a short while. I gave them an overexcited update while no one was around. A little later on Wally and Donna met Aleck and they were shocked to hear his story about putting bleach in his eyes. They were also there when a nurse came back to give me extra medication for no apparent reason. I had questioned why I was getting more because I hadn't seen the doctor but she commented that I had to discuss it with him at the next consult. I was glad Wally and Donna were there to witness some of the inconsistent practices of the ward. They couldn't believe what went on! Donna mentioned the book and I quickly shut her down because I knew it would be misconstrued.

One person who was surprised that I was being detained in the ward was a consumer rights worker who was conducting surveys. I was happy to spend time with her and highlight most of the inconsistencies. She actually commented that I was too smart to be there! It was nice to know that some people had an open mind and weren't over critical of mental patients. I completed two surveys during my time and received a text notification that they were acknowledged. It will be interesting to see if any changes have been deployed as a result of my feedback. I hope opportunities are addressed. If they aren't, what purpose does this service provide? Is there any value in the resource and where is the benefit? Time will tell, I will be advocating for better care and this book creates the awareness to commence that journey!

I also had the pleasure of meeting and discussing my position with a medical student. Unfortunately she told me her name but I was too busy providing her with my "big" story and a bit of what I was doing, so lost track of her name. I didn't want to ask the second time she visited, as I didn't want it to appear that I had lost my memory or seem rude.

I told her that I was at a loss with the system because they failed to understand what, when, who, how and why. Basically we were on different mental channels and our perceptions/perspectives were not aligned so I had to work through the process. She had an open mind and understood my position. She also asked me to draw a clock with numbers. She didn't have to tell me but I knew this was because mental patients don't have any concept of time. Again I was different; I knew the day, time and year and provided many examples of this on my holiday (I passed the test). She was very friendly and had a great demeanour. I'm sure she will blitz in her field of studies. I hope I get the opportunity to see her again, as she appeared to have the attributes to treat patients effectively and she might be able to assist me on my journey to help others.

I was a model patient and I couldn't even go to the cafeteria and buy a healthy sandwich under the escort of a nurse! I assume the only difference between prison and the hospital was that at P-Block you had an endless supply of drugs and no resources or activities. In prison, you had all resources and activities but have no direct access to drugs. Imagine if every person in prison wanted drugs and appeared mentally displaced or challenged, would our prisons become hospitals or would they all filter through the hospitals? Interesting?

Party time in P-Block – no food or drink! Guess the event? The Olympics of course! For once it wasn't a crime to dance and sing when the opening ceremony was televised. I asked the nurses to refrain from adding anything to my file. They said I should be right because there was a reason to celebrate. I thought can't every day be a celebration. It was quite obvious to me that it was a crime to be your happy self but then they were treating most for depression.

Where is the logic? I must have rare sense because common sense is obviously a thing of the past!

I had also engaged a few patients in hospital about a terrorist attack at the Olympics because I wanted to determine if any were easily influenced. Aleck for one strongly disagreed that there wouldn't be! But most had an open mind and didn't agree or disagree but were happy to accept it at face value. I found this extremely interesting because it was a total different reaction compared to the "outside" world. Mind you when I was probing, Donna (a nurse) questioned whether I still believed that there was pending doom. I thought that's going to add another couple of days for sure and quickly replied "It's been on the news, haven't you been watching the reports or reading the paper? We were just in discussion about the different theories!" Seriously unless you have experienced this environment first hand, it is very difficult to get a full appreciation of what transpires.

So with nothing to do other than chat, smoke, drink hot chocolate and challenge staff, I thought I'd create a P-Block Olympics event. Some of the events we collectively created were:

- Block Dash
- Block Relay
- Magazine Hurdle (for safety reasons obviously)
- Plastic plate discus
- Long Jump Mania
- Shot put ball (with a tennis ball)
- Pencil Javelin

Unfortunately it was difficult for me to coordinate my mates to conduct these events. Maybe patients stuck in transit can use this in future, if they are bored and need an activity. Or it may be some cheap family fun for home!

Friday 27/7/2012 9:40am – Second consult with Afea and a social worker Stephanie. A nurse always attended my appointments too. (Mick also attended every appointment after the first as it was vital that he witness what transpired first hand and was there for support.)

After answering the general questions, I asked "what have I been diagnosed with?" I was told "manic episode". I then asked about the symptoms. Afea said in my situation it was an elevated mood. I asked, "How was this determined?" and her reply was "It is from what we call observation". You may deem me mental but I'm not fucking dumb! (Just as a side note, I laugh because I was constantly monitoring them and they had no idea. I found her condensing manner comical! She also didn't know I was recording this consult so I had proof of what transpired - albeit half because a call interrupted the recording. I had to fend for myself whilst my rights were denied).

She continued to elaborate highlighting it is also the nursing staff and the police that brought me in that provided information to draw these conclusions. I asked whether they spoke to the police directly and she said "yes when they brought you in." I said "I came by ambulance" (no police present). Had she not checked her records? Did she assume I lacked memory? Or was she fabricating the truth to suit herself? She changed the subject by adding "you had very very fast talking and your thoughts appeared to be racing". Mick did advise that I naturally talk fast and was quick to think.

She said have you had unusual thoughts. I was testing her and said "Is a terrorist attack or a tsunami strange?" She replied "yes" and I asked her "why" (because these events have occurred in the past). Afea responded with "because it is not controllable". I brought these up knowing full well they had recorded my rants. She didn't understand where I was coming from. I was acknowledging what had transpired indirectly. She didn't ask me what those so-called strange racing thoughts were. I had not mentioned anything about control. Why did she assume this? How could she possibly know how I think? I replied with, "how you perceive and what you interpret is different. I don't entertain how you think and what you feel and you're entitled to your opinion." (People would be shocked to know how much I actually did in that time and what I researched. I was processing too much information on a heap of adrenaline and wanted to keep going. I did become addicted but for a good cause. I wanted to share my knowledge to help others but inadvertently got to experience the other side first hand, which has supported my original findings. In the last statement to her, the 4-dimensional thought process was evident – perceive, interpret, think and feel.)

She proceeded to say "And it sounds like it was a little different for you as well!" I responded with "No". (She had no knowledge of what I had been researching. What metaphors I used in the early phase and how my brain interpreted those during the surge of adrenaline.) I responded with "how can you articulate that when you are not in my mind?" She decided to change the subject and ask if I would have thought like this 8 weeks prior.

I told her that we were deviating but happy to head that way. I said "how can you make a true assessment if you don't understand me, what had transpired and the research I was conducting?" She deflected and said "What else do you have?" Going back to the elevated mood, I asked whether it was deemed in a positive or negative manner. She said negative and that I was agitated, irritable, up and down in my mood (I didn't respond because I knew what was right! They weren't going to change their minds so why bother fighting it). She proceeded to say "you were proving your points and doing strange things like taking your clothes off". I asked "has anyone taken the opportunity to get my side of the story?' I kept going back to the symptoms because they weren't giving me a condition, so what were they treating me for? Having a manic episode or being manic for one point in time is not a condition alone. (Otherwise how many drunken or drugged up people would be clinically labelled mentally ill after doing extreme things?)

She expressed that I still had the symptoms and was going around in circles. Why? Was it because she couldn't directly answer my questions or didn't want to be honest with me? I was trying to obtain satisfactory answers to my questions and this was deemed part of my condition! She advised writing on your own walls isn't normal. I advised I could use whatever forum I liked to communicate. (I was testing her to determine if she gave me the opportunity to explore that further but she didn't.) So I elaborated about writing on the wall and highlighted that I was trying to communicate. (I also knew that she would not have accepted what, how and why. I was in a different state of mind. How could I tell her that I inadvertently put myself in that state of mind doing research for psychology? It was quite obvious they had already drawn their own conclusions). Processing too much information and wanting to communicate is very different to having racing thoughts!

I proceeded to highlight the events leading up to being admitted and what transpired in hospital. I explained I was making observations. For example: only having 3 pieces of poor quality fruit in the tearoom when there are 30 patients. I also asked why I was given more drugs when I hadn't consulted the doctor. I tried to find out why I was mistreated when I hadn't put myself in danger and I was resisting being moved. I asked why I had been woken up from a deep sleep for a blood test at 7.30am in the morning. There were many things I covered in that consult but it fell on deaf ears. They continued to ignore me and not give me any credibility. I didn't get frustrated. I assume others would have, trapped in that situation. I needed to have control otherwise it would have worked against me. More meat for my bone – book!

I told them that I was testing the boundaries and using reverse psychology. The nurse made mention that I was defying what was required and irritable. I asked, "How did you draw that conclusion?" Because what you perceive (what each individual wants to see and hear) can be different to reality. Apparently by continually questioning my treatment and making observations, I was consequently deemed irritable and having racing thoughts. Go figure, damned if you do and damned if you don't. I told them that I didn't swear in their presence, had not shown any violent behaviour and yet they still failed to acknowledge my "normal" good behaviour. Pity the fool! They weren't me so how could they be sure I was irritable, suicidal or whatever else they believed? They never once viewed it from my position. Miscommunication and misinterpretation, failure to acknowledge or accept my position, double standards at its best! In every consult they wanted me to acknowledge I had a mental illness and I kept telling them I had sleep deprivation. I could have agreed but I would be going against one of my core traits of being honest. Why should I change to suit them? Plus I had to confirm what, who, how, when and why in the medical profession for my research given that I had an opportunity to explore this area unexpectedly.

I was deemed guilty before charged! I told them I could articulate and recall the reason why I behaved in that manner and the purpose. I highlighted that terrorist attacks and natures force were evident in today's world. Yet people who believe in god are not deemed crazy when there is no physical proof. I expressed, "I shouldn't be crucified for my beliefs". However due to current practices, boundaries and perceptions, I was treated in what society believes or perceives as to be right and normal. (Fucking crazy!! Every person is different that's what makes us an individual – logical!!! Sarcasm helps occasionally).

In summary (nothing is ever short with me), I did not receive a satisfactory response for my diagnosis, the symptoms and the drugs that were prescribed and why. I asked for alternative treatments and *surprise*, the subject was changed. They confirmed that I had improved but did not establish how the treatment contributed to that! They were quick to advise what they believed my mental state to be but failed to acknowledge any emotional state. (They asked how did you feel and my reply was good, that was it!)

I questioned why I was admitted as an involuntary patient when I was not violent or aggressive (I was deemed involuntary at Casey Hospital mind you). I further added I was happy and had not harmed or threatened myself or anyone else for that matter. My questions on what are the expectations? How will they be met? Will the voluntary status change? When will I be discharged? What medication do you think I need and how often? What conditions do you want me to meet and let us discuss them? Where to from here? All were unanswered except for the involuntary status and it would not change. It was evident that they had already decided what was best for me in their eyes. I just played the game and rolled with it!

I did challenge every nurse and doctor in a constructive manner. I knew by their tone, language and body language how they perceived me. I could tell by some of their behaviours that they were confused and frustrated. It was only natural because who was I to mentally challenge them?

Poor Tony a nurse, who had been assigned to me once, was telling me that when I'm high and then get depressed, it wasn't normal. He proceeded to say "and when you talk fast it suggests that you are unwell." I told him that I haven't been depressed and I'm always happy. I kept interrupting him and he was becoming frustrated. He then said we would catch up later as he had to attend to other things. I found him later that afternoon and he was busy! He was talking fast and highlighting his duties. I said "you appear to be stressed and you're talking fast, are you sure you don't have a mental illness?" Of course he didn't see the funny side and was a bit reluctant to engage in conversation after that. By default his change in behaviour highlighted to me that I made him feel uncomfortable or maybe I was too mentally challenging for him?

After a week I asked Gary (nurse) if he worked at Mitre 10 and if he had a brother called Jordie. (I'd previously met Gary once at Mitre 10 when shopping with Mick but I knew Gary didn't know me). Gary looked shocked, like I spooked him. I then proceeded to tell him I was Gazelle's wife. I didn't get any special treatment but I'm tipping he was relieved that I didn't have any special powers!

The placement nurses were a breath of fresh air. They were very friendly and always assisting others. At times they were a little confused, especially when I gave them a rundown of why I was there. Julie-Ann was my favourite and it was nice that they showed some emotion on their last day. They expressed the tears were because they enjoyed their time and were sad to depart but they had to move on! I'm sure they will all be great nurses and hopefully I get the chance to see them again!

A nurse's day consisted of administering medication and accounting for them (at least 2 resources required and a mountain of paperwork), unlocking doors continually to the storeroom or linen cupboard, handing out meals (minimum 2 nurses required for breakfast, lunch and dinner, plus they cooked toast!), taking observations (blood pressure and temperature), attending consults and updating patient files.

Generally it was 4 patients to one nurse during the day. I changed my sheets daily because I could and had nothing to do. As I had 2 showers a day, I impeded on their time at least 3 times a day for linen and supplies. I did bulk up on items on the odd occasion but I still went back for something else. I was testing the system to a degree they couldn't appreciate. At night it was around 4-6 staff for the ward.

They had no time to talk to their patients amongst all the standard procedures. I could never understand why a nurse was needed in the consult either if the doctor was present. If it was for support, it was clearly ineffective and wasted use of a resource.

Bubbles inspired me to write something else on the board, so on Saturday 28/7/2012, I came up with this:

> Like a flower, we started from a seed,
> A seed of love is how it should or was meant to be!
> Some may blossom, bloom, shine for whom they should be,
> Others may wilt, from a lack of a nurturing need!
> However from that precious seed that flower will grow,
> It will evolve through cycles, up and down, so we learn and appreciate that we are all here as life should be!
> Teaching, learning and growing as one, living in the moment and doing what we need or please,
> Enjoy your time and empower yourself to be that beautiful flower of rich colour and soul,
> Because you my friend have heart and soul!

Sunday night 29/7/2012 after a full day in the office, I thought I better get my ass into gear and work out how to escape P-Block. I read my rights for the first time and thought wow I did have some but they weren't adhered to. I immediately thought this was great and I can work my misfortune to my advantage.

As per Southern Health's RIGHTS pamphlet:

According to section 18 of the Victorian Mental Health Act (1986) act gives specific instructions regarding the rights of patients. These rights include (this is not a conclusive list):

- *To receive best possible care and treatment* **(failed on all accounts)**
- *To have your religious, cultural, language, gender and any other special needs respected*
- *To be told you are a voluntary or involuntary patient* **(I became aware of this after I was sedated)**
- *To be given written or oral explanation of your rights when you are admitted* **(This didn't happen!)**
- *To ask questions and receive answers you understand* **(I understood the answers but I couldn't get satisfactory responses.)**
- *To be told about your diagnosis, treatment and risks* **(I never received any satisfactory details and they only provided a diagnosis after more than a week.)**
- *To negotiate with your doctor and nurse about your treatment* **(I never had the opportunity to negotiate and they were prepared to inject me against my will. As far as treatment and risks were concerned, they were never discussed and I was forced to take drugs without knowing the side effects or the benefits.)**
- *To request a different psychiatrist, nurse or case manager* **(I tried but this was denied.)**
- *To not take experimental drugs* **(How would you know if they didn't tell you?)**
- *To complain about your treatment or anything that you are unhappy with* **(Clearly that worked for me, not! It was deemed part of my condition.)**
- *To talk to a lawyer and have legal representation or an advocate*
- *To see your file before a mental health review board hearing* **(They never allowed me access to my file even though I engaged the Chief Psychiatrist.)**

Armed with some more knowledge, I completed the "Appeal to the Mental Health Review Board" stating the reason for the appeal:

I have never had a history of a mental health challenge (illness). I did not do anything illegal. I had not taken any drugs nor was I induced by alcohol. I have a "clean bill" of health. The psychiatrist only visited once, I had been sedated, denied proper care, was abused and unfairly treated. I have photos of those injuries. Doctors prior to sedation were attempting to force me to take drugs without a diagnosis. I had and have continued to provide logic however current procedures and processes were not adhered to and the hospital denied me of my rights.

I requested the nurses to fax the appeal at midnight 29/7. They said they would but they had to complete the task because I requested the transmitted confirmation. (I think they were planning on doing it later.)

Monday 30/7/2012 I rang Mental Health Legal Aid. Unfortunately there were set times to seek advice from a lawyer. Tuesday night was the next available time from 6.30pm.

Mick arrived not long after and we attended another appointment. I recorded this consult as well. (I'll try to keep it brief.) After the standard questions, I asked if it was possible to re-cap on Friday's consult. I expressed that I haven't been given a diagnosis other than an elevated mood. Dr. Hughes advised that I had Bipolar. I told him I didn't agree and that I had sleep deprivation. He told me I had disorientated thoughts. He highlighted that I previously had written to Barack Obama and that wasn't normal behaviour. (I laughed to myself because not once had anyone asked for evidence that I had, yet they were willing to accept that I did.) He advised that I was talking about the world destructing and asked me why. I said I could have been talking about financial destruction. He advised that I could appeal at which point I said that I had submitted that request. I also told him that my rights have been denied and I have proof of my injuries. He then proceeded to read the form and try to assess that. He added that I had aggressive thoughts. I questioned if he had records of what was said. He said "no" and I said "I have recalled every detail of what transpired in hospital". He went on to say that my thoughts weren't logical. (Hilarious really, if someone was in a dream-like drunk state mindset, of course it may be difficult for others to understand! They were logical to me at that time.) He didn't want to see my injuries when I offered to show him. (What sort of doctor was he? Obviously he only dealt with minds!) They had administered at least 5 different drugs during my stay and never once was I told what they were, what the purpose of the medication was and how it would benefit me. I guess I was no different to a lab rat!

I provided him with an insight of observations again. For example: Why is the linen cupboard locked? When I had queried Jibi, she said it was because it was a psyche ward. Graham advised it was Hygiene control and another nurse confirmed it was to control usage. He queried why I was interested in that. I replied that I was bored. I said I was fine and this is who I am.

He advised that there may be a possibility I could go home by the end of the week but I still have to take medication. There was obviously a difference of opinion and when I was trying to justify my position he couldn't appreciate it. I could tell he was not sure what to make of me. He asked me to leave the room, to provide Mick with an opportunity to discuss matters privately. I knew Mick had nothing to discuss but obviously the doctor did.

When I returned, Dr. Hughes advised that Child Protection would be involved as part of my pending discharge. Mick had apparently shown Afea some footage of what I captured the night before my big day out, unbeknownst to me. Mick didn't tell me until we were sitting in that consult. Betrayed by your husband at a crucial point in time was a great test for control. Boy did he cop an ear bash after that consult! (A major Mama tongue lashing!)

To cut a long story short, Lexi was playing on the floor and had picked up a marble from a game the boys were playing with. Mick panicked and was concerned she would choke. I said let her explore. If I was in the kitchen or in the laundry, I know she has the skill to do the right thing. It was supervised. I also thought that if you put a finger in her mouth, it could cause her to choke. I didn't give her the marble and tell her to eat it! She had picked it up and it was already in her mouth when we realised! Not one person asked why Mick didn't think to remove the marble himself if he thought I was unwell and out of control. Where was his responsibility? It was a very confronting situation for him. I had used a very aggressive tone.

As previously highlighted, I was in a different state of mind but I had reason and purpose but no control over tone/behaviour! Mick advised he was scared to act! Was it because I gained power because of my tone/behaviour? Or was it his fear to react to a situation? Mick has confirmed it was the latter even though I wasn't violent! (He also showed a few friends, one can only imagine what they thought. I didn't entertain that but Mick said he regretted showing others! Obviously there was no harm, right or wrong, it was about how it was managed and why he had shown others. There is no purpose in blaming as it doesn't solve the problem. I was over it after I released the emotion. Poor Mick, he rode the negative wave while I was on a surfing adventure of a lifetime!)

Back to the consult, I did try to highlight my reasons and purpose but Dr. Hughes advised that it was inappropriate behaviour. I said it was part of the learning process and evolution. (My thoughts I did not share in the consult were; she was not at harm and I had proof that she didn't choke! I assessed the risk and consequence for her to learn for herself. If we over protect our children, how do they obtain the skill?) Ultimately, he did not accept my view and was not going to reason with me because he had his opinion and I had mine. (It would be difficult to determine who is right or wrong for this situation because it is about choice!) He failed to accept I was in a normal state of mind.

He said I needed to be educated on how to care for my children. I said that's fine, whatever it takes to get home! A great punch to any mother! How would you feel? I wanted to rip him to shreds because he wasn't listening, he judged and assumed he was right! Luckily I'd had the experience from my childhood plus the knowledge and control to hold my composure at a critical time!

He said it was difficult and confronting to accept being diagnosed with a mental illness. I asked him why he assumed that and I don't have a problem. He wasn't sure what to say other than "well it's good that you feel that way!" I told him I was conducting a social experiment and that his failure to assess me properly would be exposed. I continued to say that this type of care wouldn't help anyone and it was unsatisfactory. There were too many inconsistencies with the *so called care*. I also added, "If you put people in a box, how can you evolve?" (Yes priceless but I never hold back and how could I change me?) I knew what I was doing and had plenty of time to articulate how I would execute and deliver my findings. Again I can appreciate how that worked against me from a medical perspective but I didn't care. Because it highlighted opportunities that needed to be addressed! I envisaged I'd be helping a lot more than I originally thought – amazing for me on my new found quest!

After highlighting that I was entitled to a second opinion, I had another appointment on Tuesday 31/7/2012. It was a total waste of time. I won't even bother sharing the details. What colleague from the same hospital would consider a mental patient's view against a peer? I was still declared mentally ill but I just laughed and it gave me an opportunity to speak with Tom my nurse who attended that session.

When I first saw Tom, I thought it was interesting that they had a priest in the ward. So I was surprised that he was my nurse. As it turned out he was a priest and said it wasn't common knowledge. I found that amusing! I don't know how but we ended up talking about World War I & II and I explained a bit about what I had researched. I thought finally someone can appreciate some sense! I respected his beliefs and he understood my belief in myself. He wasn't a preaching priest and I thoroughly enjoyed spending time with him. Nanna G was also intrigued by him as well and was planning to visit his parish.

The cleaners were always friendly. Cosal always looked after me and tried to get hot chocolate when the ward ran out. I enjoyed many chats and occasionally had a lengthy conversation with him during my stay. On this particular day, he asked about my beliefs after overhearing a conversation I had with Tom. Cosal was a Buddhist. I basically told him that I believe in myself however if I was made to choose it would be a congregation aligned to Karma. I also advised that for me, I don't believe you have to prove your faith by attending a congregation. He was fascinated and we built a stronger rapport over the days that followed.

Selena did get a bit annoyed with me once. My bathroom hadn't been cleaned for 3 days but it didn't bother me because no one was in the adjoining room. So I asked whether my bathroom had been cleaned and Selena advised that it had. I said well the floor is dirty and there is no toilet paper. She claimed that I just walked in the shower/toilet and created the dirt. I said I didn't even go into the bathroom because I had no paper and want some. I then proceeded to say, that I was happy to clean my own but obviously I wasn't allowed to use the chemicals or maybe I couldn't perform her job! Anything to pass time, I was that bored!

I was glad there was no one in the adjoining room for a good 6 days as Mick and I were able to share some quick memorable moments. A moment without kids is "hard" to come by! I'm tipping we weren't the first to have a private moment in a public place and I'm sure we won't be the last! The nurses never invaded the bathroom at least!

Tuesday night I requested to use the phone to contact the Mental Legal Aid board. Janet queried that they would be closed and I expressed that I was told that a service operates at that time. Three failed attempts and I walked off deemed more mental (as I assume it would be perceived that I had no concept of time). When I rang the following day, Fern from reception apologised and was concerned that I was not able to make contact when the service should have been available. She assured me that if I rang after 3pm, I would be able to seek legal advice. I was very fortunate and privileged to speak with Hilda. I explained that I had not taken any medication and that the medical team had deemed that I was getting better. She understood my precarious situation and advised it would be best to schedule the appeal in 4 weeks to ensure I could be fairly represented. She provided a wealth of knowledge and highlighted the best approach. I was extremely grateful for the time, attention and advice she provided, it was very professional. Finally a government service worth its weight in gold. She never once questioned my ability or intelligence and was very considerate of my predicament. At that stage in the process, no lawyer could act on my behalf prior to the appeal being scheduled. In effect, I could not even use the law to assist me in getting out of the place! What hope did I have?

I also requested to obtain unescorted leave. I expressed that I didn't want to inconvenience family and friends for escorted leave. I wanted a break from the office (not that I said that). Janet asked whether I would be inclined to take drugs or alcohol if I was granted leave. I replied, I didn't consume any drugs or alcohol and ended up here, why on earth would I start now when I'm actively trying to get back home? I guess this is another example of applying standard procedures. They couldn't even think or assess at an individual level. They had no capacity to cater for each individual because they treated patients all the same.

Mum and Dad visited for the first and only time. After asking me how I was, Mum advised that she needed a certificate because she helped look after the kids. I could see and tell by my Dad's behaviour that he did not trust what I was talking about and he was worried. He queried why I didn't ask for help and I told him that I was doing research for a book. He sternly said it was embarrassing and to think about my kids. Mum tried to smooth things as she always did and I expressed to Mum it was fine. Dad is entitled to his own opinion. If someone has already made up their mind and cannot accept a point of view, don't make it your problem. You can't control how people react. I provided the opportunity but obviously when I shared my stories of what transpired around the hospital he thought I was nuts! I was in a fucking mental ward, what do you expect to hear? I discarded my drugs in front of my parents after the nurse left. I could feel and see my dad's disappointment. He queried whether I had ECT and I replied 'hell no'. I said they were even feeding me Valium and I refused to consume that. Mum advised that she had taken those pills before and they were bad. I didn't expect him to take matters into his own hands.

As most of my friends had moved on, I found more time to write and thought I'd provide the medical staff a snapshot of my thoughts. Here is what I provided them:

Wednesday 1st August 12.35pm

Just had lunch, spoke to Mick earlier, apparently Dad wants to catch up. I assume Dad didn't believe my stories but wasn't bothered – can't teach an old dog new tricks. He always wants control and thinks he is right. (Janet had a subtle insight to this regarding the certificates – we required coz my mum has looked after my children. My Dad wanted to check them before Janet finished explaining it to my mum). He (my dad) said he was embarrassed – his problem, not mine and it was in the past. I acknowledged I had an episode due to sleep deprivation and it is equivalent to losing touch of reality "do crazy things". You can't undo the past but you can control how you react – 1st step is acknowledgement. I don't deny that my friend's plight with cancer was a trigger, maybe the diagnosis (for me) is part of post-traumatic stress – won't be able to establish that until I have access to the internet and other resources. Basically told Mick to say to Dad "no" Mick's time is better spent with my beautiful kids and to mind his own business cause he isn't helping - obviously in a nice way. Sometimes you have to hurt the ones you love to get what you need. <u>(I was referring to emotionally hurt just in case it is misconstrued!)</u>

Had the pleasure of catching up with Donna (over the phone), love her to bits, just gave her a brief update. She mentioned she had words with my sister – that was great to hear. She said Marie had noticed that my behaviour has been different over the last year that would be the perception to her for the following reasons:

1. *We spoke regularly but on a different level, e.g. more baby talk – children same age*
2. *When I was short for money, I had to sell my gold – to make do over the weekend. She who has always been selfish – I guess unintentionally, who also inherited $250K at 16, has never really needed to live life like the rest of us. Her house is fully paid, has $?00K sitting in a bank, nice cars and a*

caravan but on this occasion for example, happened to ring me before I left for the shops and I explained my situation and she said "well don't sell anything you want to keep". <u>(She didn't even offer me a hand in need.)</u> I have or never will get angry with my sister, although others do, (I'm not a jealous person so that doesn't even come into the equation) because I accepted who she is for her, you can't change people but you can think or have control of how you react. Again this is a technique I have used throughout life. It also keeps me emotionally in "check" because anger, hatred and all the negative traits don't do you any good. Of course, I have been tested, more so now than ever but I know I'm a much better person for it, experience, learning and growing.

3. *Actions speak louder than words, I have got a lot of love, knowledge, kindness etc to give and have always put others first because I don't expect anything in return. However for my sister, I tend to treat differently because of who she is, I feel a little hypocritical coz she believes we have a solid relationship yet I know it's on false pretences. I still love her dearly. But now her telling others what she believes to be correct will ultimately be her undoing and she may or may not learn from that.*

Again I don't entertain what other people think, as we are all entitled to an opinion, keep what you want and discard the rest. You can see how each individual can contribute to what they believe is right but essentially not helping overall.

Again I can only control and request others especially my husband to trust himself and me whilst working through this process. I will now request a photocopy of this and ask it to be added to the file.
12.55pm 1/8/12 to just give the medical team an insight to the follow on effect of what I will need to manage post my discharge, along with managing the involuntary order to ensure that appeal is overturned and more importantly, get back to my much loved family and into the normal routine. So on reflection, I came here to rest and will now have to manage a whole lot more but I know with my positive mindset, insightfulness and control, I will achieve this and will

continue to become more enriched by life for being the best person I can be!!

Thank you!! xx

Just thought I'd mention I don't know if the doctors read my notes but they were added to the file. If they did read it, they would have known I was not the type that would be trying to commit suicide! They would have known I had my wits about me on a number of matters, concept of times and dates for one. The letter alone highlighted what my thought process was at that time. How did they interpret this letter? There is a great deal in that letter, if you can read between the lines and consider many angles. For me, anything I said or wrote was of no relevance! In fact they consulted with my Dad and ignored my husband, totally contravening all privacy laws too.

The doctors were evaluating you on the present to a degree but then questioned your behaviour on that one point in time. I had acknowledged what, when, who, how and why! They didn't know me or want to get to know me! They just wanted to pump me with drugs that I knew I didn't need. Some that came with quite serious side effects. I wasn't going to be placed in a box and be treated like the rest.

Anyone deemed with a mental illness especially in a psyche ward has no rights or freedom of speech. No one gives you any credence! I experienced this first hand with a clear mind. If I had taken any of those drugs, I would have been screwed.

That night I started to re-connect emotionally with my family as I assumed I would be released soon. I had written individual letters to all of my children and Mick. Tears were streaming down my face as I wrote; it is only natural when a mother hasn't seen her children for so long. Especially when they are your life and vice versa! I did speak with my children on the phone but it was limited and not enough to break-me! Whilst I was detained, I treated my P-Block mates as family. They were there with me!

Thursday 2/8/2012 – I was rudely interrupted during my lunch for an unexpected appointment but I had almost finished so I took my water with me. Again the door was unlocked and as I went to sit down Dr. Hughes asked what was in my cup. (I thought, like fucking hell, why does it matter to you what's in my cup?) He asked me to drink it and I complied.

Obviously he had been 'christened' with water before – I wouldn't have been surprised. Anyway he asked the standard questions, same reply. Then he said "well we have decided to change your treatment and we will be giving you an injection". I knew I had no rights whilst I was on the order and I also knew my dad had contacted their office.

I didn't panic, I asked the dickhead "Is that because you have spoken to my Dad or family member? Dr. Hughes was diplomatic (really it was gutless) and he didn't deny or accept but rather said it was best to manage my condition. I quickly fired back with "Well if that was the case, why wasn't I treated like that in the first instance?" The doctor could not respond, instead he changed the subject. I then proceeded to ask what the drug was and the side effects. He said I may get dizziness and tremors. Do you think if I was mentally challenged I would have thought to respond so quickly and articulately? I could tell by the doctor's body language, tone and language that he was uncertain of what to make of me!

I was so angry with my Dad and rang my husband and vented. I told him to tell my Dad to "fuck off and mind his own business." I knew my dad was only doing it out of love and care but he had no knowledge of what I was doing and when I explained he didn't want to listen. He was always right, always wanted control, could never be told and only heard what he wanted to hear. Again, just like my childhood! Anything I said would not have mattered – he in essence became the doctor! Only the doctor's intentions were out of a duty of care. If that didn't send me crazy, what would? (Oh and the reason I requested Mick to make the call is, I knew he wouldn't and there would be less to clean up later.)

I then rang Donna and was most upset, with valid reason. She felt for me as she had never heard me so emotional and sent a text to Mick. Mick was already on his way and I was all settled by the time he arrived. I dealt with the emotion then and there! I assume most people would have gone berserk in the appointment, if they were in my position.

Next came my plan, I had to remove the drugs from the premises. I needed to validate my side of the story when the time was right. I couldn't compromise my position whilst in the system, as I had no rights and they could have taken the evidence. Mick took them home and funnily enough they are currently sitting in fishing tackle boxes.

When I received the information of the toxic injection, the first thing that caught my eye was the second point, "This should only be used after at least 4 attacks within 12 months". It was my so called first episode, so why would they give me this injection? The side effects were enough to fucking disable and almost kill you! They were going to intoxicate me! All patients said "Don't get the needle man!" One patient claimed he couldn't walk for 9 months.

Even if I did experience the mild effects, how the fuck would I have cared for my kids. And then they were going to happily send me out the door with an extra few pills to manage the ill effects of the side effects! There was no way I'd be getting that injection, will there is a will, there is a way!

Now on reflection, did I suspect or know that my father was going to compromise my position? I did request for the note to be added to my file a day before the doctor decided to change my treatment. My note highlights a sequence of events that lead to Dr. Hughes changing the course of treatment. The doctor did not answer my question. Had I acted subconsciously without realising? I'll leave it with you to ponder and let you work it out.

Friday 3/8/2012 – Show time! I was well and truly ready for my doctor's appointment with Dr. Julian Hughes. I was about to eject him out of his chair rather than him inject me!

Transcript of the recorded consultation:

DH: Grab a seat, so Annette how are you today?

Me: Very well thank you

DH: Good and um how did you sleep overnight?

Me: Very well

DH: Ok..Now did you um, have any suicidal thoughts?

Me: No

DH: Have your thoughts been racing?

Me: No

DH: Now Annette you didn't have your medication I understand

Me: Yep

DH: OK ..Why was that?

Me: Um I guess the ball is sort of in my court at the moment

DH: Hhmm mmm… in what respect?

Me: Um I needed to seek legal advice and um I'm not in a position to discuss that with you at this point in time

DH: Hhmm mmm

Me: Um again I guess this is going outside of your normal domain, I have not taken one tablet since I've been here

DH: OH really (significant change in tone)

Me: That's correct

DH: ah hah

Me: So it pushes all boundaries, I guess in a sense

DH: ah huh

Me: I don't have any racing thoughts but you've probably got some now!

DH: ah huh

Me: So you can understand the position I'm in

DH: So you are claiming you didn't have any medication

Me: Ah I have proof, it's not about claiming

DH: What do you mean you've got proof?

Me: I have every tablet in a tissue that's in a safe place and photos of that. (Although I said every tablet, I meant from when I could store them as I had no means in AMA and there was one or two that slipped through)

DH: Why have you done that?

Me: because I wasn't here for bipolar. I had sleep deprivation. No one listened

DH: ah huh

Me: I have been very patient

DH: ah huh Can you show me the pictures?

Me: Yes I can – not till I speak with my solicitor

DH: Where are the pictures?

Me: I don't need to disclose that

DH: Where are the tablets?

Me: I don't need to disclose that

DH: Well you know having tablets lying around is a hazard

Me: And it's a hazard giving me tablets for something I wasn't treated for properly

DH: Hmm mmm

Me: You were prepared to give me a drug this afternoon that even if I had bipolar I haven't even had 4 relapses in 12 months. So you can appreciate my position, I'm in now! And I understand your position is compromised

DH: In what way?

Me: Well trying to drug me for something I don't have that has been misdiagnosed and has legal ramifications

DH: hmm mmm so um

Me: Again I don't know how productive this conversation is going to be. I need as I said to contact my lawyer

DH: ah huh so can you show me the tablets that you have allegedly retained

Me: Yes I will do that

DH: Can you go get them now!

(As Mick and I left the room, DH asked the nurse to escort us and I said, I'm entitled to some privacy when I need it and said that won't be necessary. This was so I could find the photos on Mick's phone.)

Me: There is a picture of some of the evidence

DH: So what are these tissues? Is it?

Me: With every drug, there was one or two that slipped through the cuckoo's nest

DH: Ok so you still got the bag of medication

Me: Yep and I'm not at liberty to give you any more details at this point in time

DH: hmm mm why is that?

Me: Because I'd be compromising my position

DH: So you feel you've improved despite not taking medication

Me: It's not a matter of being improved. I came in with sleep deprivation. I've tried to explain that so I had to do what I needed to do um in that respect. So again not going to say anymore

DH: Well um yeah did you take any drugs or speed or anything beforehand?

Me: Check your records (I then turned to Mick and said "Don't say anything hun!")

DH: OK so you're claiming you haven't taken any medication

Me: Again this, this is unproductive the way I see it is, you discharge me immediately. You keep me on the order and look at it (the drugs) at the appeal board in 4 weeks time as my solicitor suggested and understood my situation. And 2 weeks is not enough um or you can proceed with giving me this drug and further becoming negligent in your role as a psychiatrist

DH: (was rapidly flicking through the medical file) so ok we'll see

Me: I'm happy to give you time to digest anything that you need to

DH: I'm just having a look (silence for a few good seconds) you did have an intra-muscular injection?

Me: That was when I was sedated. And I had the leisure or pleasure of seeing a physiatrist at that point (I didn't want to lead on that I knew it was him) and that involuntary could have been overturned within that 24 hours but um I was drugged up without warning or giving my husband the courtesy call to say that was what you were doing to me. I had no one here. So there is enough breaches of the act. Due diligence has been compromised

DH: (interrupts in a raised tone) But you were unwell! You were mentally ill when you came in!

Me: That's your perception and again this needs to be argued I guess outside of this one room and I appreciate that

DH: Ok um let's see so

Me: I came in here with sleep deprivation. First thing I said, if you want to help me, I need sleep. No one listened

DH: (a few seconds passed) um (after 40 seconds he said) ok (he continued reading and then said) so (and continued flicking through the file)

Me: And if you checked the nurse's notes I actually told them my situation last night and I wanted to speak with Janet because I have a good rapport with her. And she understood where I was coming from, she didn't take me as a psyche patient as such

DH: (after about 20 seconds) so you have been spitting them out in tissues

Me: It's irrelevant at this point in time. I think I have shown you enough. You write down what you believe is correct!

DH: mmm

Me: As you can tell there is not a lot on my mind. I'm talking slow and am very calm if that's one of your observations. If no one listens or I'm passionate about something, I will talk fast. Because in that 15 minutes after my first appointment you were obviously not listening to me! Actions obviously speak louder than words sometimes even when you don't have any rights.

DH: hmm mm so you don't want to take any of your old medication now?

Me: What purpose would it be when I haven't taken it for the whole period of time? I'm telling you that I am fine

DH: So that photo shows about 4 tablets

Me: That's fine, you make your assessment on that

DH: But you're saying you've got the whole supply of medication

Me: (I interrupted) I'm not telling you more,

DH: So

Me: I'm not telling you any more

DH: so yes you know it's not totally convincing that you've got all the medication

Me: (I interrupted) That's you're at liberty to make judgments. You've made judgments on my so called mental state. I'm entitled to that in reverse.

DH: So so you are not prepared to show us at present

Me: Not now, god no! Would you, if you were in the same position? That's why I need my lawyer. (They wouldn't even accept Mick's opinion because they decided to consult with my dad. They ignored Mick's comments even though he was my next of kin.)

DH: mm mm

Me: I understand the ramifications, I understand how this will unfold.

DH: mm mm

Me: and I'm probably 10 steps ahead of where you are probably thinking now and that's not being ignorant (I asked Mick to go and get me a water – the doctor didn't say anything about having water in this consult! Did I miraculously gain some control?)

DH: (After a few minutes silence) do you think that there is something happening sort of - like people

Me: (I interrupt) you draw your own conclusions

DH: No I'm asking you a question. Do you think people are plotting against you?

Me: I'm not entertaining any more of this, so you write down what you think is right.

DH: Any thoughts of hurting others?

Me: Are you playing me for a fool? I've just explained my situation

DH: I've just asked you a question

Me: I don't need to answer that anymore

DH: OK (after another minute) and in terms of voices, you haven't answered that question, are you prepared to answer that, are you hearing voices?

Me: I'm hearing your voice

DH: Yeah but what about when no one is home

Me: It's irrelevant; I've told you I don't need to keep playing these games. You need to trust yourself and what's best in your professional opinion and things will unfold in due course

DH: Do you know what day it is today?

Me: The 3rd of the 8th, it's Friday

DH: um month um 8th - what about the year?

Me: 2012

DH: Do you know where you are?

Me: At a psyche ward at Monash Medical Centre

DH: And do you think you have any illness at all? Or any other kind of illness

Me: You haven't listened to me for the last 17 days so

DH: (interrupts) I know you said you had bipolar

Me: I'm not answering anything other than tell you what I want to tell you. It is irrespective because you haven't listened

DH: So you haven't changed, you previously said you don't have a mental illness.

Me: I didn't say that. I said I had sleep deprivation. So you can write that down

DH: OK

Me: And no one had taken the time to listen and you made an assessment on your current practices and procedures. I've highlighted that you can't make a full assessment unless you appreciate the full picture. Um again that's the current procedures/processes.

DH: mm

Me: That's fine, I appreciate that!

DH: mm

Me: I've played the game as best as I could. But I was not going to allow myself to be drugged involuntarily. So even though you denied me of all my rights and neglected all my acts (I meant "the" acts) I have found a way. Someone that doesn't have the correct mindset, insight or intelligence wouldn't have been able to do that. So write that down

DH: mm

Me: And yesterday you weren't honest with me when I said were you giving me that injection because of my father. My father compromising my position, you chose to be diplomatic and not answer that! Actions speak louder than words. Why would you give me an injection now when you didn't start at the start? So you can see where I'm coming from hopefully. If not, you will in the not too distant future.

DH: So we will need to observe you. See how you are off medication

Me: I haven't been on medication

DH: But that's what you're telling us but we have no way of verifying that

Me: I've given you some evidence

DH: But you've only given us a photo

Me: That's fine I'm not going to show you anything until we go to court

Mick: Why don't you do a blood test?

Me: Yeah check your blood test

DH: Umm

Me: Check some of the other observations. I haven't had constipation yeah check the blood test

DH: Umm that's a good idea

Me: Thanks Mick now you are starting to think like me

DH: Ok would you would you, we'll do a blood test now

Me: Yeah do a blood test and check the ones you did last Friday when someone woke me up 7.30 in the morning when I was in a deep sleep.

Mick: That would prove that she didn't take any other drugs

DH: We can do the one for the drugs that we are looking for

Me: By all means and I refused to take that oral one you tried to give me yesterday so Demitrix never came back cause I explained my situation then

Me; So this is how I'll do it, I'll speak to my lawyer who is available at 3 o'clock. I'll do the drug test and get the pathology back and if there is not one drug in my body you can release me. Or you can keep me here against my will and it will go against you in court.

DH: ah huh OK

Me: That's my plan.

DH: mm mm

Me: You are entitled to do or think or at liberty to do what you need to do

DH: OK so what will do um we will keep you here to observe how you are

Me: Yep

DH: We will stop your regular medication. And see what happens to your mental state

Me: I've just told you, you can take a blood test

DH: But we can only do that for one of your medications (thought to myself you can only conveniently test one but if it was an autopsy you can test a whole lot more! Maybe the tests are different?)

Mick: Can I ask a question? When is she likely to come home?

DH: Look umm

Me: Well if you are keeping me here against my will

DH: (interrupts) We need to observe you. Hopefully we can, you know we can get you home next week

Mick: This is not going to help

Me: No that's alright hun, we'll stop it here. I'll speak to my solicitor at 3, they are already negligent, I've proven that. They can take the blood test. You can actually check your notes, I have not had constipation, I have not been sick! A lot of others have. Symptoms that a lot of other people have experienced and not just one or two, I have a list of 10! And I've kept record of that.

Me: Now you might find it hard to believe that someone who is not educated in medicine is able to go down this path but I actually used logic.

DH:	Right
Me:	I've kept every note.
DH:	Good
Me:	And you won't find any on this premise
DH:	ah huh
Me:	anyway I have had enough time, we'll get going

Mick asks about the blood test and I say that they will find me. Mick says thank you and we walk out. I did say at one stage to Dr. Hughes, are you having racing thoughts? Can you hear my voice? How do you feel? But that there were parts of the audio that were interrupted by a frequency and it wasn't captured. Mick looked in shock as if to say you're game! I guess I was being arrogant and ignorant throughout the whole consult because I had had enough. Being arrogant is not part of my core traits but is used when required.

Now what I wanted to do in this consult was call it how I did but when I asked him if he needed more time, I would have liked to start singing – you got to know when to hold them, know when to fold them, know when to walk away and know when to run! I also had envisaged that I'd be leaving the ward singing Frank Sinatra, I did it my way. I was at least smart enough to know that had I behaved in this manner they would have kept me in longer but at least I can share what I wanted to do. (Another example of assessing risks and consequences with needs and wants from a mental perspective.)

Just before lunch, Afea stopped to talk to me and Mick. The doctors never stopped to talk to anyone in the corridor so I knew I had rocked the boat. She proceeded to ask how I was and mentioned that she had heard we had a "major" meeting. I said there was nothing major about it, I needed to do what I had to do and you should check your notes. Her reply was ok and we walked off. Why did she call it a meeting? Normally it would be referred to as an appointment or consult, was I breaking down the barriers? Why did she approach us and engage in conversation? Instant change in her behaviour!

I was asked to go to the ECT room for my blood test. I said to Mick you better come with me in case they fry my brain. I couldn't trust them! I had the blood test there because the nurse had poor eye sight and the light was better in that room. Mick was paranoid about the ECT room which I found funny.

After listening to the recording, I also noticed that Dr. Hughes was trying very hard to get me to concede or admit that I had a mental illness. Wasn't he the doctor? He tried to misconstrue that I deemed I had bipolar – I know for a fact I consistently said I had sleep deprivation and also captured a recording of this at three consults. My account of what transpired and what I said never deviated because I always told the truth. I just had to be patient, something that previously didn't come naturally. (A great learning curve for me though!)

I also found it strange that he introduced new questions, like do you think someone is plotting against you? Did you take any drugs or anything? Do you have any other illnesses? Why suddenly did he explore these avenues? Was it because he didn't take the time to assess me properly? Was it because he needed to validate what had transpired? Was it because he needed to protect his professional integrity? Did he doubt himself or was it a lack of confidence in his own professional opinion? He admitted I improved and yet this was without the so called treatment! Many questions have remained unanswered. Do I deserve the right to know? I do for the purposes of my research but I will cover this in more detail as we progress.

Mick and I attended the "relationship" session that afternoon to kill time as previously mentioned. We also sat in the lounge and I was observing what was happening in and around the nurses' station. Files were being reviewed, nurses were actively making calls and there were more doctors present. You wouldn't normally see that many at that time, especially on a Friday afternoon. Dr. Hughes was even in and out and at one stage he paced up and down – very unusual behaviour. I don't know if I caused a flurry but I enjoyed thinking it was me. Other patients noticed this as well.

I spoke with Hilda and she praised me for my actions. She basically said "you don't need a lawyer you have the system worked out, you just need to take it one step at a time." I was so grateful to have

Hilda as she gave me hope and direction when I was presented with difficult challenges.

They didn't want to give me my results and they had no intention of releasing me. I did think about calling in the media or starting a friendly protest but chances were they probably would have just considered me mental! Plus it would have tarnished my credibility and case. I did contact a journalist from The Age a few days prior so I could share my story but obviously it wasn't meant to be! The journalist I called had written an article about suicides in the Cardinia shire (18th June 2012).

Jibi and Tina (nurses) advised that they needed to do a bag search to confirm there was no accessible medication. I explained I had the pills from the night before and removed them from my pocket. I asked whether I could take a photo of the evidence that the nurse was confiscating. They weren't sure what to do. However they reluctantly allowed me to take a photo. I pulled out everything in my suitcase. I showed them where I hid my loot and also offered if they'd like to sniff my makeup bag, as there was a lingering odour of the meds.

They didn't even check the drawers nor did they look under the mattress. The drugs weren't on the premises but you would have at least checked. It was also amusing that I was allowed to take a photo when phones were banned, should they have confiscated it until my husband left? (We didn't question, it was their rules, again another example of using their system to my advantage).

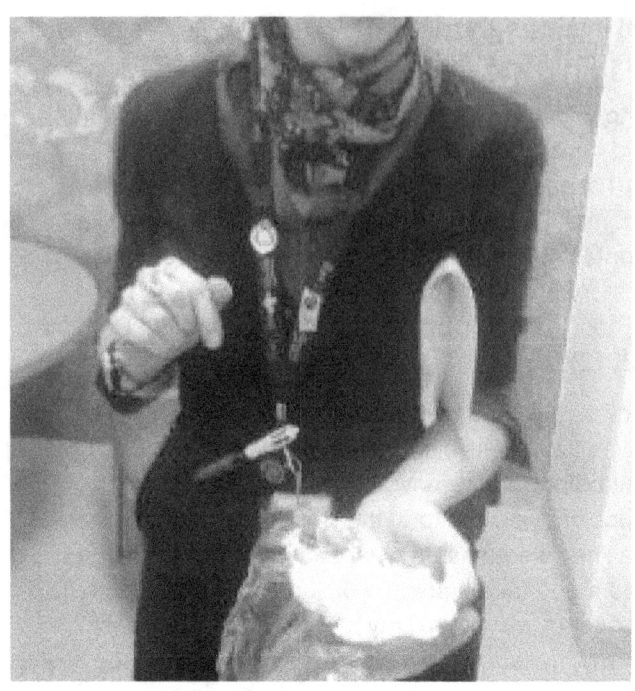

Above: a nurse holding the tissue containing medication from the night before. (Not a clear shot of the tablets but evidence none the less!)

I guess they were focused on making sure no one had the potential to overdose. Funny really, because if a patient was thinking about suicide and by passed the system like I did, how many Valium, Epilium, Seroquel pills and any other drugs they were dishing up, would allow you to successfully make that attempt? Obviously the doctor didn't consider this in his observations. 17 days of pills in one hit would have permanently put me to sleep! I never mentioned suicide or put myself at risk but had the opportunity if I did! Reverse psychology, different perspective, trained or untrained mind? Or was he in denial? I assumed he thought I was suicidal because he kept asking me those questions. Furthermore there was no evidence that I tried to take my life (at any stage) so I was totally perplexed by his logic or thought processes in treating me for this condition.

I requested to speak with a higher authority, Dr. Barton but staff refused to allow me to contact him. I then rang the hospital board requesting to speak to Dr. Barton (on behalf of a patient) and they transferred me through to the Psyche ward nurses' station. (They were sending me around in circles!)

I then contacted the Chief Psychiatrist (governing body) to determine if there were any options available for release. However they were in a board meeting and on a Friday afternoon a mental patient would not have been a priority. (They did call me back on Monday to their credit.)

Mick was running late to return home for the kids and I needed someone to relieve Mick's sister who had another engagement. I didn't want my parents at home because of what happened; Mick was livid. I explained to Mum that I was fine and that they didn't need to be at my house and I needed my own space for the time being. (She misinterpreted what I said and thought I meant I didn't want to see them at all.) I rang my sister to see if she was able to fill the gap! She said she couldn't but then started to abuse me over the phone. She yelled "You're the fucking one in hospital and you should be taking your medication." I just hung up her. I didn't have time to even bother about her and even today I have kept my distance to avoid conflict. I tried a couple of friends who weren't available. Fortunately Mick's other sister was able to fill the gap!

The most amusing thing for me was that I was emotionally and mentally in check. However other than a handful of patients I was there the longest time! Bad Mama – if you don't play their game, you have to bide time while they work out what's going on in your head! I'm lucky I got out really!!!

Mick was furious, angry and frustrated. He expected that I would be released. I was fine, although I didn't get to go home, I did avoid getting that toxic injection and I was taken off all medication. I didn't have to pretend or be bothered by the staff. Mick rang me at 11pm that night and he was most distressed. He was physically and mentally exhausted. Here I was at the nurses' station trapped in a psyche ward coaching my husband and reassuring him that things will be fine soon. I told him not to get angry or stressed as it would not do him any justice. I bet the nurses didn't record that conversation on my medical file. It would be interesting to determine if they recorded anything positive on my file. This would prove how extensive their observations and analysis were to determine if they made a fair and accurate assessment of a patient.

After speaking to Mick, I asked Gary whether the results from the blood test were confirmed. They were in that afternoon but clearly I didn't receive the courtesy of being told (even though I asked). Apparently there was a slight trace of a drug. I assume this was because the nurse who administered the pills had decided to chat to me for a few good minutes and question how I managed to avoid taking my medication. I couldn't believe it! I was sitting there talking to her while they were dissolving under my tongue and she didn't even think to ask me to open my mouth to check. I said I couldn't disclose that as it would be compromising my position. (I had previously rejected the oral Resperidone (liquid formula) hence why the nurse questioned my position.)

I never lined up for the drugs at 10pm as all patients were required to do. The nurses had to find me. On three occasions I didn't even receive my pills. Wonder who scored them? Maybe their strict protocols of administering pills were unsound? Or it could have been overlooked! (I have actual dates but won't publicly share them as I need to contain some information if the Medical profession wants to investigate this matter further! If I provide details now there may be an opportunity to rectify the inconsistencies which wouldn't go in my favour to substantiate the facts!)

I also explained to Gary that I slipped pills into the pillow cases in AMA and seclusion because I failed to mention that in my consult. He told me not to worry about that because it would have been discarded in the cleaning process. Now we all know that there are strict controls when dealing with medication in hospital. Was my admission added to my file? I was highlighting a potential risk! I could have easily popped them under the mattress and that would not have been lifted off the floor/bed. The pills could have been dislodged and fallen on the floor. The cleaning I saw was by no means thorough! Irrespective of this, shouldn't all pills be accounted for, that's why they searched my bag! If there is a potential risk, shouldn't the hospital have procedures in place? Furthermore they would have been able to determine if a patient did not consume their medication! Maybe I was the only mental patient to think and act in this manner? I know I won't find myself in that position again but for anyone else protecting themselves, I hope I haven't made it too hard if the process does change!

Sunday 5/8/2012 - Mick and the whole family came in to see me! My children hadn't seen me for 19 days. Max, my eldest born, was suffering emotionally. Normally an angel, he was becoming unbearable for Mick. He was yelling, throwing furniture and smashing glasses. Anyone would have thought he had a behavourial disorder if they encountered him during that time. Therefore I had to relent and let them visit. As previously mentioned, I was trying to protect them and keep them settled at home, as best I could.

Beng - a happy beautiful nurse (who was on my side and trying to teach me to say less, so I'd get out) ensured the back lounge was made available for us exclusively. I couldn't even go to the cafeteria because my leave form, from the previous week had not been signed. I did ask daily but it was overlooked. I didn't get angry as that would have spoiled my day! One excuse I received was my doctor wasn't in! I replied "If my doctor dies, would I be stuck in the system forever?" I did use their lack of processes to my advantage when I needed to, more on that soon!

I told Mick to bring in the footy and some bubbles, so we enjoyed those activities. We made things out of paper/foam cups and sticks. The kids loved the hot chocolate machine and we basically made the best out of the hospital confinements. Beng brought in a heap of food around lunch time and the kids loved the novelty.

Max said it was the best day ever after about 10 minutes but I knew he meant seeing me. He asked whether I could return home and I said I couldn't. He then asked if he could stay. I didn't want to break his heart but I suggested he ask the nurse but highlighted that she may say no because children couldn't not stay in this part of the hospital. I preferred to share the burden! Obviously the nurse said no.

After a relaxing day with my family, the hardest time was saying good-bye. Especially for Max, being older he understands and is quite bright for his age. He held on for at least 15 minutes. Michelle another nurse told me not to prolong the situation. I told her that I wasn't going to push my child away when he needed me the most.

Nanna G had given me a crystal ornament when she left the ward. So I took Max back to the room and told him to take that special gift home and make a wish that night. Although he was most upset and reluctant to go, he did head home.

Monday morning 6/8/2012, my family returned, Max wanted to see me and I thought I'd take the opportunity to introduce my beautiful family to the doctors. I asked Max if he made a wish with the crystal ornament and he said he didn't because he didn't want to get upset if it didn't come true. (It is uncanny how much we are alike.) I wasn't going to disappoint him. My children were very well behaved but Dr. Hughes recommended that they leave whilst we proceeded. I accepted and Mick attended to the children.

There were an additional 3 people in the consult and I found it rude that they were not introduced. Was it because I was deemed mental or was courtesy a thing of the past? (I always made observations; I don't have to think about them, they happen naturally.)

I immediately apologised for my behaviour on Friday. I advised that I felt trapped, threatened, frustrated and my survival mechanism kicked in. I then highlighted that the extra time allowed me to view the situation from their perspective. (I was trying to break down the barrier to get what I wanted.) I kid you not, a couple of questions later Dr. Hughes asked if I was suicidal. (Did he hear me? I had previously said my survival mechanism had kicked in. He never once believed me because he had already put me in a box and labeled me with Bipolar. I guess he only wanted to see and hear what he perceived). I responded with "I find that question offensive but I can appreciate your position and it's in your duty of care (again managing the barriers).

Basically after the standard questions, the doctor advised that I wouldn't be discharged and would not give me a date. I knew this was breaking the family. I then advised that Mick needed to return to the consult to allow him to ask questions. Mick's first question was when will I be coming home?

When Dr. Hughes told Mick I wasn't coming home, Mick rubbed his head, his face turned red, he took a deep breath and I knew he was too upset to talk. So I intervened and said "Look you're actually causing more harm than good. My son and family are suffering. My husband is worried about his new job so I'm willing to compromise.

Dr. Hughes said although I appeared well I should take medicine to prevent a relapse and I would have to abide to that. He advised it was his duty of care. (I thought where was the care when they physically abused me but I never said anything because I knew it would hinder my departure especially after I threatened going to court). I thought that his intent for forcing me to take the drugs was to protect himself but I had no other choice. I couldn't put my family through the emotional pain and suffering, they came first. I was told that I would have to take 2 epilium tablets in the morning and night. (Pharmacy actually made a mistake so I only had one in the morning and one in the night once at home.)

Dr. Hughes advised that I may be discharged at the end of the week. I then proceeded to say well can I at least go home tonight? He said no. I then replied with, "I completed a leave request one week ago and I still have not been granted any leave, can that be approved?" (Fucking got him in front of his peers). He said well yes he could arrange that but we need to monitor you on your medication. I quickly asked how is that different from me attending the local doctor, being prescribed medication and having an anaphylactic shock at home. (Best ball I'd thrown!) From no discharge, I was able to obtain overnight leave and discharge the following day as they failed to meet their own standards. (Would someone of unsound mind be able to articulate this, in an instant?)

He further added that part of the condition was that the department of human services will be involved. If I didn't comply with the recommendation of being supervised with my children 24/7 for a period of time then my children would be removed from my care. I thought you fucking arsehole, clearly he was making it very difficult (maybe because I manipulated the situation in front of his peers to get what I wanted and embarrassed him). It could have also been a mental test but I happily said "that's fine, I understand your position."

I requested that it would be beneficial for the family to seek the services of a psychologist and they said they would arrange that, however it never happened! Again the entire time, I had not consulted with a psychologist. I didn't need their assistance but thought it would be beneficial for my husband. Clearly the hospital's duty of care is partial and drugs are the only answer!

That afternoon, I received calls from Diane, Anita and Yvette. I rarely received outside calls but was happy to finally get in contact with more friends. Diane in particular said that I sounded my old self and advised that she didn't think I was myself after the first CAT team made their assessment. I found this interesting. I assumed she noticed that I changed. Understandably so because she didn't have the full picture! I briefly filled Anita in and she asked whether she could do anything. I requested for her to keep our conversation private as I was mindful of my sister's reaction based on the previous Friday's conversation. I was able to fill Yvette in and she was shocked and explained she had tried to call to no avail. She didn't know what to really do or say. I said "You don't need to explain yourself, I know who you are and you're busy with your family etc."

Whilst I was on the phone to Yvette, I did find it interesting that my sister sent my husband and me a text:

> *"You should make sure you have the correct information before you accuse the wrong people. It was me that told the doctors not mum & dad! People don't like associating with those that continue not to tell the truth & be taken advantage of. Hope you both can be helped!"*

Who was lying? My dad had called Mick and said he called the doctors. I hadn't spoken to my sister since the Friday when I hung up on her? Was my sister trying to protect my dad? Where did she get her information from? She hadn't spoken to Mick? Would her comments be assisting someone that needed care? (I didn't need it but what if I did have a problem?) Who was she thinking of? Sometimes when people are trying to help, they are actually creating more harm. This was a classic example of only thinking from one angle.

Before I left to go home, I was given my leave request form. I couldn't believe that Dr. Hughes back dated the request. The form actually stated I was entitled to leave from 2/8/2012 -12/8/2012 for a period of 3 hours. He didn't even check the details on the form. Lucky my husband and children can validate that I wasn't even able to go to the cafeteria when they visited on Sunday 5/8/2012, if he or the staff attempt to fabricate the truth.

When we were organizing certificates for Mick's work, the nurse advised that she had to notate that I was in psychiatric care. I said I don't have a problem with being deemed mental, write what you think is correct. I did feel like saying, what hope do patients have if the people that care for them, have a stigma! For me, it was a great place to work! (It would be interesting to determine if other sections of the hospital include the condition on the medical certificate; e.g. colonoscopy, circumcision etc.) Just publicly vilify your patients; that will make them feel better and integrate into society!

As we left, Michelle, a nurse wished us well and advised that it wasn't standard procedure to be sedated on your first admission in psychiatric care. I thanked her and advised I will be doing everything in my power to improve the system.

Has anyone tried to change their whole self (in my case 39 years) in a matter of three weeks? I didn't change, I used different strategies and assessed the situation from different angles throughout my informative holiday for the purpose of my book! I remained true to myself and did not mentally break in a very depressing and difficult environment.

Some other memorable moments (good and bad) in P-Block were:

Nanna G, Flynn and I were watching the Blues (my football team) and Richmond play (Flynn's team) Nanna G liked both, in the back lounge. I'm very loud and get right into my sport! During the game a couple of sheepish nurses who I didn't get to know, opened the lounge door and told us to be quiet. Directed at me really, as the others weren't making much noise. I said, "There is a door there and every room has a door, so just close them" I also said "It was my religion" and jovially added "What do you fucking expect? It's a psyche ward!" Gee we had a good laugh! I said to Flynn and Nanna G, if they come back, I'm going to sing "Who let the dogs out? Who? Who? Who?" I was spewing they didn't come back.

One time in band camp, (just kidding), in the courtyard, a pigeon attempted to nose dive me and landed opposite the yard in a bin. Erin, Axil and I were contemplating what we should do! I said "Knowing my luck, a nurse would catch me shaking an empty bin and I'd get another 10 days!" As we approached the bin, it did fly away.

Doing my laundry was never fun! But I got over people moving my clothes. Anyway on this particular day the dryer had overheated and it hadn't before. I checked with the nurses and they said it did happen occasionally. Sweet! Three hours later it still wasn't going, so I hung all my clothes up in my room. I told a nurse that just so they didn't think I was crazy. You are monitored the whole time, actions and behaviours are always misinterpreted so I was mindful of that. After speaking to the nurse, I thought I'd check just one more time and the fucking thing started just as the nurse passed! FOOK I laughed but was thinking, man I'm looking crazier by the day and I'm the most mentally stable of all – including doctors and nurses.

Another night in the back lounge, Bubbles, Nanna G and I were watching TV whilst Madrid was sleeping on one of the gym mats. Well fook me, he let out the most toxic, nose scorching fart I have ever come across and had to bolt to the public loo. I nearly broke my toe on my way and had a good hurl! The girls could hear every motion but laughed none the less! I'm a very bad 'chucker' and I can't stop myself from making it sound better!

I had a great laugh with a few of my mates, as I told them you have to always be careful of what you say! I said "Take me for example, I said to Mick's Ex, other than your brain, which is suffering from a mental condition, you should consider donating your organs as they are a wasted resource! And look where I have fucking ended up! Talk about eating your own words and karma biting you in the arse!" (All for a good cause!)

Now the pompous warden administration clerk, Kym wouldn't give anyone the time of day. She was in charge of all the nurses including the running of the ward. The only smile she could have cracked would be the one that came out of her arse when she farted. I always delightfully said hello because I knew it would irritate her. Her response was as dull as her personality – pity the fool! But on one occasion, I had the fool looking for a ball around the ward.

The patients found this amusing as they knew and loved watching me work the system. Anyway, she told me there was one in the games room. I then returned and said the games room was locked. So I followed her to the games room, and she unlocked the door and then the cupboard – no ball. Then proceeded to another cupboard – no ball, and then checks the store room – no ball. Last check, nurses' station and yes – no ball! She said "We don't have one!" But I had a ball/blast watching her do things that she clearly hated, so did my mates.

Two days later when I noticed she was in the booth, I asked if there was a ball, knowing full well she was going to pull the memory card. In her sarcastic manner she said "Don't you remember, we don't have one". I politely said "I thought you'd have the courtesy to order one!"

With that, Vera was heading out that day, so I got her to get me some balls! She came back with three tennis balls. I should have brought everyone one if I knew how much joy they were going to bring. That afternoon there were three of us, roaming the block bouncing balls. I'm sure it would have driven them crazy or at least some. I'd occasionally just go "I'm just doing my rounds". I didn't care if it was working against me because I knew I'd get myself out of the shit eventually.

I was having lunch on one particular day and Jibi came to give me my drugs. I said "Why am I taking these drugs in the middle of lunch? No-one else is but I'll do it just this once." Next day, same time, she tried to pull the same stint. I said Jibi (I say pet I say love - is what I was thinking) I told you yesterday I wasn't going to take drugs in the middle of lunch, so you can sit there and wait for me or find me later! My mates enjoyed a laugh at her expense, but she asked for it!

So I had fun with the nurses! Two weeks into my interesting holiday the need to shave my legs became apparent. I walked up to the nurse's station and asked if I could have some Nair to remove my hair, before I needed a whipper snipper! They said I could have a razor! I'm like what? Firstly, if patients are suicidal, why are you giving them razors? I asked if they were any good because I didn't want to cut up my white silky legs! The nurse replied that they weren't great but would do the trick! They did request that I return the razor after I used it! I waited to see how long it would take before they came searching. After about 2 hours, I decided to return it. I could not see any logic in the whole process! Someone could have cut up rough in that time. If there was a change of shift, it would go unnoticed; it wasn't as if they signed you up for a disposable!

Poor Geoff should have been in a place more suitable for his needs. He was close to 70, couldn't talk properly, was in a wheel chair and needed more assistance than the others. On this occasion, Geoff wanted to eat his dinner in the ladies lounge but the bastards wouldn't let him. They forced him to dine with the others. I intervened and said, "Let the poor man eat where he wants, where he was comfortable and happy". I got the "he needs to integrate" I thought fuck me, how do you know what he wants and needs. Geoff roared and I piped up and said "Geoff you tell them, with that roar you'd make Jeff Kennett proud but he probably got you into this mess as well!" with that the dining room erupted with laughter!

Another time, same place, I found Lyn sobbing and proceeded to gently rub her back. She was distressed, painfully expressing that her husband had done mean things to her! She kept saying "I don't want to tell you! He did horrible things! He did nasty things! I don't want to tell you!" I just reassured her that she didn't have to tell me and to let it all out. Then Connie had started getting upset and I'm thinking, I just wanted to go out for a smoke. What do I do now? Lucky Tanya a nurse came past and spoke with Connie. Lyn had settled so I said, "I'm just taking a break!" – I was politely trying to get away. With that the nurse looked at me like I had a multiple personality. I walked off thinking I'll be damned if I do and if I don't; at least I cared for the patients feelings!

Sonia the little middle-aged Asian kleptomaniac provided a great laugh. Jimmy Bear and Madrid (both over 6 feet) and a couple of others were standing at the nurses' station when Sonia, said "excuse me, excuse me" to the boys and then started belting a chair forcefully against the glass! It was the polite manner quickly followed by the aggressive nature that made it funny! She used to "borrow" stuff from others, one minute she would be wearing Cristana's beanie (which she scored in the end). Next she would be wearing one of the boy's Ripcurl jackets that was way too big. Patients always had to retrieve jeans or something from her. Obviously she didn't take a fancy to my stuff not that I would have minded.

My party trick came in handy at the office! I performed a few judo rolls around here and there, displaying my skill. (Maybe that's why they kept me in longer but they never asked about that behaviour.) I was also showing a few other Judo moves; how to break an arm, how my "roll" can be used to flip a person if they were charged at and the like. They were all impressed and knew not to mess with the Mama. I never felt threatened or unsafe whilst I was in hospital because I trusted everyone (even though some could and were volatile on the drugs) however I was dubious of one!

The dubious one (I won't give him a name, just in case he comes back to haunt me!) was a heroin dealer who had no etiquette. He frequently executed the vial spit-back snort and spit. He had no table manners and left a mess wherever he was. After a few days he did settle and became more tolerable. He obviously noticed that I was happy and cheerful getting on with all. He started to engage in small talk when we were out in the yard. I was happy to do so, as everyone deserves a fair go. I did feel a little awkward when he called me Mum, the others referred to me as Mama. He also insisted that I call him son at one point. (Whatever - I am in a psyche ward is what I thought). Now this guy was obviously getting too comfortable because at the last P-Block barbeque I attended he asked "Has anyone been raped in this joint?" Erin and I just looked at each other and thought, why don't the nurses hear shit like that? The next night he suggested that we should all have an orgy. At that point, I said "that's why you've got a fucking hand, use it!" I wanted to make it clear, if he did have any intentions, not to mess with me!

Poor Geoff was left in the back lounge for a good 5 hours. I only know this because he was unable to pick up the cardboard pee bottle and I happened to be passing when he was yelling for assistance, so I handed it to him and left. Hours later I found him yelling again, this time the sheet covering his body was on the floor. I didn't want to see his package or embarrass him so I found a nurse. I was appalled especially because Geoff didn't have the capacity to move or speak properly. He was trapped and tormented and they did not at any stage make him comfortable. They forced him to do things he wasn't happy with. How would you feel if your mum, dad, grandma or grandpa where treated like this in hospital?? How would you know what went on, if you didn't spend enough time to appreciate what was happening in and around that environment?

Aiden was offered Valium pills to sleep at 3am on the 29/7. He slept most of the day as result of the drugs and they didn't allow him to go outside for fresh air! Marky Mark was forced to take additional medication because he was singing and busting a move. He asked what would happen if he refused and Janet O told him security would be called to assist! Mark reluctantly consumed the extra medication at his physical expense.

I overheard the nurse telling Sam that she needed to have a shower because she hadn't had one in two weeks. Sam power walked the block for hours and days with a vacant face. No expression and seemed distant from all! I couldn't believe it! I had no idea that some people suffering with depression didn't shower for long periods of time. I was told by some other patients that either they didn't have the energy, are too busy or don't feel worthy of one. I guess I made up for Sam not having a shower and didn't have to feel guilty about my excess use of water!

I was bailed up by a patient for about 2 hours. Zoro was normally reserved and quiet, who was always polite. However on this occasion, he was telling me how the Queen was spending his money. He said that his Dad created the television. Apparently the Russians murdered his family and were trying to steal his intellectual property. It was nonstop and I didn't want to be rude but was thankful when lunch arrived. I expressed to the nurses that he appeared manic and was disturbing others as well. They just looked at me as if to say, what would you know? I stood clear from him and retreated to my room. It was very intense. I couldn't believe they released him the next day! Crazy! I hope Zoro is back on the right path, I didn't get to really know him that well.

On the day I was discharged, I was horrified by Nick's state. Nick was quiet and friendly. He never appeared rattled and spoke clearly and fluently. However the night before Nick had the resperidone oral formula. He could not talk properly and he said he was up all night. He couldn't feel his limbs or move them. He said the whole experience was awful and advised that the doctors had given him other drugs to accommodate the side effects. He was hoping that they were going to work. I was hoping that it was worth the pain and suffering. I thought thank fuck I didn't get the injection. If that was the oral, what would have the injection done to me? A merry go round of drugs, healthy for the profit line of the pharmaceutical suppliers at the expense of those emotionally or mentally challenged. Especially once people become dependent on these for a lifetime. No wonder the world seems to be getting worse!

After 21 days, I had a great understanding and appreciation of others that were mentally displaced. I was also able to establish some inconsistencies with the health care system. I did have the ability to take control and ownership of myself in a difficult environment even when every right had been denied.

Time for another song! This is one I made up in P-Block to the Banana Boat song!

Come Mr. Doctor
Doctor me bananas
Daylight come and we wanna go home
Come Mr. Psyche Doc
Give me something good
Daylight come and we wanna go home

First assessment is not enough
To poison our system, with the drugs dayo dayo
Daylight come and we wanna go home
When will the team wake up? Come on doctor, we've had enough, can't you see what you're doing to us?

Nurses on rounds all night and day,
Still not enough resources to help the bunch Dayo Dayo
Daylight come and we wanna go home
Come on doctors enough is enough! Stick your pills up ya bum!

8. Aftermath

Chugga chugga choo choo, I hope you have enough left in the tank to finish the book! There's nothing like cleaning up your own shit! I didn't expect a rough ride in the "real world", but it was actually more challenging than in hospital.

It was great to be home with my family after so long. That night I bathed the kids, read stories and let them stay up. Max was so excited and relieved. Harley was his normal self and Lexi took a while to warm to me, she preferred Mick over me! Isaiah was his normal self too.

I came home to some changes. Some of my friends and family had a working bee which I was very grateful for and couldn't thank them enough. We hadn't asked anyone for anything. However while I was in hospital, friends and family offered their time or had brought items to help us out because they cared and loved us.

Consequently it came with mixed emotions because I couldn't find items in my own home. Things were moved, re-arranged or thrown out. I would normally roll with it but I was furious. I was trying to get ready for an appointment to be discharged and couldn't find what I needed.

All of Lexi's clothes that fitted were in bags and the clothes in her drawers were all too big. I had only re-arranged and sorted the boys' clothes 3 weeks prior and they weren't in "my" order. Max found it difficult to find his own clothes which frustrated me because it took me a while to re-sort back to normal. He would organize what clothes he wore but he was struggling. The clothes that were in bags, I had to re-wash and sort again. I had some clothes for Lexi that were in boxes with marked sizes that I was planning on storing and these were obviously shelved. In effect, it increased my work load at home and it impeded on my time.

My blanket box at the end of my bed contained the kid's blankets where I normally kept my sheets, practical and logical. My microwave was moved and not near the stove, which again wasn't practical for me. I couldn't find my brush, comb or hair dryer (still haven't found these items). All bathroom cupboards were re-arranged. I couldn't find my wedding/engagement rings for 5 days because Mick couldn't remember where they were hiding after they were moved from their normal spot. All my "junk" boxes that weren't unpacked because the house extension wasn't finished were all sorted or thrown out. Toys were discarded; a fisher price keyboard that was worth $80 was sitting in the wet trailer when I got home. There was nothing wrong with it and the kids did enjoy that activity. My bedroom which I normally kept tidy had 7 massive bags and other stuff in it including the rumpus room rug!

Not one person thought to ask me whether I minded. I could act and think for myself and yet no one checked. I don't mean to sound disrespectful or ungrateful but can you imagine your friends and family going through your personal items? Especially without your knowledge or permission! I felt that my privacy had been violated. It was very frustrating not to be able to locate things in my own home.

Mick copped another spray. I had to release the anger and frustration because I would have carried that attitude to my appointment. I asked him whether anyone went through our secret stash that contained Picture Magazines and other stuff. (I brought the mags in the early days of our relationship. We would read these together because they were a great laugh and they came with handy tips too!) I didn't mean to keep pounding him but he was the only one there! (Poor Mick!)

On the flip side, there were just as many great things that had changed. Isaiah's room did need a clean out and had to be re-arranged. Curtains were installed in the kid's room. Friends helped gather wood. The house was cleaned after the mess I created. They covered up my graffiti. Jane who has the biggest heart again brought some other items. Friends and family dropped food around and looked after my children. They erected a clothes line on the back deck. The trampoline that was under the deck for the last 18 months was erected. And I'm sure there was plenty more that I'm not aware of.

I then pulled my head together realising that my frustration was over trivial matters. My friends and family had acted with good intentions and were trying to help. It was the thought that counted and it stemmed from love and care. In comparison to the victims of Black Saturday, I shouldn't have been whining about anything! I quickly reverted to my old self without realising and then back to my improved self (wider perspective).

I was contemplating not to include the above in my book because I didn't want to offend my family and friends. But I thought it was a valuable example of the positive and negative theory. In addition, it was something that Rose experienced amongst her chaos. Oddly, we had something extra in common to talk about. Another reason, it was difficult to determine what support I could have provided Rose. Hopefully this will offer some guidance or insight for others in a similar position. I have faith that my family and friends who helped will understand my justification.

Jan was able to help us out again. She was able to drive me to the hospital and look after my children while I waited to be discharged. I had my final appointment with Dr. Hughes which was short and sweet around 10.30am. After I provided an update on my status, he advised that I had to wait until the CAT team had met with me before I could be officially discharged. (I have included the details of the consult with Dr Hughes in the next chapter). Dr. Hughes advised that I would have to remain in the ward until such time and that it would probably be late afternoon before I could leave.

As a result I spoke with the nurse after the appointment to obtain approval to go to the cafeteria. Jan was waiting for me there with the kids until I could confirm what was happening. Just as I was about to walk out of the doors (behind Dr. Hughes) he quickly turned round and said in a stern sharp voice "No Annette you have to go back in" and slammed the door in my face. I bit my tongue and headed back to the nurse who said it shouldn't have been a problem and allowed me to leave but suggested for Jan to meet me at the door. I highlighted to Jan that she would be late for school pick-up so she left and I made alternative arrangements. (They were prepared to discharge me but I was still treated like a prisoner and had to waste a nurse's time twice to seek approval on that day, fucking ridiculous! It wasn't a formal approval but still, where is the value? How rude of Dr. Hughes to behave in this manner. What goes around, comes around! Hopefully the book serves him well!)

The CAT team (2 resources) basically confirmed requirements and highlighted the process post discharge. I couldn't understand why the nurse or doctor couldn't perform these functions. I guess it keeps someone else in a job. I ended up leaving P-Block around 3.30pm. If they put more resources into people rather than paper, we would see better care!

I was discharged on a community treatment order (CTO) with involuntary conditions on Tuesday 7/8/2012 effectively spending 21 days in hospital. If I failed a blood test at any time, as a result of not taking the drugs, I would have been thrown back into hospital! The CTO was to last a full year until it was revoked at an appeal or the hospital performed a full discharge - non-conditional. I was now a prisoner in society!

When Child Protection services had called Mick, they advised that I had to be supervised 24/7 with my children. Donna was able to assist on my first day back into the real world. I didn't dwell on the conditions because it would have affected my mood. I just accepted that I put myself into that position so I had to deal with the situation.

My case had been transferred to Casey Hospital as it was closer to home. I received a call at 10am Wednesday 8/8/2012 from the CAT team to advise I had an appointment at 12pm. (It takes 30 minutes to travel from my house to Casey Hospital). I expressed that no one had contacted or advised me of this appointment but I would attend. I didn't want to give them any excuse of non-compliance.

Dr. Paul Ng was my new psychiatrist. He asked me the standard questions. When he asked me about suicide, I told him I have too much to live for; my kids are my life. However I elaborated and said I was suicidal around the age of 12-14. (I was giving him an opportunity to explore this. It should have been something new to add to the file because I had not mentioned this before). He didn't ask if I tried it but asked about each family member. I gave him a brief on all. I tried to justify my actions and why I stripped. He said that wasn't normal behaviour. I said that I have done this before drunk and I was in a drunk-like state of mind, does that count? Dr. Ng clearly didn't believe me. (I've seen heaps of people drunk and nude and not just me! Maybe they are mentally challenged too! Can't people have fun without being punished these days?)

I asked him what conclusive tests were performed to prove I had the mental illness. He advised research had not established that and was years away. There were no pathology tests to measure an imbalance. I also knew that other factors could cause an episode. E.g. after trauma, brain tumours etc. So I asked him, are there any other factors that can trigger a manic episode? He replied yes and then asked me whether I had a brain scan. I felt like saying check your notes. I could have also brought this up in hospital but I wanted to determine when all options are considered as part of a diagnosis. If I hadn't alluded to other factors, they would not have considered them. I did have a brain scan so I know I have no tumours! I asked whether the medication could be reviewed and he advised not at this point. No harm in trying, I didn't expect that it would be. It was clear that the medical profession couldn't appreciate any other angles. They didn't even consider other options before treating me with the one they assumed I had. The brain scan proves this! (I'm surprised Dr. Hughes didn't order one, he was probably still in denial!)

Dr. Ng confirmed that I would need to have a blood test in a couple of days and provided the relevant form. He advised not to take the drug on the morning of the test. I guess it would affect the results!

It was very difficult to find friends and family who could assist with 24/7 supervision especially when Mick left for work at 4:30am in the morning. Mick was paranoid that if they did visit and I wasn't supervised that our children would be removed from our care. Mick wasn't sure what the actual criteria was and how long I needed to be supervised. They refused to speak to me, I guess they assumed I was unable to think or act for myself or maybe they didn't trust me. Therefore he contacted the Child Protection agency to confirm on Wednesday 8/8/2012. No surprise they had nothing on file. They said they would investigate and would be in contact. They called back later and advised there were no details. Mick expressed that we would return to our normal lives and that everyone was well. We were satisfied that we acted accordingly and there was no threat to us or our children, if they decided to conduct a visit unannounced.

It would have been a wasted resource anyway but what happens to the children that are in desperate need of this service? How many suffer due to a lack of processes/inconsistencies? On the flip side, how many people are unnecessarily investigated? I guess it all comes down to judgment, assessing the risks and consequences. However if the protocols inhibit the agency to act in an efficient and effective manner, then it highlights a serious problem for the welfare of children that are vulnerable. I have heard of many cases where the system has failed to act accordingly. I have also heard stories of where children have taken advantage of this service. It does become evident that there is a lack of resources (both time and people) to assess the situation in its entirety to be able to determine the right outcome.

Child Protection Services did eventually make contact and were going to visit on 12/9/2012 (5 weeks post discharge) but cancelled due to extreme weather. On the 21/11/2012 they advised that the case was closed and there was no requirement to visit. Although I was happy to have them at my home because I wanted to find out more for my book, I'm glad that they didn't waste their time.

Thursday 9/8/2012, the CAT team contacted me to advise that I had another appointment on the Friday and I was required to take the blood test. Prior to arriving I had been vomiting and had 5 bouts of diarrhoea due to the drugs. I was concerned that it would affect the results of the test and they would throw me back in hospital, so I resorted to taking photos. Thank goodness I didn't have to use them. When I arrived at Casey, I advised that I was going to have the test and return. While I waited at the window for the staff to complete their duties, I was annoyed that they were spending time on their personal mobile phones instead of actually attending to people. When the blood test was being conducted, the other office rang to remind me to return. I thought to myself, what a bunch of idiots. I had just told them I would be returning and they are reminding me!!! Who had a memory problem???

I met Joanna (I'm not sure of her position) and assumed she was a social worker. She didn't ask any of the standard questions. I advised that I was well. I told her that I hadn't been appointed a case manager and I was working through the process in order to resolve my predicament. I expressed that my appeal was scheduled for 7/8/2012 and it was adjourned. Not that anyone advised that I was scheduled for an appeal on that day. I was at the hospital at the time and there was no mention of it there either. She advised that my case manager was Geoff Neill and he would be in contact soon.

After the appointment I met up with Rose and Yvette at a play centre. This was the first opportunity I had to see Rose since the incident in the car. I had been in frequent contact via text and had left messages since that moment but it was so good to see her in person. I didn't have the opportunity to contact her whilst I was in hospital so we had heaps to catch up on. Our friendship had not faulted. We didn't even discuss that day. I was busy filling her in on my adventure and she provided an update on her last few weeks. My experience had not affected my relationship with Rose or Yvette because they knew me, understood what had happened, accepted that I had a moment and didn't judge. I was still the same person albeit with a different passion and crazier outlook! True friends, I was ever so grateful and privileged.

I didn't feel privileged to meet Geoff, in fact I deemed him an enemy. My understanding of a Case Manager was that they were essentially there to assist with your treatment, process and integrate you back into society. So when Geoff arrived a week after I was discharged (15/8/2012 3.25pm), I was excited to tell him what had transpired. I advised that the Mental Health Review Board had contacted to say that my appeal date was the 28/8/2012 at Monash Medical Centre. He questioned that, so I called them in his presence. I was told that all details were correct for the appeal. I quickly noticed that Geoff had no interest in what I was saying. He continued to stare at the TV and on the odd occasion only turned to me when he had a question. For example: He asked if I had a reply to my email regarding my book when I was giving him an update. I said that was my business and then he turned to look at the TV again. He did not make direct eye contact and I thought he was quite rude. He said to keep things simple or it would be considered to be an elevated mood. How could I justify my complex position simply? Also how could I control my passion? (I didn't sound as passionate as Steve Irwin but I was energetic and enthusiastic about my project.) I basically had no right of reply and couldn't be myself! No different to hospital! He also advised that I wouldn't be successful in the appeal however he noted that I was interacting well with the kids and attending to their needs. He said I still spoke fast and it would not be viewed favourably. I couldn't believe that each assessment was made by a stranger who was able to dictate and attempt to control you as a person and your life without getting to know you. However I let it go. I did make him a coffee and provided some biscuits upon arrival which I regret because he didn't even deserve the smell of my shit!

Not long after Geoff left, Stephanie from the Mental Health Review Board rang to advise that my appeal date had changed to the 30th of August and would be held at Casey. I was flawed by the fact that in a space of 30 minutes it could change. I expressed that it would be in the best interest of both parties for the treating doctor and myself to attend the original appeal for a fair trial. As the new psychiatrist did not know me and did not have direct knowledge of what transpired in hospital. Stephanie understood my position and was going to investigate. Stephanie called at 3:53pm to advise that Dr. Hughes was no longer placed at Monash and the appeal would take place at Casey. I thought how coincidental that Dr. Hughes will not be available and has since moved on 8 days after my discharge! I later discovered that Afea was no longer working there as well, she had left a short time after Dr. Hughes.

I rang Geoff (4:11pm 15/8) to advise that the hearing had changed to Casey. I also requested access to my medical file. Since I was on my order, I was entitled to these records without charge. Normally you would have to spend $25.10 and seek the doctor's approval to gain access to details. Therefore information was limited and the so called freedom of information was conditional. If your doctor didn't approve you couldn't get access. That's not fair! Geoff advised that

"Julian" the person responsible for collating the file had left and he would get back to me. (Thank goodness I didn't hold my breath because I wouldn't have been able to write this book, I'd be dead!)

Since I required a script for more drugs, I attended an appointment with Dr. Stephen Newman our family doctor. He is a great fantastic diligent doctor who is very thorough. (They are very hard to come by, so I'm very grateful.) He is reserved nearly to the point of introvert, well-spoken and has a great deal of knowledge. He will not provide prescribed medication unless he feels it's absolutely necessary, as doctors should. When he has attended to my children, he is considerate of their needs and always provides a detailed analysis of possible causes and appropriate treatment. He even performs follow-up calls when he receives hospital reports. (Not many doctors take the time to extend their care that far.) Dr. Newman had only treated me for my coccyx and the odd cold prior. As I previously mentioned, I've generally been pretty healthy so rarely consulted him for myself.

He had obviously received my file from the hospital and I gave him an update. He asked whether I was normally this lively. I replied that I'm normally a concerned mother attending to my children when I visit his office. I expressed that you behave differently in different circumstances, for example: at work I was professional and at home, I was quite an extrovert. I suggested ringing Mick so he could confirm, at which point he did. He appeared satisfied that I was being myself. He mentioned that according to the file, I should have been on double the medication and advised to continue with what I was on. He was obviously aware that I had to remain on them due to the order. I asked him some questions regarding my treatment in hospital at which he replied, he couldn't answer but he advised they were all valid points/queries. I confirmed what effects the drugs were having on me and said "If you told me your dog died, I'd tell you to get another one!" (I guess the so called mood stabiliser affected my emotions pertaining to empathy and compassion. Mick would call me heartless but I couldn't control what the drugs were doing, I just accepted the repercussions of my social experiment).

It was also great to see another side of Dr. Newman. For the first time, I witnessed a big chuckle. That was after I explained my naked stunt in hospital. Dr. Newman didn't appear to judge, (he obviously knew more about me and my venture) and wished me the best for the appeal. He was also very interested in reading my book so I knew I had his support. (Thanks Dr. Newman, you're truly a great doctor!)

On Monday 27/8/2012, I met with Dr Claire McNaught the registrar for Casey Hospital. I answered the standard questions briefly and as always, honestly. Claire was not condescending and treated me more like a person rather than a mental patient. After the standard questions, she asked how my mood was out of 10 and I replied 9. I said I had been a little irritable due to the effects of the medication (headaches, nausea, diarrhoea and vomiting). I also highlighted that I had experienced irregular periods and was subject to a considerable amount of blood clots. I assume this was a result of medication affecting my hormones, as this had not been evident in the past. She suggested lithium and seroquel as an alternative which I quickly declined. I didn't want to experiment with harsher drugs. I was better off preserving with the ones I had.

She asked me whether I thought I had a mental illness. I said I don't deny that I had an episode. I further explained that my episode was caused by sleep deprivation because I was caring and doing too much for others. Ultimately I forgot about myself and paid the price for neglecting my needs. I explained my friend's diagnosis with inflammatory breast cancer had triggered the event.

I told Claire that I didn't satisfy at least one of the criteria for the order to apply because I had not taken any medication in hospital and the doctor had taken me off the medication. I was never sure how much each new consultant read of my file so I always provided an insight to what I wanted them to know.

Claire was the only person to enquire about my previous work history. I explained that I was a Project manager for 11 years of my 20 year career before I decided to stay at home with my children. She seemed very interested in my role. I told her that I was on

$133,000 a year and didn't think twice about taking a package as it was more important for me to spend time with my children. You can't get those precious years back and money can't buy that time.

When I requested access to my medical file according to section 26 of the act, Geoff was very defensive. I was entitled to view this in preparation for the appeal. He said he didn't have time to sit with me whilst I accessed my file. I said I had spoken with my solicitor and she advised that I could review my file unsupervised and I should have the opportunity to photocopy any records they deemed I was able to view.

Geoff said it wasn't the hospital's policy and irrespective of what section 26 defines, he didn't want to be held responsible. He advised if I had a solicitor I would be granted access. I replied unfortunately Government resources were stretched and I was unable to secure one prior to the appeal.

I asked whether I could have access to them at least 24 hours prior as per my rights. He again said he didn't have the time to sit with me and suggested moving the appeal date. I thought that's not conducive to my needs. I could have said why should I be inconvenienced for your lack of resources? Who are you trying to help? I advised that the review according to the process would need to occur within 8 weeks and that time was fast approaching.

Geoff appeared to get very frustrated and agitated. Claire even looked at him strangely because of his tone and behaviour. He actually stood up and quite aggressively noted that it was outside of his control. Geoff was very arrogant, ignorant and unnecessarily defensive whilst I kept cool, calm and collected. He had no intention of helping me even though it was part of the act! I asked him to at least give me the courtesy of following up my rights and allowing me to review the file. (I'm glad I made notes along the way because originally it wasn't a problem for Geoff or that's what he led me to believe. However he provided the contact that supposedly managed the records at Casey in our first conversation about the file. Hopefully it further validates my side of the story from a medical perspective if Geoff denies the claim).

Following Geoff's outburst, Claire asked what my plans were if I was successful in my appeal. I said that I would wean myself off the medication because I didn't want to shock my system. She thanked me for attending at which point, Mick and I left.

Mick wanted to knock Geoff out. He couldn't believe what he heard and saw. Mick felt sorry for any patient that had the displeasure of being assisted by Geoff. I perceived Geoff as a tyrant who only tried to hinder my progress and only thought of himself.

When I returned home, I contacted Hilda. She couldn't believe the practices of the hospital and suggested I call the Chief Psychiatrist again. The Chief Psychiatrist office was concerned that they were not adhering to the policy. They were going to investigate and confirm the outcome.

The day before the appeal, I contacted Geoff to determine whether I could review my file. He returned my call and advised that he was instructed to grant me access. He offered 2pm and 3pm that day or 9am on the day of the appeal. I explained that the times were not appropriate because I had to be available for my school aged children. I asked if I could attend at 4pm. Geoff advised that he didn't get overtime and it wasn't possible. We agreed to a review of the file at 11am, one hour before the appeal.

Mick and I arrived on time to review records before the appeal. Geoff handed me an envelope that only contained the Report on Involuntary Status for the Mental Health Review Board. He conveniently made himself scarce. I therefore did not get the opportunity to review my file, another violation of my rights at a critical time. It stated in the board report that I did have the opportunity so they were prepared to even falsify records to suit themselves. Lucky I didn't waste my time attending the day before, obviously they had no intention of granting access to my file.

I noticed I had been appointed another psychiatrist. I thought to myself, how on earth can the medical profession accurately assess a patient if there was no consistency in treating doctors? Obviously the new doctor didn't attend the appeal because I hadn't met him. Claire and Geoff were present for the appeal.

There were a number of inconsistencies with the report. Some were quite amusing but I didn't take any of the information personally because I knew better.

The report highlighted that I had 'Bipolar Affective Disorder – recent manic episode with a significant disturbance in thought, perception and mood'. My husband and my closest friends all knew I was back to my normal self yet the medical profession were not interested in anyone else's view.

The report stated that I 'recently presented as elevated and irritable in mood, disorganised, agitated and hostile, with pressured speech, tangentiality and loosening of associations, expressing delusional beliefs' for the descriptions of symptoms leading to or justifying current diagnosis.

My current mental state (including observations of treating doctors and case manager and relevant dates) was described as follows:

Annette was reviewed at Casey Continuing Care on 27/8/12 in the presence of her husband, two youngest children (aged 1 & 2 years – Harley was actually three so they incorrectly noted that) and case manager. She presented well groomed and appropriately casually attired, with good eye contact and no abnormal involuntary movements. She was calm and cooperative with the interview. Her speech was normal in rate, tone and volume. Her affect was bright and reactive and her mood was euthymic (self-rated 9/10). There was no formal thought disorder. Annette denied any delusional ideation. Nil suicidal or homicidal ideation was elicited. She denied any perceptual disturbances. Annette demonstrated minimal insight into her illness – she felt that prior to her admission she had become overtired and stressed secondary to psychosocial stressors (chiefly, a friend being diagnosed with inflammatory breast cancer) and that she had needed a rest, but did not believe she had a mental illness. Annette stated that if she was discharged from the CTO, she would cease the medication (albeit gradually).

I found it amusing that my recollection and Claire's were vastly different to a degree. Working from the bottom, I was asked what I would do post the CTO discharge? I answered honestly as per my account. Claire had misconstrued these details by claiming that I stated I would cease medication. I did not state, I was asked a question. Had she said it is recommended to continue with medication, I would have obliged for the interim to satisfy the medical profession for the order to be revoked.

Claire claimed I had minimal insight of my illness. Throughout the entire process, I confirmed I had sleep deprivation and that created the episode. I could have provided proof of my time spent at home but no one was interested. I had audio, visual, notes and internet usage/history that captured how much time I spent on my project. I had explained that I was writing a book and I was compelled to collate research for that purpose. Obviously as a full-time mum, the only time I had the opportunity to pursue my studies was when everyone was asleep. Who lacked the insight? They did not have all the details nor did they want them. Quite ignorant of them to claim that I lacked insight! A classic example of perceiving a person from their point of view only! I guess it was their way or no way! Lucky I found my way! We also didn't discuss any delusional ideations. I guess that was her perception alone based on previous reports.

I also found it odd that they commented on my attire. What does that have to do with being mentally challenged? I should have rocked up in a pair of fluoro-spandex tights with a leopard skin top! I'm sure that would have confirmed that I was mental!! The medical profession should not be judging any person on their attire!

Details pertaining to the circumstances leading up to the most recent admission to involuntary status were also inaccurate. The report contained the following:

The police brought Annette to the Emergency Department on 18/7/12 after being called by a friend of Annette who had visited Annette's home and found her acutely unwell (Annette had reportedly written all over her walls). In the ED Annette was found to be floridly manic, elevated, irritable, disinhibited, disorganised, agitated and hostile, with pressured speech and thought disorder (tangentiality, loosening of associations). Annette expressed beliefs regarding the impending end of the world, stating 13,000 people would die at the Olympics in a terrorist attack or natural disaster, and had apparently written to US President Obama to advise him of this. She also reported grandiose beliefs of having the power to manipulate other people's minds. Annette had slept very poorly over proceeding days and had minimal oral intake. Her insight was very poor, she insisted that she was not unwell and refused treatment. Annette was recommended under the Mental Health Act and admitted to P-Block at Monash Medical Centre. On admission, she required nursing in the high dependency area of the ward and had a brief period of seclusion after she became agitated and disrobed.

I laughed when I read the last line of that section. Firstly the friend who called hadn't visited. The police were the first to arrive after I instigated that scenario! I wrote on some walls trying to communicate with the police, not before. If you are trying to determine what transpired and make an accurate assessment, information needs to be correct and presented in the correct sequence or it could be misinterpreted or misconstrued. They didn't ask what I had written on my walls but were quick to comment on my emails to the US President. The adjectives to describe my mental state where presented collectively when in actual fact I didn't behave in this manner for the whole time. I was reacting differently throughout the course of events depending on who I came into contact with, what was being discussed and how I felt.

I did not claim to have the power to manipulate other people's minds. I apologised to the police for infiltrating their minds (by mentally challenging them) while I stimulated mine. I had stated that I had a greater depth to language and an acute skill of reading body language. I know I manipulated situations indirectly through my responses/actions but I never verbally admitted to this. The most rewarding was when I was able to prompt my own discharge. Clearly they failed to appreciate that or maybe it was not recorded in that light. Again open to interpretation and very misleading. They were blind sighted by only considering their angle or perspective due to their perceptions.

I didn't consider approximately 40 hours as a brief period for seclusion especially when there were a lack of amenities. It clearly stated it was because I was agitated and disrobed. Did this satisfy the criteria for being secluded? I have read my rights and I know that it doesn't. Yet they formally admitted that in the board report. I assume this was an oversight on their part and will assist me if the matter is investigated further.

On admission I refused medication without a diagnosis. I was well within my rights. If I had been told they were sleeping pills I would have consumed them. They failed to act accordingly and yet were quick to judge who I was, what I had and treat me poorly.

For earlier admissions or outpatient treatment the report highlighted the following:

Annette's first contact with psychiatric services was on 28/6/12, when she was assessed by CATT. This occurred in the setting of multiple individuals contacting the Phone Triage Service to advise that Annette was unwell. PTS had spoken to Annette and assessed her as having poor sleep, mildly elevated mood, racing thoughts, ideas of reference from songs and delusional ideas about the impending end of the world. CATT visited Annette at home three days after PTS had first been contacted, and found that whilst Annette had some odd beliefs and had experienced a period of 7 days of poor sleep and mildly elevated mood, the beliefs did not appear to be delusional, her mood returned to baseline and she had slept well for the previous two nights. Annette and her husband reportedly stated that Annette often experienced these symptoms for a period of 5-7 days and then returned to normal. CATT recommended that Annette be reviewed by the psychiatric registrar, however, Annette declined this offer and there were no grounds to utilise the Mental Health Act. Annette did not receive any treatment at this time. Prior to this contact with CATT, there was no other psychiatric history. However it is possible that the brief episodes of elevated mood, poor sleep and unusual beliefs reported at the time of the CATT assessment represent short hypo-manic episodes.

Again there were a number of inconsistencies with this section. When I spoke to PTS I was my normal self. I hadn't made any reference to songs and I did not admit or deny delusional ideas about impending doom. After being asked a question, I highlighted that an attack could be plausible based on events that had transpired in history and what had recently been reported in the news. Mick and I didn't stipulate that I had experienced these symptoms before. I had confirmed that I worked well under pressure and often performed tasks in a quick timeframe. For example; I prepared a 30 page Fairwork report in 7 days, while my children slept. I developed a parent agreement, log of events and collating other documentation in a matter of days for Mick's case regarding his children. I also highlighted I completed a 10 page response to Mick's previous employer's solicitor across 2 nights. These are not symptoms; these are actions to perform a desired task. If information is misconstrued or perceived incorrectly then it does result in an inaccurate assessment. Ultimately these inaccurate/misinterpreted claims hindered my position or status.

Under the other relevant medical or other history section, the report contained the following:
There is no forensic history. During her initial review by the psychiatrist on the ward, Annette gave a history of drinking 1-2 bottles of wine per day (but it is unclear if this was accurate given she was severely unwell at the time). There is no other known history of substance abuse. Annette's family history is significant for Bipolar Affective Disorder in her parental grandmother and parental uncle.

I don't drink daily nor is wine my preferred drink of choice. I do enjoy the odd glass but I prefer bourbon or vodka. I never said I drank 1-2 bottles of wine a day. First of all I couldn't afford to and secondly I don't have the time. I did say to the first CAT team that I could drink one bottle or more of bourbon in a night, as many friends can attest to that. I also mentioned this to Dr. Hughes but obviously he didn't capture what I said accurately. I don't lie and I have an impeccable memory, I guess it's his word against mine. Irrespective, why would they report that if they didn't validate it? I was grateful that my binge drinking didn't constitute as substance abuse or maybe they failed to recognise that! (Imagine how much brighter I could have been without all that excessive drinking! Sarcasm or humouring myself, it's my book I'm finally able to express my right of reply - freedom of speech, considering it was neglected when I needed it!) They did not query my husband. He would have been able to validate the claim. Were others misled by inaccurate reports? I have no doubt because not one person gave me any credence and continued to label me as having Bipolar. Just because family members have been diagnosed with a condition doesn't mean everyone is susceptible to that condition. As previously highlighted, I managed to break the cycle in terms of how I was treated, knew how to control my life and could determine what was right for me.

The report stated that I was treated as an involuntary patient to maintain a current level of wellness and ensure ongoing compliance with medication, in the setting of being willing to continue treatment whilst this is enforced with a CTO. Under Patient's attitude the following was recorded:

Annette does not agree that she suffers from a mental illness, and is currently accepting treatment only because it is mandated under the CTO.

Details of collaboration/consultation with patient to ascertain their wishes (including explanation of discussions and/or disagreements about the treatment plan, reasons patient consultants did not take place) stated:

Multiple consultations with medical staff when Annette was an inpatient. (I couldn't make sense of that statement but have recorded it as per the report). Annette was primarily treated by Dr. Hughes, but also received a second opinion from Dr. Wong, who agreed with the diagnosis of Bipolar Affective Disorder. Since discharge from hospital, Annette has been comprehensively reviewed by the CATT Consultant (Dr. Ng) who agreed with the diagnosis of BPAD, explained the diagnosis and discussed the necessary treatment.

This section does not ascertain any actions to include my requests. In fact it didn't even satisfy the requirements of that section. I had a short appointment with Dr. Ng which lasted all of 15 minutes. I called Mick directly after the consult so I have a record of that. Dr. Ng did not discuss treatment and the appointment was not comprehensive. Obviously his perception was different to the one I experienced in that consult. I wonder if he recorded my questions regarding conclusive tests. If he didn't, actions speak louder than words and the brain scan proves my side of the story. Or did the registrar incorrectly interpret details for the board report? Again I couldn't be confident that each person had the correct information so I generally reiterated my position.

It claimed that I had not objected to section 19A (2) (b) to the treating team taking into the account the wishes of the patient's guardian, family members or primary carers? I was not even asked so had no opportunity to reject. I would have opposed my father's input for obvious reasons. They didn't even admit to speaking with my father even though my dad had confirmed this. They disregarded any privacy laws and failed to act honestly. How would you feel? Would you trust anyone who behaved in this manner when you are trying to prove your status? I did not make it an issue because they would have deemed it part of my *so called* mental illness. I had to be patient.

Under *risks* it stated:

Annette has indicated that she would cease her medication should she be discharged from involuntary status, and hence is at high risk of relapse. She is at risk of the cognitive and social decline that may accompany multiple psychotic relapses, and there is the potential for her condition to become more difficult to stabilise each time she becomes unwell. Annette is at risk of becoming physically compromised should she become unwell again, due to poor oral intake (when she was admitted to the ward, she reported that she had not eaten for four days).

Well I hadn't eaten in hospital for 3 days, they should have reported that! They didn't conduct any tests to determine if my physical well-being had deteriorated. Were they negligent? I hadn't eaten the Tuesday prior to admission and 3 days post, yet they stated I had reported it. If they were doing their job, they should have recorded that I hadn't eaten! Technically, I was deemed severely unwell and not able to think and act for myself! I was in seclusion so it wasn't as if it would have been difficult to account for! I can guarantee I'm not at risk of relapsing. I also believe the medical profession appear to be delusional as they have ignored possible and plausible justifications throughout the entire process. (As I spin my record for the record, I'm content on returning to sender! Oh whoa ah whoa it has been a long time between songs!)

The report also highlighted that I was incapable of giving informed consent to the necessary treatment. This was evident because they believed I had poor insight, had disagreed with their diagnosis and apparently I needed treatment. The report further stated I lacked understanding of my illness and the necessary treatment required. I assume they formed that conclusion because I would not succumb to their standard procedures and practices and admit I had an illness. I did ask if sleep deprivation alone justifies being mentally ill and obviously they said no. My consistent answer was I had an episode due to sleep deprivation. They failed to acknowledge and accept my account of the situation. They never gave me an opportunity and I had no grounds to object to treatment or negotiate alternatives because of the CTO/IVO. No respect for any human rights! I wonder how many patients have been subjected to this type of treatment and if it has had an adverse effect.

Mick, Geoff, Claire and I entered a room at Casey hospital for the informal appeal proceeding. There were three representatives, a lawyer, a psychiatrist and a community member. They were all ladies and I have since labelled them the three blind mice! (Hopefully they won't have to run!)

After being introduced, the lawyer slowly explained the process in very simple terms, similar to how you would speak to a child. I assumed she thought I had very little mental capacity. Her tone quickly changed after I started speaking.

Firstly I advised that I did not receive access to my medical file but I was happy to proceed. They did explain that it was unfortunate and that it was due to a lack of resources. I thought this was a load of bullshit, I had highlighted this 2 weeks prior. Also, if it was a patient's entitlement, shouldn't they ensure that their rights are fulfilled? It's not as if a patient can walk in and grab their file!

I highlighted that there were a number of inconsistencies with the report. I queried if anyone had reviewed the police report. The lawyer said it was irrelevant. (Maybe a police report had not been completed! I tried to obtain one from John on two occasions but he never got back to me! I wonder why?) It wasn't irrelevant to me because I wanted to highlight what had transpired and the reason/purpose for the way I behaved. I wasn't given the opportunity to do that in the appeal and if I had persisted, it would have been deemed as part of my *'so called'* condition.

I then asked if factors that affect behaviours have been overlooked at that point in time, can a true and fair assessment be made? They asked me to elaborate. I proceeded to tell them about my work history and my recent research for the book. They assumed my book was about cancer because that was my original research and trigger. I expressed that it was a book covering many aspects and cancer was not a feature of the book. I expressed that it was more to do with psychology and encompassed many matters. Clearly they didn't believe me. I again reiterated that I had an episode due to sleep deprivation to no avail. I briefly spoke about what transpired in hospital as well (no point repeating it again).

Claire gave her view which was similar to her report. Geoff advised that he had only consulted with me twice prior to the appeal. But it didn't stop him from suggesting that I should be treated via injections instead of taking medication. He believed I was at high risk of not consuming the medication. I had complied with taking the drugs post discharge because I knew the consequences. I complied with the blood test. He wasn't even a doctor and he had no right to impede on my status. They even failed to provide a treatment plan as per section 19 (a) (6), so in effect, what was I complying to? Obviously my case manager didn't help and was of no assistance! From what I experienced, this resource failed on every level or maybe I was unfortunate to experience an unacceptable one!

I advised that I was not satisfied with my case manager and asked how I could acquire a new one. They said I would have to speak to my case manager (I nearly fell of my chair laughing, how fucking ridiculous! He hadn't helped at all and now he was going to help me find another one at his professional expense/integrity!) They further advised that Geoff was a very good case manager and was competent in his role. I was encouraged to be more understanding. It was a total farce. I guess everyone is entitled to an opinion but if you haven't experienced situations first hand, it would be very difficult to pass judgment or draw accurate conclusions!

I highlighted that under section 14 (3) (a) that the CTO/IVO order should be made for the minimum period considered necessary to achieve the objectives of treatment and asked what the objectives were. They had sentenced me to comply for the maximum period of 12 months but there was no treatment plan hence, no objective. Why would they enforce the maximum period without objectives? (I have the paperwork from the board meeting to confirm it was not provided! Just thought I'd mention that if they plan to cover their tracks).

I enquired as to whether the criteria for the involuntary status had been met. According to the conditions, all of the criteria must be met (if one doesn't apply technically nor does the involuntary status):
- You appear to be mentally ill
- Your mental illness needs treatment straight away and you can get treatment if you are put on an order
- The order will stop your physical or mental health condition getting worse or will keep other people safe
- You said no or were not well enough to agree to treatment for the mental illness
- You cannot receive the treatment you need in a way that would let you keep your freedom

I highlighted that since the doctor had taken me off the medication in hospital and I didn't consume any medication whilst in the ward, the involuntary status should not be enforced.

Just before they deliberated the outcome, I placed the two tackle boxes which contained the drugs administered in hospital on the table. The psychiatrist eyes bulged, Mick and I weren't sure if it was shock or disbelief.

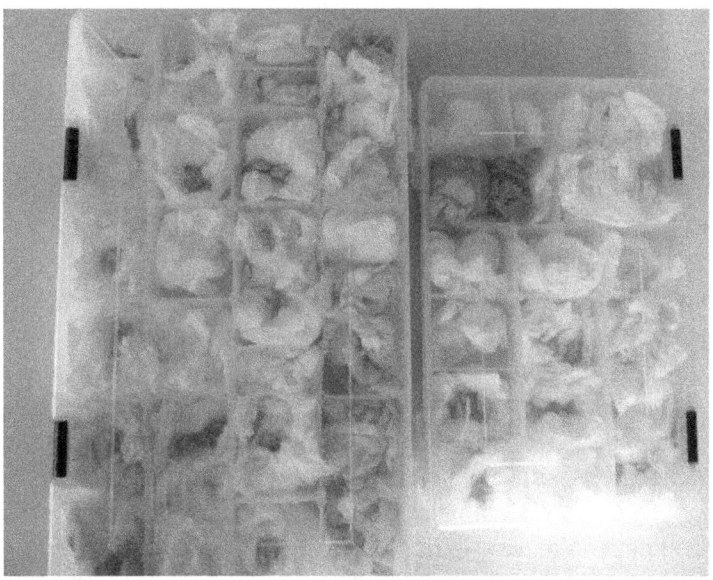

Upon returning to the room, the lawyer advised that although I wouldn't be happy with the decision they felt it was necessary to keep me on the order because not enough time had elapsed to prove I was well enough. I told them that I understood their position and was happy with the outcome. I further added I don't have a problem being deemed mentally ill but I do have a problem with taking drugs that I didn't require. I was also thankful (not that I said it) because I was able to identify another flaw in the process. It highlighted that the law or act was not worth the piece of paper it was written on, if it is not applied as per the conditions. How could they deny the actual facts to suit themselves? The doctor's records plus my evidence was enough to disprove the second point. Injustice!! I thought if this is how the law could be applied, it's no wonder some innocent people never seek the justice they rightfully deserve.

After the appeal, I contacted Hilda and provided an update. She was astonished to hear what had transpired, however she advised that I had the opportunity to re-appeal as many times as I liked. (No wonder our taxes are so high, another example of ineffective use of public resources and funds). Hilda was able to re-arrange the next appeal date and was going to co-ordinate a solicitor for the next hearing. She also advised to seek an independent opinion.

When I attempted to source another psychiatrist I was surprised that in some cases I had to wait months. I was also concerned that most would not book an appointment without having a summary of the details. If they specialise in all avenues of mental health (for adults), why are they being selective? This proved to me that there is a serious lack of resources. What happens to patients who urgently need their assistance? No wonder there are so many incidents of suicide, violence and death! I didn't end up requiring another opinion plus I couldn't afford it anyway!

I was concerned that Geoff may influence the doctors in terms of treatment (injections), especially when I didn't have any consistency with the treating doctors! Given that I had no rights to object because of the order, I needed to resolve my predicament as soon as possible. Hilda recommended that I contact the Chief Psychiatrist again. I also highlighted to Hilda that I had recorded 3 consults and had not used them to-date. She expressed to be very careful because it was illegal to record someone without their consent. I was obviously aware of this and asked her if she could determine if the same standards apply if I was deemed mentally ill.

I explained the situation to the Chief Psychiatrist and highlighted the number of rights that were denied. I also expressed that I had compelling evidence to support my case, in the form of recorded consults. She was also very concerned and also expressed that I should be very careful. She was quick to refer me back to the director of services for Southern Health, as I had many complex issues that needed to be resolved. I asked whether that would be of assistance because I tried this avenue whilst I was in hospital. She assured me that I would be able to actively lodge my complaint in an attempt to resolve my issue. She had obviously been in contact with them regarding access to my file and advised that Dr. Barton was on leave. The acting medical program director for Mental Health was Dr. Michael Gordon.

Dr. Michael Gordon was very responsive and promptly returned my call. He was very thorough in making sure he captured most of my issues accurately. He even called back to confirm some details. I felt relieved because he gave me the time of day and it seemed that he would actively investigate my case.

The other concern I had was that Geoff had arranged an appointment for 3pm on Monday 17/9/2012. I asked whether he could find a time during school hours because I could not attend. He basically said I had to attend the appointment and it was in my best interests. I had already advised that these times weren't appropriate and he didn't even try to accommodate my request. I therefore told Dr Gordon that I was not able to attend the mandatory appointment and he said he would follow it up.

The following day I received a call from a Consumer Rights representative for Mental Health. I again highlighted my issues and requested that the hospital review their practices. My main concern was being forced to have injections under the order. I didn't trust my case manager or any other doctor because of what had eventuated. Unfortunately they couldn't help me with my main issues but they were able to secure a 12pm appointment on the 18/9/2012, which I attended. Ironic, because according to Geoff there were no other times available!

The week prior, Geoff had scheduled a home visit because I advised that Lexi was ill. I was not prepared to travel to Casey for my one on one appointment. (Lexi had a chest infection which resulted in laboured breathing. She was admitted for a night for observation and was discharged the following day 11/9/2012). However, on the 13/9/2012 the day of my appointment with Geoff, Lexi appeared to relapse so I called the ambulance.

I didn't have Geoff's direct number to advise him of the change of plans and of course he arrived when the ambulance were attending to Lexi. Obviously he was concerned that an ambulance was at my house because I was deemed mentally ill. I explained that Lexi had trouble breathing and I was attending to her needs. He had a good look at the house (it was spotless) and wished us well!

Clearly the ambulance crew were curious to know who Geoff was. I openly and honestly said that I had a moment of madness due to sleep deprivation and he was my case manager. I could have said that was my business and left it at that but I wanted to see what would transpire.

I arrived at the Warragul Hospital and not long after there was a group of about 5 staff huddled together that stood behind the desk checking me out. Obviously they received an update on me as well. I continued to smile and thought if only you knew what I was capturing. If a person is mentally displaced, this behaviour could have created an issue. Therefore staff should be aware of their actions and avoid making patients or others feel inadequate. They were clearly passing judgment, I could tell by their facial expressions and body language plus all 5 were looking at me, at the same time – so it was very noticeable. Stigma with lack of respect! Obviously their duty of care didn't extend that far! If I had addressed their behaviour then and there, what would have been their response? It was therefore not worth my effort to attend to that matter. Ultimately it highlights that if people draw their own conclusions without the relevant facts, it can be very misleading. Unfortunately this could be at the detriment of the vulnerable!

The young doctor who attended to Lexi was nice but spoke in a very simple manner. She referred me to a paediatrician who had reviewed Lexi on the day of discharge. Thankfully Lexi was deemed well enough to return home. I guess I avoided Geoff and obtained another example (from a different hospital) of how those with a mental displacement are treated in our places of care! I'm not surprised that many continue to suffer when they are so poorly treated by many people in society! I have no doubt that this type of attitude would escalate poor behaviours in patients that are mentally challenged. Hopefully this example serves as a lesson and at the very least the medical profession will educate those that fail to accept people at face value!

Moving along, I was delighted to find out that my next appeal hearing was scheduled for the 11th of October. Katherine had been appointed my solicitor for my case and I provided a brief update on the phone. I also queried her on the matter pertaining to the recordings and she was unable to confirm. I expected this as I had attempted to research this online but there didn't appear to be any relevant cases. I assumed I was setting a precedent!

I met with my new psychiatrist Dr. Atanas Yonchev on Tuesday 18/9/2012. Geoff was also present and for the first time, another person attended to transcribe. Mick didn't attend as he needed to attend to his work commitments. Dr. Yonchev queried where Mick was and I advised his employer had been more than accommodating during the course of events and he needed to work. (Mick's employer allowed leave of absence to attend to family matters. We were very thankful and fortunate that they understood our position but we were also mindful of not taking advantage of the situation).

I answered the standard questions. I gave them some insight of my book and research. I provided more details about my history. I explained my analogy pertaining to the doctor and my dad. I said I know what caused the problem and therefore I can control how to avoid it. I gave him a subtle insight to my research relating to the chemical imbalance and used an example regarding the use of alcohol. Dr. Yonchev seemed interested in what I had to say. I again reiterated that I didn't have a problem with being deemed mentally ill but I did have a problem with taking drugs that I didn't require.

I advised that I live a stress free life because if it's not life threatening or changing, there is no point worrying about matters – it is wasted energy.

Dr. Yonchev seemed to be concerned about the welfare of my children. I asked what the concerns and risks were. He highlighted that I may lack concentration and not be able to manage my family accordingly. I expressed that I was able to drive to the appointment so clearly my concentration was intact. I said I appreciated their concerns but unless you live in my house it would be difficult to validate. I invited them to speak with my children. I highlighted that my local doctor would be able to confirm how competent I was as a mother. (The marble incident wasn't brought up and I didn't mention this either!)

I advised that in the last couple of weeks I had started typing and the document was at 21,000 words. He asked me whether it was in my nature to write a book. I replied I have always talked about it. I have the skill and had produced many training manuals in my previous employment. I guess it would be difficult for a stranger to quantify and if they deemed you as having grandiose ideas, it's even more difficult! I again told them my tax file number and proceeded with other details when he queried my memory capacity.

He asked whether I believed I should be on medication. I replied I'm mindful of how I respond because of past experiences. If you are recommending that I need to continue taking medication for the order to be revoked, then I would agree (to give them peace of mind). When he asked me how I felt about taking medication for a year. I said if I thought about what I have to do unwillingly that would not serve me any justice. I live in the moment and accept it so it doesn't become a problem. I focus on what I can do, not on the obstacles.

Geoff kept saying that I was mentally ill and that I had sent a letter to the President. I reminded Geoff that I was in a different state of mind due to a lack of sleep and it was dream/drunk like. I said my intention was to ensure that there were resources. If the forum wasn't available I wouldn't have had the opportunity. Geoff also mentioned the ambulance. Obviously Dr. Yonchev queried this and I advised that like any mother who has a baby struggling to breathe I did the obvious and ensured my children's needs were attended to. Clearly indirectly highlighting I was a responsible mother.

The consult lasted 45 minutes, a Mama "world" consult record! Finally they took the time to appreciate and understand my position. Dr. Yonchev said he was interested in my book and wouldn't mind reading it. I replied "I'd be more than happy to share it with you but I'll let you know when you can buy it, because you have more money than me and I could use your dollars!" With that he laughed and I was on my way! (After saying thankyou of course!) The main bonus from that day was that my medication remained unchanged (and I wasn't forced to take what the doctor originally prescribed).

The following day, Mick received a call to advise that I was going to be fully discharged from the hospital under the care of Dr. Newman. Amazing!!! At least one doctor was able to acknowledge and accept my view. I understood his reasons for pursuing the medication but I did say to him that would change once my book was published.

I had my final appointment with Geoff on October 9, 2012. The purpose of this appointment was to arrange official discharge. Another doctor initially attended the meeting to confirm that he would be in contact with my local doctor. He advised that I would be discharged under the care of Dr. Newman. (Why another person needed to advise and confirm, is beyond me! Maybe it keeps someone else in a job?) After the doctor left, Geoff basically advised that he would send through an official discharge notice in the mail. (I still haven't received it and it is December! Technically they could throw me back in hospital.) He mentioned that I would have to remain on the medication for at least 12 months. I said I guess you know what's right. Then he proceeded to say, well I'm not the doctor but I have experience in many cases. (I thought so he finally admitted he wasn't a doctor but was happy to act like one!)

Geoff seemed to have changed. He was justifying his actions and mentioned that he hoped that there were no hard feelings! I said I don't hold grudges. He even asked for a signed copy of the book. I thought you won't want anything from me after you read it! But I said I'll be happy to sign a book after you purchase one! It was a very strange meeting. Maybe he was glad to see the back of me! Maybe his opinion or view of me had changed? Regardless, I know I was glad to see the back of him! Seriously, there are no hard feelings and

I've had my say! Whether Geoff chooses to learn from the experience has no bearing on me! I can't control how he will react to my view. I'm entitled to my opinion. He could have behaved in a more appropriate manner and I would have only highlighted positive feedback. I guess this is an example of how I constructively managed my predicament all for the sake of research! Obviously the October appeal was cancelled, mind you I had to inform the Mental Legal Aid myself. I assumed there is no communication between the government agencies.

Believe it or not, managing the medical and legal implications of my predicament was easier than managing interactions between family and friends. As most will be aware, family and friends can be the most critical of you because they care and don't want to see you get hurt. Or it may be they are afraid of an undesirable outcome and the consequences as a result of actions. In any event, their concern or worry can hinder you from evolving and could cause unnecessary friction/conflict. I had to manage this carefully because I didn't want to create angst and damage any friendships or relationships.

My Dad and sister were my greatest mental challenge. But when you consider my past, it was expected.

As mentioned in an earlier chapter, when I was in hospital my sister said to Mick, "Who is the smart one now?" referring to me being locked up in the psyche ward. My sister told others my behaviour was embarrassing that was also unjustified. She accused me of being a liar and taking advantage of others, which was also uncalled for. I did not take these comments personally but I also wasn't going to accept her behaviour. If I had mentioned anything, I know she would have misinterpreted where I was coming from and just assumed it was part of my *'so called'* condition. I know her too well. I had to keep my distance. If she honestly cared, she should have been more understanding of the situation. She had direct contact with some of my friends and they could have been misled by her references. Her behaviour created division between us and I had to manage it in the best way I could.

Both my dad and my sister were telling Mick that we should sell our caravan and they gave their ideas on what we should be doing with our finances. Who gave them the right to start dictating how we chose to live our lives? I guess they were worried that money may contribute to the stress. Money was of concern previously to a certain degree but there were always other options. Stress was not the catalyst for me having my epiphany! Ultimately it was our business how we chose to live our lives. They had no idea of what I had been doing and were jumping to conclusions. They didn't want to accept my view when I tried to explain. I can't enforce that so I had to retract.

Was my sister's comment of "continue not to tell the truth & be taken advantage of" an underlying issue for herself? Or was she jealous? I am very honest and I never take advantage of anyone, she knows who I am and I have never given her any reason to doubt me. Is she true to herself? Don't get me wrong, I still love my sister dearly however I'll let her draw her own conclusions. It's a life lesson that she needs to explore!

I basically told my sister (via text message) that I didn't need to prove anything to those who didn't trust us. I also told her not to contact me for the interim because I had enough shit to sort out. A week after being discharged, I also sent her a text in respect to all the changes because I needed to vent. She apparently had assumed control to manage my personal belongings in the working bee and I guess because I was frustrated I needed to let her know where I stood and why. If I didn't explain, I would have held on to the emotion and it would have affected me.

She has since called me once and we spoke briefly. I didn't actively engage in conversation because she hadn't recognized her poor behaviour. If she had said sorry I would have been more receptive. If she queried why I was being distant, I would have told her. I don't believe it was my position to bring up matters because I had enough to deal with and I didn't create the "aftermath" issue. I didn't want to make matters worse. She said that I had everyone worried. I let her know, I was fine and if people don't have all the facts and jump to conclusions it can be quite damaging and I left it at that. I guess I do feel betrayed but I haven't been emotionally impacted because of the way I manage myself. Time will heal and I will forgive her. I know she did help and has done some great things in the past but I also know she could have been more considerate. She is a good person, is caring, thoughtful, kind and does have a good heart. Hopefully we can prosper from previous experiences and share a genuine sister relationship once core issues have been addressed. It's up to both of us! I still love and care for her but at the moment time out is required until she is ready to understand the implications of her actions.

I had not heard from my parents. I suspected that Mum had misunderstood the phone call when I explained I didn't need their assistance after my dad compromised my position. I was angry at the time but I had dealt with it. I didn't actively contact anyone in the month post my discharge because I needed time with my family. I also had to manage my predicament and could not afford to be consumed by other people's concerns. I needed to focus on myself and my immediate family.

After a month I was ready to make contact. I knew both my parents would have been suffering as a result of what occurred. Especially when they had no control of the situation! Dad happened to answer the phone. I was only expecting my Mum to answer because he should have been at work.

Dad asked how I was going and I replied we are all good. He said are you sure you are okay? I thought to myself, are you deaf? I said Dad I'm fine. He asked whether I had been taking the medication. I told my dad that I was but I shouldn't need to. He then proceeded to tell me in an aggressive tone that I needed help. "You don't do those things. People cleaned up your house. Blah Blah Blah…" I tried to explain again that I didn't purposely put myself in that mental state. He gave me the "I'm telling you!!!!" (I hate that phrase and it sends me wild!) "You have a problem!" I responded with you are entitled to your own opinion. I felt like saying you are becoming my problem and you have one.

He then said "I've got no respect for Mick. Mick is fucking useless and he is an idiot. He should have helped. He has no brains, I fucking don't like him. He is a hopeless father and he is a liar." (He called Mick a liar because he didn't believe what my sister had said. I also said I had a text to prove some of the things she accused us of, just so he was aware.)

It was very confronting and I had to really control myself because I knew it could cause irreparable damage. I guess he was blaming Mick. Blaming wasn't going to achieve anything but that's the way my dad deals with things. We are very different on that level. I sternly said, "I don't need to hear your thoughts. Mick is my husband, the father of my children and your grandchildren and if you feel that way keep it to yourself." I felt like saying who are you to judge, Mick never bashes his children, Mick changes and bathes them when required, Mick takes them to swimming and sport, Mick helps around the house, Mick works hard, Mick plays with his kids, why on earth would you attack my husband? But I didn't, I kept my cool to save face. My dad has had a heart attack before and does get quite worked up so I didn't want to aggravate the situation. Had I gone on the attack, it would have been a no-win position for both of us and there would be more to resolve. (I guess having my vent now clears any unresolved emotion that I was holding on to!)

My dad wanted to put on a barbeque for those that helped. I told him I would manage things the way I wanted to when I was ready. He said he had been in contact with Afea and knew that my care was transferred to Casey. I thought to myself it was great the hospital had the courtesy of managing me through my dad- not! I'm sure his input would have been effective in my treatment. Again I let it go! I was annoyed but had I made it an issue – it would be deemed that I was agitated and they would have tried to give me more drugs at my next visit. I was better off saying nothing and waiting for things to unfold. It was extremely frustrating to say the least!

My mum was on annual leave and due to fly out to Queensland with a friend. Obviously they wanted to see me. They hadn't seen Lexi or Harley for their birthday either. They didn't call, I would have answered the phone and spoke as per normal. I guess they were afraid to make that move. I asked dad to tell mum to return my call and said it was fine to visit the following day.

Mick was furious when I told him and rightfully so. Mick knows my dad quite well and those comments were very hurtful. But I wasn't going to protect my dad if it could potentially affect my husband. If my dad did say something directly, at least Mick would be prepared. I believed he needed to know in the event something was said out of context and caused another issue. I had to vent, I was compelled to share it with Mick. My dad is volatile so we sometimes need to tread lightly to avoid conflict.

Mum returned my call and after a brief chat I explained what happened with Dad. I basically told her that if dad behaves in that manner when he visits I'd be asking him to leave. He needed to respect me and my family. I obviously couldn't say this to my dad because he doesn't like being told but I know my mum would have provided some guidance.

That night and up to the point of my parents arriving, I was contemplating on how to behave and react. Sounds funny but I was emotionally charged and needed to control my frustration. I thought to myself if he mentions a bad word about Mick, I'm giving him the truth, i.e. highlighting his fatherly flaws. I then thought well, that's not going to assist anyone and it's going to create more issues so I'm better off just saying we'll agree to disagree. Basically I was working through all scenarios to identify what the best approach would be if I was presented with a challenging moment. In the end, I decided I was going to treat my dad like he was the doctor. I would only answer questions and wouldn't actively participate in conversation. This would at least minimise conflict! My strategy worked! I didn't mention the previous night's call and thankfully my dad didn't either. They have since visited numerous times and he has engaged in conversation with Mick. (Mick could have responded negatively but true to his great traits he kept the peace!)

With respect to my dad, I am very careful of what I say because I don't want to be questioned, as we do have a difference of opinion. Our thoughts/perceptions are not aligned and it could cause conflict.

Will things return to what they were? My perception is that our relationship has been restored in the past because of how I manage myself in these challenging situations and this is no different. But I can't answer that for my parents! Each individual needs to manage that for themselves.

My relationship with some of my friends did not change. Just to name a few, Rose, Yvette, Lu, Donna, Mich , Sally, Veronica, Jan, Angel, Mon, Grant, Robyn and Wally as they knew me, took things at face value or accepted my position. I didn't need to explain myself because their behaviours, conversations, actions or reactions did not change when I interacted with them post my discharge.

Other friendships did vary and it was mentally challenging for me! I still value those friendships and in time, they will come full circle and hopefully they will return to normal.

A few weeks after I was discharged, Diane called to see how I was doing. I gave her an update and of course that included some of the recent events. Diane was concerned that I would relapse and was spending too much time on my book. She said I didn't need to justify myself to her. I explained that I wasn't writing a book to justify myself and I was attempting to help others. I said the book was essentially about psychology. She highlighted that she wouldn't be interested in that type of book. I explained that not everyone likes all books and I was prepared for that. (I didn't want to say you don't have to read it or you haven't read it, so how do you know whether you are going to like it or not, because that's not how I would treat a friend.)

Prior to my episode, Diane and I always spoke of writing a book. She was inclined to write a children's book and I always talked of writing a novel (because I always had so much to say). I thought that it was unusual for her to change her view when it was acceptable in the past. I didn't know if it was because she found the situation confronting. She would have normally embraced my project but now she was rejecting it and I couldn't understand why.

I sent Diane an email after our conversation, explaining that after being constantly judged and having to justify myself in hospital, it would take me a bit to re-adjust. It would be very hard for people to appreciate my position because they didn't experience what I did and they are not me! I couldn't help but notice changes and therefore had to manage this accordingly.

I also attached my work in progress, which was only 17 pages at that stage. Normally she would respond but she never replied. I therefore understood that she wasn't interested. It didn't bother me. I wasn't going to force people to read my work but I wanted to at least give her the opportunity to know where I was coming from. I don't know if Diane was influenced by others and I couldn't control that anyway, so I didn't entertain that.

I know she would not intentionally discourage me from obtaining my goals. I did implicate her unknowingly so maybe she felt threatened by that. Maybe she didn't accept the change. We have engaged in normal conversation since but I don't mention the book or my crazy phase because I sense she is uncomfortable and not interested. Normally we could talk about anything! So I guess I've realised that I need to give some friends time to digest what has transpired to regain their confidence, trust or whatever underlying issue they may have with me!

Friends that I had made through Max's kinder/school were pretty much the same. Normally we would engage frequently on Facebook, chat on the phone or catch up in person. Most kept their distance. There was no active communication. It may have been because I said I needed space however after that initial break I did try to restore contact. They were happy to provide support when I was in hospital but when I returned, everything appeared to have changed.

Some may have misinterpreted how I managed to get into that state because I said I was collating content for my book. My sister had been in contact with them as well so there could have been mixed messages. I avoided trying to determine a reason and I had to accept that I was on the outer.

Generally I would have been invited to weekend trips away but I was excluded. I was invited to parties or catch-ups at the last minute, if invited at all. I was surprised how many suddenly changed as a result of what happened. I didn't read into things, I could tell by their behaviours and actions/reactions. Mick noticed and so did Max. For example: Max was asking why we couldn't go camping with the rest of the group. (I just explained that we couldn't do everything).

Originally when I caught up with the school mums, I tried to justify myself but that was making matters worse. I had the impression that no one believed me because I was deemed mentally ill. Maybe they didn't understand! Some of them had viewed some confronting footage and may have been scared. I guess they didn't know me well enough, maybe they didn't know what to say/think or maybe I needed to regain their trust. Anyhow, I continued being myself and had confidence that these friendships would return to normal in time! I couldn't force the issue and I refrained from taking matters personally.

It highlights that there are a number factors that can contribute to changes in relationships; the main one is open and honest communication. As mentioned earlier, I still value these friendships a great deal and I am taking one step at a time. I may have been misunderstood because I don't think any of them would intentionally react in a manner that was unsupportive. It is very difficult to be yourself when you witness and experience others behaving differently towards you.

Heading to another track, initially I was planning to seek legal justice for my poor treatment, misdiagnosis, negligence, malpractice, incarceration etc. However after consideration, I thought it was difficult to highlight my status in hospital and if it is unprecedented it would be even harder to seek formal justice. There is also a lack of resources in the legal fraternity and it could take years. In addition, if the law could be manipulated, how could I guarantee I would receive the justice I deserved? I also thought of those that could be suffering and wanted to help those in a reasonable timeframe. I wouldn't have been able to do this effectively if it went to court. I also didn't need the extra stress or want to waste my time, hence why I continued pursuing my book. I believed it was an effective way to achieve my goals and a more constructive approach! I do however reserve my right to undertake this path in the event that I need to action any changes that are required. Time will tell!

It's long a long way to the top, if you want to rock and roll! No different to my train. I hope you are enjoying the journey, please remember to take time out for yourself and have fun! We are about to break unchartered ground but you are in safe hands! Choo choo choo……

9. Opening a can of worms

HELLO no surprise a brain resembles a can of worms! Now we are going to dissect them! But wait there's more and I'm not giving you a free set of steak knives on this trip either! I hope to be able to provide you with so much more, with the power of knowledge! Hang on to your seat, as we may derail a few over the next couple of chapters!

In essence, my determination to help a dear close friend enabled me to explore so much more for myself. This was evident due to a lack of sleep. As I drifted into the sub-conscious, I articulated all events, thoughts, emotions, actions and behaviours. Has anyone done this before? Could this be a catalyst to broaden our research into mental health and other areas?

In sequence, the events that transpired were:

- Research (initially cancer, religion, history and politics)
- Developed theories and performed "brain dumps"
- During the 2 week break, more research and testing on self/family
- Applied theories to everyday life, "untrained" my brain, conducted more research and performed more brain dumps
- Tested my mental and physical ability/capacity

I knew I needed to break the cycle however the adrenaline that my body naturally released caused an addiction to a degree. No different to any other addiction. The progressive adrenaline and the surge produced a chemical imbalance. No different to taking drugs or alcohol.

I have performed extreme acts, so I know what "adrenaline" provides including the feeling of euphoria. Consequently I "turned on" all functions of my brain concurrently! Total recall with all senses working collectively in unison, is the best way for me to describe it. I was awake and functioning in a 'dreamlike' state. I was able to prove for myself that my ambition to test my physical and mental boundaries at the extreme, created that chemical imbalance which is contrary to how the medical profession view it today. I have the knowledge, experience and evidence to substantiate this for further research.

I never imagined that I would have to prove I didn't have a mental illness. Especially when everyone thinks you are mental! Even more difficult, when every right has been denied to disable you. Other than the right, to think and act on behalf of yourself!

How does this sound? A Mental patient tells, shows, and explains they are not mental to the Medical profession? Fucking hilarious! I'd broken many rules to prove points. I gave them every opportunity to assess me fairly however their current practices did not cater for someone who naturally thinks quickly and very differently to most. Basically we were on different mental channels. How could they understand, if they didn't get to know me or what I had explored?

I was forced to play a mental mind game for the elite! I was trapped in an environment against my will for 21 days. I didn't see my children for 19 days. I was also amongst all other diverse and interesting people who were suffering. I did not mentally break. I did what I liked doing, helping others so I focused on the positive aspects. Surely this is testament of a mentally sound mind!

I was inadvertently able to link the medical aspect to the psychological component of my research. I did not ask to be there. If I focused on what I couldn't do, I would have become angry, frustrated, agitated and moody. I would have been injected with toxins my body didn't need. I would have been fucked if I consumed those drugs. I know that for sure from being sedated and what I had seen.

Not one nurse or doctor had any inclination that I was gaining material for my book. I had even said to Dr. Hughes, the longer you keep me here, the more information I'd collect. I indicated that my incarceration was a social experiment. I assume he thought I had grandiose ideas or was it ignorance/arrogance? Maybe he didn't believe I had the capacity or he didn't have the time to care? I guess they weren't prepared for an abnormal (patient) patient!

Where was his duty of care when I didn't eat for 3 days? (One 600ml bottle of water was all I consumed at Casey Hospital.) I didn't have a blood test. I had not used the cardboard cowboy hat! Why was I in seclusion for 2 days when I wasn't violent to others or harming myself? What was their motive for treating me in this manner? My first blood test was on the 27/7/2012. I thought that I would be exposed for not consuming the drugs. Did they check the results of the blood test? It appeared not.

When I highlighted observations about the hospital, Dr. Hughes deemed this as having racing thoughts even though I said I was bored. He didn't ask or want to know my history. Analysis and observations were second nature to me. One it was a strategy to cope when I was young and two, I had refined these skills as a Project Manager/adult. Again processing information is very different to having racing thoughts. Personally I don't read into things as some may perceive; analysis/observations happen naturally without much thought for me.

When they deemed me to have bipolar, they did not check any of the behavioural attributes experienced with this condition. I may have been singing but I do that all the time! I did not mention the book in hospital because I knew it would have worked against me. I even told Donna to zip it when she said "you have to write this book!", when her and Wally visited. Other attributes like excessive shopping, adventurous sex and thinking I was God was not part of my nature at any time which are quite common for people with this condition! (Sharing two moments in hospital with my husband doesn't constitute adventurous for me either!)

When I returned to the hospital, to be formally discharged under a CTO/IVO, Dr. Hughes advised that it was unusual to experience headaches, nausea and diarrhea on the medication. He asked if I was pregnant and said that they would perform a test. He also advised that the drugs had serious side effects and cause birth defects. Why didn't he tell me that when they first started administering them? Or contact my husband? What if I was pregnant when I arrived at the hospital and I had consumed them? Isn't that negligence?

When I researched the effects of the drug, 30% suffered from these symptoms. Did Dr. Hughes fully appreciate the drug he was prescribing? By highlighting that it was unusual and requesting a pregnancy test, leads me to believe that he didn't. How can he treat someone effectively if he can't appreciate the side effects? Did he care or where was his duty of care? Given that most, if not all patients were served these pills, he clearly lacked knowledge regarding them. Was it possible that this was a drug that attracted pharmaceutical benefits personally or corporately? Just for the record, they did not complete that pregnancy test.

Dr. Ng only arranged for a brain scan after I questioned what conclusive tests are performed to confirm the condition they said I had. A tumor can cause episodes as well. I knew I didn't have any but again it is another marker to highlight their lack of competency. That scan was performed on the 8/8/12 and I was admitted on the 18/7/12. Imagine if I did have a tumor and their treatment contributed to a permanent injury or fatality?

I knew what caused the episode, why it happened, how it occurred, when it occurred and who I impacted. If I know what, how and why, I certainly know how to avoid it. I never once heard voices or had racing thoughts. I was processing too much information when I overloaded and received a surge of adrenaline. For me, I need to obtain the required sleep to function normally to avoid that situation. I definitely don't need a pill for epilepsy, a *'so called'* mood stabilizer, for a condition the medical profession believe that I have.

The doctors refer to a chemical imbalance for matters of the mind. Some chemicals have been proven to manage the symptoms of mental challenges. However there are no biomarkers or pathology tests to provide any conclusive results. Therefore in basic terms, there is no cold hard proof of a measurable imbalance and it is all based on behaviour. This is open to interpretation which can lead to a misdiagnosis and create potential risks!

There are a multitude of influences that affect your behaviour.

- Emotions
- Thoughts –e.g. perception
- Attitude
- Personality
- Values and Beliefs
- Experiences/events – e.g. trauma, abuse, survival
- Alcohol/drugs
- Sleep deprivation
- Culture/Social environment
- Habitat
- Family, friends, peers

Can a true and fair assessment be made at that point in time or period, if factors that influence behaviour have been overlooked or not considered? Everyone is different and should be treated individually. The doctors did not make any effort, appreciate my view or take the time to understand me, in my case. All they wanted to do was feed me drugs. Appalling! I was really shocked that this could happen in the 21st Century. If this happened to me, how many others have been negatively impacted by their experience? I would hate to think my own children could be subjected to this treatment. As a parent, if I didn't attempt to highlight and resolve this challenge I would have failed them. I'm strong and I'm actually all the better for it. I have the chance to help others in my new found venture.

There is a misconception that someone deemed mentally ill is unable to think and act for themselves. I was able to do both even at the peak of my episode albeit with extreme behaviour. I was breaking boundaries as part of my research. There are two sides to a story and many angles to view it from. How could I substantiate my findings and write a book, if I haven't explored most angles?

Has any psychiatrist or psychologist put themselves in a patient's shoes? Have they mentally and physically tested themselves to understand their patients better? My knowledge was derived through experience; at least they can't deny me of that!

From my research, I identified that many factors can simultaneously form an imbalance. If Rose didn't find herself in a dire situation, I would not have spent extra nights performing comprehensive research. If I didn't attend the 40th party, I would have caught up on my sleep. If Harley didn't have a random attack of severe croup, it would not have manifested. If I didn't care or want to help I would not have experienced what I did. There were a series of events that eventuated and I kept going. These events were the driving force into the sub-conscious. However this "opened" my mind and allowed me to evolve and explore from many angles.

Firstly I identified that my purpose in life was to help others because this made me happier – my top core trait second to love. Essentially it was my ambition that created the imbalance along with the emotion of receiving positive feedback. I also felt guilty receiving praise, the negative aspect from shaving all my hair off in support of a friend. Due to my past, I sub-consciously sought recognition. When I did receive an influx of positive feedback, I couldn't deal with the emotion of guilt. I became off balance. There is a positive and negative to all matters, our physical and mental composition is no different.

To provide another simple example, when I drink irrespective of the amount, I'm always happy. I believe this is because I'm naturally a happy person and have an overall great attitude (you can still have bad days). I know some people who are emotionally charged and have poor attitudes/values or beliefs that display aggressive or violent behaviour when they drink excessively.

When I drink too much wine or champagne – my memory is intact but I suffer from headaches. I suspect when I drink wine, chemicals in my brain change the balance and this causes dehydration. When I drink excessive amounts of vodka – I forget things or lose my memory – the chemicals obviously create a different imbalance and therefore a different result. When I drink bourbon which I have a high tolerance for, I'm an overexcited, happy and very expressive. I'm also a greater extravert who talks a lot of shit and sings a whole lot more. The chemical allows me to retain a complete mindset. Clearly if I drank way too much, my body would dispel any excess. I'm not prone to vomiting when drinking! I suspect people that are and who often vomit may accelerate damage to their bodies. Basic logic prevails if your body does not cope with those chemicals, then it rejects them as fast as possible.

I know for a fact and have provided many examples in my book, how my emotions, experience, attitude, values and beliefs affect my behaviour and consequently the outcome of the matter. If I'm happy my whole mind and body are in tune. I believe that's why I'm generally healthy even though I am overweight (or obese). Therefore it is highly plausible (and has been proven to some degree in the medical field), that these factors can drive behaviours and not solely the chemical structure of a person's mind. When emotionally detached, you are not influenced by the "feeling" and can deal with the core issue/challenge more effectively. Considering all of the above, logically the chemical imbalance could also be amplified when other factors are added to the mix, like substance abuse or drugs (prescribed or illegal), trauma, survival, lack of sleep etc. If you deal with the emotion/feeling, I'm pretty certain there would be a better outcome for people who are mentally challenged or displaced.

Patients may still require medication but the overall outcome would be better. It may also remove the dependency for prescribed drugs long term. (Obviously it depends on the extent of the issue/challenge!) How each individual deals with their emotions and feelings is entirely up to them. The medical profession can only provide guidance to assist them to obtain their goals. Strategies need to be tailored to the individual because everyone is different.

Exercise is known to promote good health! I know when I completed the Muddy Buddy event, I felt like a million dollars. The main reason was because I accomplished something that I never thought I would (mind). The physical component was that my body produced those good chemicals to restore the body (matter). If an untrained person suddenly participated in excessive exercise, it could have a negative impact on their body and may result in a heart attack. The physical impact may harm the body because it has not built the required endurance. Everything in moderation is the key, and to a degree you determine the right balance for your body! Mind and Matter, Mind over matter or Matter over mind? I believe it is mind and matter collectively and it's not how it is currently viewed today. More research in this area would be able to determine conclusively.

I have a full appreciation of people who have survived in extreme circumstances. Not because I've endured a life threatening situation but I understand what my mind did when I put myself in a different mental state. In essence, I can comprehend how components of the mind function at a deeper level.

Aron Ralston who severed his own arm to save his life in a climbing accident endured 127 hours pinned between a rock and a hard place. After 5 days, he was able to find a way to help himself. He stated that he treated his arm like an enemy which allowed him to perform that lifesaving procedure. I know that he would not have considered severing his arm on day one because his mindset didn't allow it and it would have been a 24-hour ordeal. This is basic logic.

Aron was forced into a dire position and I'm assuming the will to survive combined with a lack of sleep, the natural adrenaline created by his body would have been at a premium. Was it the feeling (physical sense) that triggered the adrenaline or mental courage required to cut or was it the change in chemical structure brought about by the adrenaline or sleep deprivation? All scenarios could have created a different chemical balance that allowed him to explore other angles and ignore the physical aspect of losing his arm which in turn allowed him to perform the procedure. It is plausible that your senses both physically and mentally (emotional feeling) play an important part as well.

His account of the experience was he felt "The intensity of emotion, the euphoria…It was ecstasy. Think of it like this. Every instance of joy, happiness, pleasure, delight and fun you've ever had in your life and pack it into one moment." Personally, I felt the same on my day. I did not think or feel like I was dying and I wasn't stressed but I received that surge at the optimal level.

Given that I was not injured but lacked sleep, the adrenaline allowed my mind, body and senses to work at the optimum level in unison. In fact, I was able to see a reverse image at some stages. The only evidence of this was how I wrote on my wall, which was plastered over when I was in hospital. (One of the first things I asked Mick was did you take photos of the walls, unfortunately he didn't.) I was working in the sub-conscious so my episode could have also been triggered either by my memory or physical requirements? Again further research is required.

If I had an addictive behaviour, I'm pretty sure I would be compelled to do it again, that's how good it was. (Obviously I wouldn't put my family through that again!) I therefore can understand why people take drugs and become addicted. I do know that my brain transmitters and receptors were all working simultaneously in an order that has not been quantified to-date. But to others this was deemed a "manic episode". Once I had rested, I returned to my improved self (greater insight/outlook, better foresight, perspective and perception, overall more positive and happier). I'm not surprised that people often say they have changed for the better when they are forced to deal with extreme challenges in life and consequently lead happier/positive lives. As I don't abuse drugs, it is difficult to quantify if the transmitters and receptors have been altered permanently for others, as a result of consuming excessive chemicals. I know mine are operating as required.

Memory is the key component of the brain that allows us to function without thought when required. E.g. riding a bike or driving a car. However to acquire those skills initially requires thought (think of what you need to do) and experience to capture and store that learning to your memory. Therefore no surprise it is all interconnected! If you are changing the natural chemical structure through drugs or ECT therapy (which zaps memory) then logically it may interfere with previous established skills, values & beliefs, attitudes, personality and everything else that has been absorbed through your mind. The overall impact could affect your judgment and/or ability! Another way of explaining it, the whole brain is the conductor and different components of the mind interact for the performance. If the transmitters and receptors (instruments) are faulty, then a discrepancy becomes evident!

I guess that's why I have grave concerns regarding ECT therapy and extensive use of chemicals. It may assist with managing the condition short term but if there are no conclusive tests, how can the profession know for certain that this doesn't develop harmful long term effects and when do they stop? The recurring problems of patients could be the adverse effect of the drugs causing a permanent change to how the brain functions. Others may view it as the individual becoming immune to the current medication. How can we be certain? Again without the correct tests to substantiate, it is very much trial and error. This therefore requires additional research.

It is also a known fact that some terminally ill patients appear to get better before they pass (catch a plane). I believe that adrenaline is released and as a result of the chemical structure changing, the receptors and transmitters allow a flood of memories to surface. Some details expressed by individuals at that point in time, may be incoherent or absurd. This may be a result of our lack of understanding or misinterpretation. I am able to explain what I was communicating and why but others thought I was illogical and manic. Is there a test for natural adrenaline? It may provide some vital answers!

Another aspect that I have considered with respect to adrenaline is that it could be the key to understanding Chronic Fatigue Syndrome. In Rose's case, her symptoms disappeared or have remained dormant since being diagnosed with cancer. Was it because her mindset had shifted to survival mode or has her body produced adrenaline to help her fight cancer? I just thought I'd mention it for any potential future studies.

I was nowhere near death or I'm sure the medical staff would have attended to me more appropriately (and not abused me). All past events shared in my book I had memory of prior to my realisation (and I have thousands more). However, what I was doing leading up to and during the day was processing this from different angles for different reasons and purposes. I believe it allowed me to fully appreciate my life, experiences and learning's. I would not have been able to do this without the release of adrenaline. No wonder adrenaline is used to assist many patients for various conditions!

(Mick can confirm I covered all bases as it was very confronting for him! After viewing some footage of my brain dumps, I was surprised because what transpired and what I thought at that point in time were conflicting. It was very strange but also aligns to the theory of every action has an equal and opposite reaction!)

I did become addicted to the adrenaline but for the purpose of writing a book in order to help others. Had I not pushed myself, I wouldn't be a better person today! There were no "ifs" for me in life, including this whole experience. It was my destiny. I was able to validate and fully appreciate my entire life to-date. I had to ride through the shit to get to the good. Unfortunately I impacted those around me as part of the process. It wasn't my intention but it was unavoidable because I couldn't just vanish for a period of time to complete what I needed to. Personally, the overall experience has been a miraculous journey/epiphany!

Being happy should not be a crime! Some attributes for bipolar are comical because aspiring to write a book or singing should be acceptable. Why is it extreme to have grandiose ideas? These patients may have the talent and if not, is it harmful to dream? (It's a different story if they are at harm to themselves or others). Maybe society needs to accept differences rather than rely on conforming!

The medical profession should remove its 'blinkers' and explore other plausible avenues to evolve because they have not been able to advance in years with respect to mental challenges. **If something is incomprehensible, it doesn't mean it is not feasible**. How else would we have evolved? Logic would suggest that we have not been looking in the right place, we may have only factored the physical or based theories on what society perceives! (Well that's my view for what it's worth and I'm sure there would be other possibilities as well.) Many influential people are deemed crazy (in a negative light) or eccentric (in a positive light) why? Primarily it's because they did not conform to society's boundaries. I'm happy to be one of those people!

I have many theories in respect to other illnesses but if I explored them now I would never finish this book. I'm also conscious of not delving right into the clinical aspect because I don't want to lose or confuse anyone. Hopefully what I have covered provides a satisfactory insight at a high level. Ultimately if studies are only conducted from a single perspective (predominantly physical) there is a high probability that important aspects are not considered or remain unfounded.

Attention passengers, we are about to change direction and review the past! Did you know that beliefs have influenced and misguided the medical profession?

Homosexuality was considered a disease but was declassified as a mental illness in 1973. People received medication and endured shock treatment in an attempt to cure their illness. (Although I only had a small amount of drugs, I can appreciate their plight.) Many patients were emotionally and physically abused as a result of this treatment. No wonder people were afraid to be their true self. I'm pretty sure there are still many that can't find the courage or freedom to find peace.

It is inexcusable that this occurred in the first instance. Obviously these people did not conform to society's expectations and were therefore deemed mentally ill. This is outrageous! How could society be so blind sighted? Religious beliefs are all based on theories that have remained unsubstantiated. (They have not been scientifically proven nor has any evidence been obtained over time!)

Our beliefs can be so powerful in providing direction in life but can also be very misleading, as I have highlighted. How many lives have been affected as a result of people being forced to live double lives? How many people are unhappy and can't be at peace with themselves? How many negative beliefs impact on society? When I first developed my theories I immediately thought of people who were purely true to themselves in society. Given attitudes, behaviours, values and beliefs, homosexuals came to mind. They were courageous because even when presented with so many challenges in society, they were not scared (minimal inhibitions and fears) to be themselves. Got to love that spirit!

Even if the above didn't eventuate through religious beliefs, again why would you have a problem with someone being happy? If it's not for you, you don't need to engage in that activity or entertain the thought. People who express adverse views have obviously been mentally conditioned to a level that impedes them from being true to themselves. Because if you were happy within yourself you would accept everyone at face value! (This also extends to anyone who rejects a person in society for race, colour, culture, physical ability etc.).

We should openly acknowledge and accept differences and embrace the good in people and what they can offer. As opposed to rejecting, neglecting or harming others for the sake of indifferences. You don't have to like everyone you come into contact with. We all have differences of opinion because we are all different. In essence, it is about respect and understanding each other by treating others how you would like to be treated.

Choo choo choo – exploring the mental or psychological components are more intriguing. I will mainly cover an analysis of what transpired at the extreme level. There was so much that I did, said, thought and processed in that phase (month) that I'm sure will take a few years to unravel and comprehend completely.

In basic terms my mind instinctively went from operating on a simple level (say/think and action/do – how the majority currently function) to a complex model which was to perceive (many angles), interpret, think, feel before I acted/reacted/did. The way I processed information changed significantly. It didn't happen overnight; it eventuated through an intense and extensive process. At the time, I didn't fully appreciate what I was actually doing until I was rested. The process was completed in two cycles.

Initially the two week break (between the 2 phases) allowed me to assess what I was capturing, that is the what, when, who, how and why from a psychological aspect. Initially that formed the basis of my book. I did however, want to test, implement and execute these for myself in order to complete my research and substantiate my findings for this book. Unexpectedly, I was able to evaluate the medical side because I exerted myself to the extreme.

During the sub-conscious stages, I was functioning with my current mindset, my changing mindset (transition) and my improved mindset. My mind was operating at three different levels. At present, I bounce from old to improved and vice versa (as per some examples previously highlighted) because this concept has recently evolved for me. I did consider many angles when I was presented with personal complex challenges in the past but that was on rare occasions. It was never the norm and it didn't include the 4-elements collectively (perceive, interpret, think and feel). I may have sub-consciously thought this way in the past, without realising it.

Sometimes we do or say things that we don't realise. This is because they are instigated sub-consciously/instinctively. Logic prevails; if we are not aware of those sub-conscious thoughts/actions then it would be difficult to control, interpret or understand. (I'll explore this in more detail soon.)

I had control of all except behaviours to a degree and I believe it formed part of the learning. I effectively became rebellious to "un-train" my brain and my physical actions/behaviours were part of the process. I haven't articulated the exact changes as I climbed into my sub-conscious mind but will conduct this analysis in the near future. I believe it will uncover more of how the mind functions at different levels and could provide answers to explain how we function at a greater depth.

I know for a fact that in my different state of mind, my memory was complete. I found it interesting that the people I engaged with on that day, I had recently been in contact with or had thought about. I was either trying to help or find closure to unresolved matters. I was behaving the opposite way to how I would normally behave. At some stages, my mind was operating adversely. Considering I was functioning on 3 different levels, processing my life experiences, feelings/emotions and a whole lot of information, it's no surprise that my mind became disordered. From what I can gather, I mentally traveled from my base mindset and went from one extreme to the other. I can quantify every thought, action and conversation.

People that suffer bipolar may appear to be dishonest or may be unaware of their behaviours/actions. I believe this is because their memory has been compromised and they cannot recall what they may have said or done. It is similar to hearing a message. For example: You can't respond if you don't hear an instruction. The sense of hearing transfers details to your mind in order to process or store items to your memory. When you are mentally displaced and things are disordered, the mechanism to collect and store information to your memory could potentially be distorted creating an anomaly.

Unlike most that suffer a mental illness, I had concept of time. I believe others don't because in that frame of mind, time is of no relevance. My understanding is that the individual is more focused on a matter or subject and the mind neglects everything else. Anything that impedes an individual from addressing what they are processing or thinking would be considered a distraction in their view. As a result, they lose track of time. They ignore day-to-day tasks. They could become irritable, moody and sleep deprived. For me, I reprioritized. I didn't ignore my requirements or duties. Instead, I just managed them differently. I had a different objective and was performing research for my book when my episode was triggered. I can substantiate where I was at mentally and why.

Given my experience, it is quite plausible that the mind could be reset or retrained to a more suitable state. Early intervention is paramount, especially in children. Logic prevails, the longer the problem exists, the more complex to rectify. Basically a more intensive training program would be required for those that have suffered long term. The concept for retraining the mind would need to be tailored to that individual for the most effective result. Techniques on how to achieve this would need to be explored further as it is more about how each person functions. I believe this would complement current treatment and provide a better outcome.

I prefer to use mentally displaced or challenged when referring to those suffering. I believe that if a patient is continually told they are mentally ill, their mindset would not allow them to try and acquire a better mental state. If you are constantly told you are ill, chances are, you are going to be ill. There is no incentive to improve. It is similar to being overwhelmed or consumed when you are surrounded by negativity. Those that associate themselves around positive/neutral people are more inclined to be happy and healthy. People should be aware of those interactions to keep them balanced. As for doctors and case managers, they should attempt to ensure that the correct support is provided.

Once the medical teams are able to fully appreciate my position and validate details, it will provide some answers to what happens to a person that is in a different state of mind – call it a manic episode or it could be a matter of survival.

It may explain or provide a greater insight as to why people murder others, behave extremely or harm others. People need to be aware of behaviours and actions. Significant changes or unusual behaviours may be signs that a person needs help. This help should be tailored to that person. Treating everybody in the same manner will not assist the individual effectively because everyone is different – especially when it comes to their experiences and events in life. If you don't intervene then obviously situations can become fatal. This could be as simple as someone falling asleep at the wheel because of medication or more tragically murder or suicide. I am not condoning any harmful and deadly behaviour but obviously people are ignorant to a degree of what is happening around them, their family, friends and society.

Liam for example has been failed by the system since he was 10. Early intervention is a key for all behavioural challenges. Where was the support when he needed it? If Bob Hawke, one of Australia's ex-prime ministers was successful in his promise of assisting the homeless and declaring that no-one will be living on the streets by 1990 – especially children, Liam may have had a better life! Is the government full of empty promises that are ultimately affecting us all in some way, shape or form? Is it a lack of resources that affects those in dire situations and conversely impacting society in a negative manner?

Marky Mark had childhood issues. In one of my recent phone calls with him, he expanded on how he first became a prisoner of the system. He had been smoking a fair bit of pot. This surprised me because he was so anti-alcohol. He clearly used drugs as a relaxant or a distraction due to his troubled past. He misunderstood a great deal of the questions upon his first visit (he was probably high or stoned). He believes he was misdiagnosed whether right or wrong, he strongly feels that the medical profession is trying to change the person he is. (I can appreciate his situation as they attempted to do this to me!)

Consequently the prescribed drugs have affected him more than the plant and for him, he believes the situation is now out of control. When he takes his medication, he sleeps up to 16 hours at a time and is still physically exhausted upon waking up. He is at a loss to rectify his situation because no one has taken the time to listen or effectively help him. Are there tests to determine how behaviours have manifested for these conditions? The medical profession knows the symptoms but they don't validate the cause. If they don't validate the cause, how can they effectively treat the person? Logically you are only addressing half of the problem. Therefore, the issue for the individual would still be evident.

From a different psychological aspect, some friends were acting differently even though my core traits had not changed. I was still the same happy go lucky person. (Just like when someone gets cancer, a number of patients will tell you, people treat them differently). Some of the reasons may be that people don't know how to manage change or are scared of:

- What to say or how to react?
- How to say things?
- When to say things?
- Asking inappropriate questions
- It might be too confronting
- The inevitable – reality

It could also be that we can't be totally honest or we need to be honest to a certain degree. This may be a strategy to avoid upsetting or confronting others facing a difficult situation. For me, it is finding the right balance. This includes assessing the consequences and risks. Ultimately I am my true self, what you see and hear is what you get – no hidden agenda!

Exploring further, some may not know how the person is going to react and is mindful of that. Or maybe it's a case of feeling for them (just to name a few):
- Pity
- Sorrow
- Guilt
- Sadness
- Embarrassment
- Hurt

Whatever the reason, if you do not communicate openly and honestly, it is mentally challenging for anyone. This is more apparent with someone that is mentally displaced. People suffering mentally need to be heard and establish trust before they would be willing to accept help. In most cases, they wouldn't be in that position if they were treated acceptably in the first instance. Hence the reason patients may reject offers of help. It is a defense mechanism. By only providing drugs and failing to discuss core issues, it could be perceived that the health/medical system does not care!

Threatening the mentally displaced with drastic action is also not conducive to assisting them. I was told that if I didn't take my medication I would be forced back into hospital under the CTO. (Police are often called in these situations). How confronting would that be for someone who is mentally challenged? It would make matters worse! Especially if you had no power to defend yourself and no one listened. I'm sure others that are not as strong as me would be scared, trapped and helpless. It would be interesting to find out how many have suffered the same fate I did and how it impacted them. I was denied many rights and was treated inhumanely. It is very frustrating to know that this happens to others and they don't have the capacity to help themselves! It is deplorable and sickening!

As I have mentioned before, I'm not a doctor nor do I claim to be one. My experience enabled me to inadvertently obtain some valuable knowledge and create an opportunity to help others –

initially it was to provide an opportunity for others to help themselves. Personally it's now ensuring that people are treated humanely.

Other than the recommendations I've already highlighted, I believe the psychiatric and psychological faculties should be combined and form the one specialist function to improve the system. More patient time and consistent care is required. Consulting with 4 different doctors in a space of 6 weeks, does not help a patient that is mentally displaced. Consistency is of utmost importance.

Doctors need to get to know their patients better to be able to treat them effectively. Some doctors may not have the time to read their own notes from consult to consult, as was evident with Dr. Hughes (the audio captured 'minutes' of flicking pages). How are the doctors providing the best care with so many inconsistencies? Current practice and procedures need to be reviewed urgently for the sake of all. If this treatment is common practice across most hospitals, I'm not surprised by the number of deaths, suicides etc. It is clearly evident that there is a huge deficiency in resources and it needs to be addressed. If patients are treated more effectively, they may be less inclined to return and could restore their lives.

Prevention is obviously better than cure! For the severe mentally displaced, they need special care and attention. They need to be taught how to function in the real world and become independent to the best of their ability. Education is the key. Their needs should be respected and heard. It would be interesting to determine how many have suffered or are suffering due to the neglect of proper care. Not to mention the cost to society and I'm not just referring to the dollars. It is easy to forget those that can't speak for themselves. Therefore I would not be at peace with myself if I neglected these issues.

As you are aware, I was not granted access to my medical file even though I had every right. I did want to analyze both sides to articulate any other opportunities. I guess I'll have to wait until matters are investigated further. In the meantime, hopefully Dr. Newman can provide some of those notes so I can progress on my journey.

Heading down another track.........The excessive use of drugs and alcohol seems to be more prevalent in society today. I believe this is because people are becoming more frustrated, trapped or depressed by many issues that are manifesting in the community. These substances provide an escape. I don't have a problem with natural plants being used for a stimulant but chemicals can be deadly. Any relaxant (legal or illegal) should be consumed with care and in moderation. I don't endorse any use of chemically engineered drugs illegally; it is toxic on all fronts and can be fatal. Ultimately, the government can't ignore that people will exert their own right to consume relaxants and it may be time to review laws to gain some control. I know it is controversial but I'm playing the devil's advocate. The drugs that are prescribed by the medical profession are just as harmful and are uncontrolled to a degree. Who has the tenacity to determine the right balance in an attempt to minimise the issues currently presented in society? Reviewing places that have relaxed laws may provide valuable insight to forming a desirable outcome to improve the situation. By ignoring the cause (individuals who are impacting their mental state through these stimulants), we become paralyzed and are unable to provide a better outcome. It's only an opinion, accept what you want and discard what you don't need. I'm only attempting to widen our perspective, as these challenges that we are currently facing will not improve, especially as our population increases.

From my experience, anyone can achieve the same effect of drugs naturally by doing what I did. I don't encourage it because you may find yourself locked up in a hospital and if you don't know what you are doing, you could find yourself in a very difficult situation.

Considering the legalities of events:

In respect to the illegal recordings (consults), my philosophy is: If I was clinically deemed mentally ill, in theory I was unable to act and think for myself. The hospital assumed responsibility for me under the order therefore technically it was their duty of care to ensure I abided by the law. I didn't have any rights, they denied them. It was their policy that no devices were on hand, not mine. I didn't sign anything to confirm that I agreed to that policy. They would not have allowed a recorded consult because they restrict such devices.

Common sense prevails, who would approve a recording when they could become legally implicated?

Consequently I had to protect myself under duress. From the very first appointment, I knew I would struggle to prove something that had not been quantified, even though I tried. I had to act to protect myself. If a person is cleared of murder on the grounds of self-defence, then surely I should be cleared of an illegal recording for that same purpose. In addition, I was still being forced to take drugs that I didn't require. I also had the potential to indirectly help others that had been inappropriately treated. What other alternative was there for me to protect myself? How could I prove otherwise when I was deemed guilty before proven innocent? Or in my case I was deemed mad/crazy/mental before sane! I only captured what I needed to, when I could. I never recorded any consults post my discharge because I was free from the ward/hospital. I believe my intentions were justified given the situation I was placed in. I did not deliberately break the law; I was forced to work outside the boundaries because of the ones I was subjected to.

With respect to using real names, it's a matter of freedom of speech. I may have been harsh in some cases but with good reason. I have been openly honest and provided the truth. I should not be crucified if others can't accept or handle the truth. If I'm challenged legally by the medical profession/individuals, I may be forced to instigate a counter claim which could result in a class action. I'm prepared to test the waters. (If they are true to their profession, I suspect that will investigate, review and implement changes rather than proceeding with the legal avenue!)

Some may have thought I was naive or stupid for exposing my tax file number. As previously stated, it holds little value to me. It is of more value to the government. I view it as testing the boundaries. How secure are government processes, if others manage to use this number? They might have to issue me with another number, hope their system copes!

Chugga, chugga, chugga, gee the train is getting hot, hot hot! Don't worry I'll keep my clothes on!

I mentioned earlier that I was able to view aspects very differently however it is difficult to explain. Therefore I've used a couple of celebrity examples just to introduce a very different insight to language, behaviours and actions!

Michael Jackson's – we are the world, we are the future, so let's make a brighter day and let's start giving! So true!

MJ produced some awesome music. I love his legacy of inspirational joy he brought through sound and still enjoy his music today. But he had a tormented mind with a tortured soul. He suffered and so did others behind closed doors. Never Never Land – named appropriately, because you should never go! It never was a place of real joy and was financially unsuccessful. Money assisted to provide a superficial blanket to cover, what he had hanging over his head! (A son nicknamed Blanket because his head was covered and placed over the balcony! Actions speak louder than words!) Sometimes we do things we can't explain or don't realise. This is because we don't consciously do them! What was he hiding or couldn't publicly face?

Gina Rinehart – world's richest woman (at the time of print) who predominantly is responsible for mining natural ores, is in a legal battle. Her family is at stake for a claim of the riches. Why? If they are your children, it's only natural to provide for them. Isn't she responsible for providing the guidance for her children to act accordingly in life? Who else wants a stake, if your own family is prepared to fight? Are her friends true friends or are they enemies? Money is the root of evil. It must be a pretty shallow life to live.

Conversely, her children may be seeking love through possessions because that is all they know, maybe they are greedy, maybe they believe they deserve more. On the reverse side, Gina may be teaching them a lesson but if that were true, a reasonable amount of money should be distributed to help those less privileged. How much does one person need?

Gina has a great influence on the market because at the moment, money is power (due to our mindset). She was prepared to play the market and sell shares in Fairfax, in order to drop the prices. This would have allowed her to buy back shares at a reduced rate to cash in later. (Similar to the great Kerry Packer – they played the same cards.) Is this business savvy, greed or exerting the power of money?

The recent news of Gina claiming Australia as "**class warfare**" is the height of hypocrisy from such an aristocrat. My view is that Gina bases her happiness on material status and there is nothing noble about it. In fact livelihoods are impacted – the workers here (unemployed) and the immigrants (exploited labour – cheap rates), there are no winners. Breaking down terminology - "**Class**" classes are based on monetary status, we are at "**war**" and it's just not fair "**fare**" - what you sacrifice to pay your way!

It is not the billionaires that are doing more than anyone to help by investing their money and creating jobs. It is raping our environment and our livelihood under false pretenses. Have we been conditioned, programmed or brain washed over many of centuries?

These are only small examples of how to view matters in real terms as a commoner. I can't control how people will react or think, each for their own. But I do know that the truth hurts because when what we think is right, is actually the opposite, we get angry or frustrated as no one likes to be wrong, be betrayed or misled.

Therefore the easiest way to manage this, is to accept pure logic, there is no right or wrong to a degree but more so how to react. (Harming others is not defined by the laws of logic, i.e. treat others the way you would like to be treated. Therefore it is excluded from the right and wrong theory.) A positive reaction ensures more benefits and a negative makes for a more challenging trip – you still get to the same spot irrespective!

Just one more thought in regard to the above example. One of Gina's comments was "If you're jealous of those with more money, don't just sit there and complain. Do something to make more money yourself – spend less time drinking or smoking and socializing, and more time working!"

My current reply would be, "well we can't make any more money when all of it and life is sucked out of you (us), we have to make the most of it!!!" How many more would be suffering from depression if they didn't have an outlet?

As you are aware, jealousy is not in my DNA and by the time you finish reading this book, you will realise that her comment could actually work in the reverse! (Hope you're in tune!)

I feel for those who continually take the negative path because it will never bring them true happiness. Unless of course if individuals are prepared to change and redeem themselves for past actions or accept the consequences of their behaviour! As my dad would say, you can lead a horse to the trough but you can't make it drink! I would add, just make sure there is fucking water in it - (referring to providing the opportunity)!

Hopefully you have an open mind to learn and grow from a failing system and ignorant society ultimately derived by consumption! I have faith that my experience provides an avenue for change and acceptance of different theories/strategies.

I hope Dr. Hughes does not get a case of "slap cheek" if the book manages to hit (find) him! KAPOW be careful of slamming the door in someone's face next time because it could come back to hit you! Hopefully as I have acted in good faith and I'm only venting, karma won't bite me! Karma is tricky sometimes; you never know what will happen!

Time for another song! Doctor Doctor, give me the news? Am I crazy or is it you? No pill is going to cure my head, because I have the right mindset!

Just a side note, I found it quite ironic that the government had published a review of the mental health services just as I was completing my book. Hopefully the information contained in this book provides the insight for changes required from a patient's perspective and not a fabricated report produced by someone who has not experienced the treatment first hand. In hindsight, the $21,000 they spent on detaining me may have been beneficial and cost effective! (The cost of managing a patient is estimated at $1000 per day.) Hopefully my story assists in fast tracking some changes for the benefit and care of the vulnerable.

There is still a fair bit of steam left in the engine! We are going to pick up a bit more speed. Just remember to expect the unexpected! Chugga chugga chugga…

10. Talking about a revolution

If I told you we were all puppets boxed in a frame with strings pulled so tight that we can't freely enjoy life, what would you think, feel or say? Just thought I'd set the scene, for one bumpy, extreme ride across treacherous bridges/tunnels, well for me anyway!

Before my realization, I had no interest in religion and politics. I also wasn't very opinionated because what could one person or group for that matter, be able to do to rectify the current issues in society or the world? Absolutely nothing or very little because of many factors, those mainly being:

- Money
- Attitude
- Values & Beliefs
- History
- Population
- Government Policies/Law

For this reason and for the fact that I have already crossed medical and legal boundaries in previous chapters, I thought why stop there! It also provides an insight to what I was covering and the output of that time in my life. I will cover the top and the bottom! The meat in the sandwich (and how to initiate changes locally) will eventuate in the next chapter.

I always found religion hypocritical. I could never understand how most religions were built on wealth and yet none of the riches were shared with the under privileged. For example: locally the homeless and globally, third world countries. I did visit the Vatican and the Sistine chapel and the art, the gold, architecture was truly opulent. But although it was significant for history and symbolic, it was disheartening that it could have provided so much more to the livelihoods of those less fortunate.

In addition, there were countless reports of pedophilia that were managed behind closed doors. Who were they protecting? Were they guilty or embarrassed? Were they afraid that people would leave the congregation? By not addressing this serious and evil behaviour appropriately would have had a major impact on those individuals and would have negatively transgressed into society. Removing babies from mothers who were out of wedlock or due to race was also appalling. What gave them the right? More recently, corruption has been exposed in the highest echelon for Catholics, the Vatican. This contradicts the basis of what they were/are preaching and teaching.

At the next level, redeeming yourself by confessing to a priest or Chaplin seemed comical to me. Firstly for the reasons above and secondly, how does expressing your wrongs to an individual rectify a situation? Wouldn't the world be a better place, if you addressed any issues in an honest and open manner? For example: correcting the situation and clearing your conscience the true way. I always viewed the confession box a fallacy for the mere fact that a *so called* "God" through a prominent religious figure has cleared your conscience. How is this logical?

My dad came from a country with a high number of Muslim followers. Most Muslims are great people and integrate seamlessly into society. Unfortunately we only hear about the extremists that portray a very negative picture for the true, hardworking Muslims who do respect and care for others. The extremists (of any religion or origin) should not receive any media coverage as it adds fuel to the fire. They are the ones that should be dealt with appropriately, harshly and behind closed doors. Australia or any other country doesn't need evil violent individuals compromising the safety of others and damaging the community. Governments need to update the laws to protect the real people!

Now the burqa has always been a point of contention in Australia and other places. I say wear what you want, whatever makes you happy. I do wonder though, was it historically introduced by the males who did not want to face the guilt and shame for the poor treatment of women in those countries? There have been countless deaths by torture, stones/rocks for adultery and domestic violence against women. I wish I had a magical wand for this to cease, it is sickening. I don't hear of the men suffering the same fate. On another note, I don't recall the turban being such an issue when people from India migrated to Australia, was it because they integrated without fuss or was it because you could see their faces?

One more angle, some Australians fear that we will lose touch of our society by accommodating other religions or cultures. Multiculturalism is part of Australia and we can still wear our shorts, thongs and head to the bar! Our children can still sing the National Anthem and Christmas carols at schools and kinder. I believe that by trying to become too politically correct, we have lost common sense! As a result, we are misguided and have misinterpreted what our identity is or should be which has created disharmony. It is really up to us to define or redefine! Depends which way you swing, present or future?

Since I've explored many matters over the last 3 months, I do believe religions served a purpose in building a base and foundation for individuals to enjoy and explore over many centuries. I also believe that it was based on one fable that deviated throughout history for particular reasons and was essentially created to provide guidance.

The Dalai Lama supports this view as well. His generic teachings are testament to uniting people, not for the sake of profit or at the detriment of people. It makes complete sense and I'm not surprised that people connect with such a great passionate, humble and intelligent man.

I have and will always respect others in their beliefs, because I am respectful. I only need to believe in myself, my husband and teach my children the same. If anything a dog is the closest to offering unconditional love, trust, support and guidance, is it a coincidence that this spelt backwards is God?

This is my view with an open mind for what it is worth. I'm not encouraging anyone to do anything in respect to their values and beliefs. I'm just sharing some thought for thought!

Right, might as well take the underground track as this is no scenic route! As you can appreciate, there is a great depth to explore when highlighting government opportunities. I will therefore focus on what is relevant to me and what has been topical in recent times. Purely to create awareness and provide a different view of matters to broaden our horizons.

Education is fundamentally important for any society. What, when, who, how and why is critical when identifying the curriculum for future education. It has been suggested that literacy has been compromised due to our advanced technology. Many factors contribute and in today's society it would be difficult to determine if we have not adequately adapted to change.

Predominantly professionals are basing measurements of academics on historical indicators when times have changed. It appears that teachers have more to teach, less resources, more students and no extra hours to accommodate a portfolio that is probably 3 times as big, than 30 years ago. Logically this would compromise the overall performance of our students.

Where possible I believe once a child has learned the fundamentals, learning should be integrated and applied to everyday life. For a simple example; primary student project, how many seeds are required to harvest a crop of tomatoes for a stall at the market. Students develop and deploy tasks. At completion, I'm sure they would get a greater appreciation for technology, science, maths/business, learn about horticulture, becoming self-sufficient and dealing with the public.

On another train of thought, what is frustrating is that childhood obesity is an issue and yet regular exercise on a daily basis is not part of the school curriculum. I remember at the start of each day and afternoon at primary school, we had a 10-15 minute workout of some sort. It also provided energy for the afternoon classes. Why and when did that cease? I know play times are quite active for some children but not all, at least having a set routine promotes exercise and well-being.

Bullying is obviously another issue that seems to be taken out of proportion. One or two incidents do not constitute bullying. It is a normal experience and is part of the learning process. In fact, it is character building and provides the opportunity for our young to negotiate and establish themselves in the real world.

Max started school at the age of 5 this year and in his 8th week, two older children from grade 3 and 4 told Max to move seats on the bus. Max stood his ground and received a bit of an ear bashing. He was most upset when he got home. I explained to him that he was very brave and that it was great that he did not give in. I did let the school know in case there were repeat incidents but also advised not to follow it up unless it was happening to others or if it happened to Max again. Happy to report there has been no further incidents this year. I suspect it won't be the first and last time because it's not unusual for any of us to experience differences of opinions from time to time.

I agree that constant and brutal situations require urgent attention. In most cases, the bully's behaviour stems from home and needs to be addressed there. I know some critics will jump off the train and say, what about the children with ADD (or similar behavioural conditions). It is still a manageable condition, would be my answer.

It's great for schools to educate children on bullying. However I would prefer my children to receive information on acknowledgement and acceptance, which could provide the same outcome in a positive manner. How much is too much? Is this extra activity sacrificing learning or teaching of other important topics? The Government is quick to provide funds for failing projects. Is this bullying campaign another one? Why now? How bad is the problem? Are the majority of children *that* depressed and have to resort to *that* behaviour? If it is the case, what have we allowed society to become?

Surely this is not the case! If the school is unsuccessful in managing this directly with the parent, I think it would be more logical to include this in the human services portfolio rather than impede on all teachers and students for the minority. Obviously the bullies are not happy otherwise they wouldn't be behaving in that manner! At the very least, parents may become more proactive at the thought and may just take the necessary action that is required to rectify the problem!

All schools nationally should adopt the same curriculum for consistency and equality (special schools excluded as they require specific requirements). This would also provide flexibility without compromising a child's education, those travelling interstate or those in blended families using different schools throughout the year. Why should the less fortunate be disadvantaged even more? Are we creating division through our children and is it impacting on society adversely? Wouldn't it be more economical to operate one set of standards?

I know I would rather be spending that hard earned cash on sharing a valuable experience with my children. I would prefer this than expecting they will do their best because of how much I spent sending them to an exclusive school. Who knows, the pressure of sending children to these exclusive schools could have just as damaging an effect on them personally? (If they are not meeting their parent's expectations or deem themselves as failures, it may affect their behaviours or create unnecessary issues).

I did not attend exclusive schools, they were considered private but working class schools none the less. My parents could only provide little academic assistance throughout my school years. Irrespective, I consider myself well educated and successful in life. Regardless of whether you are spending $30,000 or $300 a year, each student will perform based on their own ambition. The most important aspect is to ensure you provide them with direction, skills and a positive experience. With that in mind, as a parent, I won't be enforcing any expectations on my children. Ultimately it is their life, as long as they are happy, it will make me happier! Guidance is the key.

It annoyed me that enrolment forms were so intrusive. You also had to complete some details three times in a series of forms. Seriously, how is this productive? Why does the government request a number of forms to be completed when all the information is available through Centrelink, Medicare or the tax department? We know that their systems are linked, that's how they keep track of us!

Why is it important for schools to know your occupation? Does this set what your school will cater for? If it does, is it a fair system? There are more lower-middle class people providing more funds through the tax system; are these schools accommodated for adequately?

While I'm at it, who keeps track of the funds we provide the Government to benefit the community? Oh that's right, we can apply for details under the freedom of information. This is flawed because they will only include information that they would like to share. I experienced that first hand when reviewing this option to access my medical records. Sorry for deviating, you can appreciate that I've had enough and this is just the beginning!

The most disconcerting aspect of education for today is now we all have to provide a police check, if we want to assist at schools where our children attend. Why are we all treated like criminals? Who are we protecting? A stranger (law enforcer) authorises a form and these evil predators slip through anyway. Some people might find that this is a good mechanism to provide a safe school environment.

It is under false pretenses. I view it as a deviation from the purpose of what the police force should be undertaking. They are wasting valuable time and resources by performing this task on the majority when they could be using this time to catch and punish the real criminals (minority). This would appear more logical and productive. It would also be more cost effective!

The predators are not publicly named and are protected. Why? Does it provide them with the freedom to target victims again? Some may be rehabilitated but should they deserve the freedom whilst we are governed to meet extreme policies as a result of their actions? It is very difficult to determine what would be acceptable but why should society be forced to accept this evil behaviour in the first place? (Treat them how they have treated others!) I know I feel uncomfortable about some individual men in places like parks/play centres and they could be innocent. We become afraid knowing that they could lurk in our community so we inadvertently overprotect our children and they can't explore. The Daniel Morcombe case was a classic example.

Pure evil should be dealt with accordingly – capital punishment for the extreme. How many more have to suffer? (Jill Meagher and her family recently endured what no person and family should). These predators' rapists, murderers and any pedophiles should not be held in prisons sucking more out of the community and harming/brain washing others whilst in captivity. Would you allow venomous snakes to slither through your house and community at your expense (emotionally, mentally, physically and financially)?

Actions do speak louder than words and could protect the majority. It would enable us to live in a less fearful world. Capital punishment does serve a purpose in our current society and will do, until those poisonous predators are eradicated. I'm happy to wear a wig and declare it!

As a result of relaxed laws and lack of resources it has created a discrepancy. It only makes sense to review this urgently so collectively we can restore what the majority should be able to enjoy freely.

While I'm on policing, it's no surprise that a number of archaic laws are still in existence purely for monetary reasons. We have a number of street police reprimanding the public on how to cross the street. Jay walking! Aren't people able to use their common sense when crossing a flipping street? People understand the risks and consequences. Surely this resource would be better spent again looking for the real criminals. Or is it assumed that people can't think for themselves these days?

Why are they issuing parking fines, how is that protecting society? Why are they baby-sitting people in hospitals? Four police men for 2 misfits of society for at least 6 hours. This is a complete waste of resources. I and the other patient were not threatening and if we were, we should have been locked up instead of wasting hospital resources. We have security and police at sporting events in the droves, how is that an effective use of resources? It would make more sense to have more security and a minor team of law enforcers.

The cost of an under resourced service and archaic laws further creates disparity in society. It impedes police from attending real incidents and compromises people's safety.

I once called the police thinking I had an intruder at my home when Lu was staying with me. We waited 30 minutes, when the station was 5 minutes away. In the meantime we were armed with a can of

Mr. Muscle in the most inaccessible room – a walk-in-robe/ensuite! (Oven spray-kills me every time I use it! One spray in the eyes gives you enough time to run or the attacker would be at very least visibly challenged to render any harm.)

Intervention orders are another issue in society, some are issued without proper investigation making it a mockery. At the caravan park, two ladies who didn't see eye to eye were involved in a verbal bitch fight. At the time, both were suffering from personal issues. One managed to obtain an order on the other when no violence, threats or stalking were evident. Because of this, others can't be adequately protected that need to be and end up worse off due to a lack of resources. How many victims have been seriously injured or have died as a result of this process?

Police should be enforcing laws that protect people and ensure safety. Any outdated laws that relate to common sense, are a money spinner or currently ineffective should be reviewed and changed. Has anyone considered the cost or adverse effect of these laws? Hopefully a review will provide better protection, be more cost effective and ensure a resourceful police force, if deemed necessary by the community.

There is nothing fair about 'Fairwork' from my experience. From what I can gather, you're fine if it's of a political nature. My husband was underpaid a significant amount of money and 9 months later we are still waiting for the government to follow-up the under payment.

I prepared a 30-page report in early April 2012 providing evidence, clauses in the award and what needed to be clarified. The case manager has claimed it is hard to validate; all she has to do is view the records and operations of the business. I did ask her how an employee can dictate to an employer how to run a business, if the company was not adhering to policies? She had no answer and it's December and we have to lodge an appeal. Absolutely ridiculous!

Workcover is not working! People who seriously need to access this benefit are doomed on all accounts. The process is convoluted and is financially crippling if you have no other source of income. Who wins? It's the lawyers if it gets to that point and the insurance companies if it doesn't. Is this building up a false economy?

Alternatively if you individually insure yourself, there are that many conditions and generally it is only for a set period of time before your lifestyle is compromised.

Those claimants that manage to get through who don't necessarily deserve it make a mockery of the system and create a stigma. Those that are rehabilitated can't find work. Why? When money is the driver, it is difficult to establish adequate protocols because of the leaches in society that seek a quick buck!

What would I do if I was the government? Support the injured in a new role by assessing what each individual wants/can do; provide training and sufficient income simultaneously as they return back to work and integrate back into society.

Furthermore families and livelihoods are affected; depression, financial stress, immobility just to name a few. Yet they have to fend for themselves whilst working through the process and if you have not recovered from your injury in a set timeframe, you're fucked!

Don't get me wrong, you will get great medical care that is fast tracked because it is funded but those that are not involved in a work injury or road accident have to wait very long periods? Hmmm is one life or livelihood valued more than another? No wonder we are all challenged when we seek medical care – we are not working in a collective environment. Money is the root of all evil and now pain and suffering!

Child support agency is another farcical! I understand there are parents both female and male who abuse the system however you would have more chance at roulette than receiving a fair chance with this mob!

My husband has never complained about providing for his children. When they were both in our care full-time, their mother didn't pay a cent in child support for the first 2 years. Just before her daughter moved back home in the 3rd year, the amount received wouldn't have covered a supply of bread for the year. She saw her children 65 days out of 940, claiming she was working most of the time. We knew she wasn't working the whole time. But she was working for cash which was not declared but there was nothing we could we do about it.

Now one child lives with us and the other lives with their mother and my husband still has to pay the full of child support amount. No different in the cost of raising a 12 year old who participates in sports all year round and a 15 year old – is this discrimination?

Contact hours are not conducive to most workers who need to contact the office. More often than not you are placed on hold for more than 30 minutes so it is difficult to contact them in your lunch break. When you do provide details and proof, it is continually ignored and not followed up. Mothers are always right, I guess!

Personally, given the complexity and issues with this service, if you can happily arrange to provide for your children between your ex-partner, I wouldn't use this service (just keep records for your protection). It is a waste of tax-payer funds. The whole community is paying for a service that clearly needs an overhaul but given people's mindset of what it should be, it may take many years.

Our government also sends valuable resources to fight in wars. How does this benefit anyone? What are we trying to prove? What are these soldiers fighting for? At what cost?

Peace doesn't come in any form of violence, it just creates more. We have lost a number of great heroes and many return mentally, physically and emotionally challenged which also affects those around them. The people in those countries are no better off with innocent lives lost and buildings/homes destroyed. East Timor and Vietnam are still in the process of re-establishing themselves after years at war! Was there adequate assistance to restore the devastation in a reasonable timeframe post war?

War spelt backwards is raw! Is it the raw emotions of values and beliefs with the misconception that money is power that leads us to war? Or is it the constitution which is based on religion? Why else would you be required to swear on the bible? I'd swear on my life or heart, that's me! Well it's my theory and my book, believe what you want!

I know that whilst we participate in such atrocities (trashing cities), we are on a path of worldly destruction that filters through all societies and countries. We are all experiencing the effects indirectly, in price hikes for one! Geez it's us (maybe shorthand …..Je - it's - us!), we need to wake up!

We institutionalise illegal immigrants from those countries and yet we try to protect them in their war torn country? Aren't we hypocrites? Why not help them here? I know people will be quick to share their views and all are valid. If you were put in the same position, such as their plight, where a terrorist regime took your livelihood, threatened your family, what would you do? You had no other option other than to run leaving all your belongings and money behind, wouldn't you at least try to find another place to live? What would be a better approach for the government to undertake?

My recommendation would be to promote workers in our society to train the immigrants in those areas where we are deficient in. (Not at the detriment of those that are already in the workforce.) Instead of spending millions to house these detainees, let them work at a cheaper rate so we can develop a competitive infrastructure or manufacturing industry. We could produce more cost effective projects/items and still maintain or stimulate growth, keeping a fair balance within the community.

Some may arrive on our shore because we do provide accommodation and food. Maybe if they have to work, it might have a different effect and less will make that journey? It seems more acceptable to make them work rather than house illegal immigrants at the tax payer's expense.

Recent news of detaining legitimate refugees has been dismissed or overlooked by the government. Why? Is it because the current processes are inconsistent? Only address what you think we want and not what should happen? How will that work for any country trying to evolve when resources both physically and environmentally are stretched?

Climate change……oh what a catastrophe! Better late than never or is it a case of too little, too late? It is a very serious matter and shouldn't be ignored so I applaud the Government for providing the attention it deserves. However our government is attempting to be world innovators with a strategy that has more holes (gaps) than Swiss cheese!

My interpretation is that the Australian Government charge people more but sell it as a benefit, while the companies strive to implement costly infrastructure to minimise climate changes that have occurred over centuries.

I agree we need to review our energy source and lessen the impact. However this needs to occur in conjunction with policy and processes that impact directly. Keeping in mind that this is only one component of a very complex issue! It also requires the public to make significant changes to their lives in order to be effective.

Logically if people or businesses are charged more, then there are adverse impacts on society. Most people won't change but will accommodate. For example: people work longer to cover the increases which impacts on your precious time. Children may be left in care longer than necessary in a system that is already struggling to cope. Children need time with their parents, have we failed to realize this? Or will the next expensive device provide that love and support your child needs?

Another angle is that there is an increase in crime in order to survive or defaults on payments, some may lose their house. I experienced those pressures first hand back in the eighties. Will history repeat itself? From a business perspective, it will result in unemployment because of the rising costs and emphasis on profit/bottom line. Overall little impact on the environment and no winners all round! Has the cost of the adverse impacts been considered accurately?

Just like the Goods and Services Tax (GST), the only benefit it brought was for the government to have access to spend more of our money ineffectively. Once the dust had settled and there was no other option, people just accepted that it was a part of everyday life.

Prices have significantly increased since that period. It is reflective in financial terms as Cost Price Indicator (CPI) from quarter to quarter and generally only compared to the previous year. Government statistics indicate that since 2006-2011, households are generally paying 20% more for goods and services when changes for wages in the same period were around 5%.

You don't have to be Einstein to work out that there is a substantial difference. No wonder the poor are getting poorer and the rich are getting richer. Something has to be sacrificed, no wonder I drink– we are continually getting beaten and remain powerless. (Well so we are lead to believe at the moment! Mama to the rescue, well not me alone! It is currently a case of wishful thinking! Does it hurt? I have nothing to lose! Freedom of speech, my greatest test to-date!)

Just for the record, I couldn't find the wage information directly on the government site, maybe because it is conveniently not available. Funny about that! (I obtained this information from an article "Australian census: not quite the US, but the gap widens" which was published on www.theconversation.edu.)

We have had major advances in technology but we still have all the paperwork. I thought technology would have replaced that, or don't we have faith in our systems/processes? It is not feasible to send a group of ozone plasterers to the sky limits to rectify a problem as gigantic as what the environment is experiencing. If we continue to have excessive wants then it will only impact our environment. Furthermore, a growing population, more consumer needs and wants, greater detriment to the environment – basic logic! How does the government change the basic requirements to effectively support a feasible strategy? Or any strategy for that matter!

Trees help sustain our environment and we butcher them for what purpose? Trees control the level of pollution, that's why people love the country air! At what point do we use all resources more effectively? Contain buildings and restore derelict/abandoned ones, like the plethora of abandoned schools around the country.

By sourcing more environmentally friendly infrastructure and creating more opportunities by varying an industry (currently lost in a one dimensional mindset), we could stimulate growth and promote a better world.

For example, we could provide opportunities to educate and retrain society. This would include eliminating unnecessary forms, building a better logistical service both commercially and domestically. Instead of issuing jay-walking fines, we could ban cars from the city. People will learn to change but ensure the facilities are available. Provide businesses with the necessary funds or assistance as a trade-off for ineffective or damaging practices that are eliminated.

If our attitude towards the environment is that it is too hard and too costly, how is that going to improve the situation long term? I have covered enough at a very high level but hopefully it stimulates others to think outside the circle. (It's always been circle for me, eyes are round, world is round and I hate being placed in a box viewing the world through a frame like a puppet!)

Other matters that frustrate me that don't directly affect me personally are adoption, sexual status and animal welfare but are all just as important. Again there are many more, I'm only trying to highlight important challenges.

We have people wanting to love, care, nurture and support children in need, why is the government making it extremely difficult to adopt? They are compromising the livelihoods of all. What gives them the right to control and then implement policies that reprimand those that explore other avenues? Are the governments encouraging exploitation in other countries by preventing great deserving people of an opportunity? But the government will send valuable resources to war and inadvertently kill those that they are trying to protect? It is insane and I'm disgusted!

If disease control is the issue, then have the necessary checks in place. We can't even admit we have an issue with Lyme and tick disease as recently reported. There have also been other cases of a resurgence of some diseases. (I'm only using disease as another example). Is this situation with adoption a contradiction or discrimination? Is it about control or finance? Many questions are left unanswered because we all accept what has been established over centuries.

All species and predominantly animals are here for a reason and a purpose. It is natural that we are all part of the food chain, whether you choose to eat it or not. A bear is not choosy when divulging a human!

Those that profiteer or inhumanely harm animals should be dealt with appropriately. Just recently, on the show '60-minutes' there was an interview with a man from South Africa who was so called protecting rhino's by severing their horns. This is not protecting them, it is mutilation. I wonder how he would have felt if someone mutilated his manly hood?

I was appalled that they considered this to protect them from the hunters yet they kept the shavings for future investment. Another company had a more acceptable approach which was to move them to isolated areas, out of harms reach.

Conversely, if animals are at natural extinction then obviously their time and purpose on this planet has ceased. There is no benefit from protecting these species as it may be at the detriment of nature. Dinosaurs were obviously not killed and hunted but ceased to exist in time. This obviously allowed for other species to evolve, this is part of evolution. Pure logic and far more feasible than what we are currently resorting too. (Also just another example of how holding on to the past may be at the expense of the future.)

In earlier chapters, I have highlighted that it is truly great for individuals to be themselves. In fact, it is inspirational that gay people can be open about their sexuality. Is it right for the government to control, what you choose to do?

Currently if you don't meet a certain criteria you cannot legally marry. Individuals who engage the same sex are labeled gay. Why? Because they are happy! I like that notion even though I'm happily engaging with my husband. Can't we all be gay? It is just another word for happy!

Why should they hide or be denied a right for being their true self? Let them marry if that's what makes them happy. We all know that the constitution does not allow it based on religion and this appears to be flawed. Is the government afraid of losing votes? Gutless! What adverse impact could it have on society? In my opinion, none but I do share another view which will be revealed later!

Are there too many complex policies? Are Government agencies under resourced? Is the government taking advantage of the vulnerable that are trying to survive in the real world? So we pay tax for all these services that don't provide sufficiently, where to from here? The government is spending far more than required, we are paying more tax to subsidize the inefficient policies and as a direct result, the majority of Australian residents struggle to enjoy their humble and reasonable life!

I'd encourage a review of all services and not a lengthy report that will take years to action, one that starts at the local level-what people want and need.

If funds you provide are not being correctly allocated and you do not approve of some projects, don't you have every right to assist in rectifying the challenges? When your livelihood and your children's are at stake, would you want to attempt to rectify the matter? When you look at it, we are all shareholders of the government and country. (I don't think any party would support my view but seems logical to me!)

Locally we can attain traction in expressing what is important or what we'd like to change! We just need to turn back time and find a way!

Before we head to that, I just wanted to highlight that we live in a depressed cancerous society that is one vicious cycle. This is an example of how matters can be interpreted differently with consideration to the physical and mental aspects for oneself and global. It is a technique to collectively view language, nature, economy, policies and self in a unique way to identify and potentially resolve social issues.

Euthanasia: the government has no right to disempower an individual who knows what is right for them. Patients would be well aware of the risks and consequences, and know what is best for them! If they do not have the capacity, surely their relatives could decide based on governed procedures, a more sensible approach than the inhumane strategy of today.

We legally and humanely put down animals that are suffering. Yet humans that have lost their dignity who can't communicate are in pain and suffering, die uncomfortably slow. They are left trapped in a depressive room prolonging the inevitable at the expense of their quality of life and others both financially and emotionally. This is a no-win situation!

If there is contention regarding members accessing estates and manipulating the system, maybe the policy ensures if a patient has not previously nominated their preference than it must be decided by a member with no financial links or the person suffers in silence.

I know if I were in the same position, I'd want to be "awake" to hear what was said and at least enjoy my final party. Is that where we get the "wake" from? Had that been taken away in earlier centuries? If you don't support the view, what does it matter? This updated policy wouldn't impact you? Seems logical that this could be a potential quick change? Keeping it simple, makes for a more cost effective approach and less complicated.

On the opposite side of the scale, as a result of Gross Domestic Products (Economic indicator): what are we doing to the "Youth in Asia" (sounds like euth-an-asia)?

We are literally killing them for an excessive want, for what purpose or need? Where is the limit? In any financial market, in excess could actually create a negative or adverse effect as recently seen across many businesses and markets. (Environmentally we create pollution and destruct the earth.)

Why? It could be that we become greedy, maybe that we lack foresight or it could be due to circumstances outside of our control – nature or terror. The reverse angle of this is others prosper at the expense of Asia (and the like) in terms of their future, their livelihoods and the vulnerable, particularly their children!

No surprise they are trying to seek a better option for themselves in educating their young in western worlds. That is their only alternative at the moment or other countries participate in scams from a negative angle.

If we change our buying habits, become more astute and aware of the impacts of over indulging, we could help them. In return, this will restore balance to their lives and level out our lives and the economy. It doesn't mean work more for less. It can actually work in the converse, once we clear out years of unnecessary policies and laws to provide a sustainable future environmentally and economically.

We are all compromising ourselves! We are all consumed by consumables. Even in hospital the assistance for patients was labeled "Consumer Rights". When did I become a product? The nurse advised it was a general term, 'patient assistance' would have been more appropriate. No wonder people have lost respect for each other and we expect it from the young!

We are also consuming precious natural resources and at this rate, it is not sustainable for future generations. If a major disaster was to occur in Asia or other areas, where would that leave everyone in terms of trade? Assuming that a large proportion directly or indirectly is produced or serviced in those places, (an uneducated guess would be 70%) for Australia; our economy would be significantly paralyzed and livelihoods here would be directly affected. Unemployment rises, defaults on debts, crime increases, it basically sky rockets…. another great depression – logical?

In fact, we are currently living in a great depression; we are a very depressed society. We are all controlled without realizing it because we have accepted rather than questioned and based our life around obtaining material possessions.

The direct opposite to euthanasia is suicide. (Breaking down the word from another angle: (sui) **so I decide** (cide). Some people are taking control of their life by ending it because they see no solution to their problem/s. We may not be effectively listening or helping those that have attempted suicide. For those that caught the plane, we may have not learned or grown from those experiences, otherwise there would be a decline in cases.

It is really sad when you think of how many people are living unhappy lives and are suffering. I know eight people (directly and indirectly) that have successfully made that choice unfortunately. There have been just as many say that they have contemplated it. Thankfully those that had mentioned it to me are still living. Blaming serves no purpose, it clouds the core issue and does not change the situation. Deal with the emotion and find a positive path to get back on track!

A major issue for society especially the young, could be that they are trapped, confused, feel unloved, unable to live up to expectations or don't have the skill because we protected them too much. They don't get the opportunity to learn and grow for themselves.

Another angle, Society has confined them to boundaries so they are unable to explore. They are damned if they do and damned if they don't. They can't explore like we did 30 years ago!

Why? People in society are misguided by the fact that money is power and want a piece of the pie. Courts are a way of managing those boundaries and an opportunity to grab a quick buck. The sharks (lawyers) feed off the vulnerable.

On the reverse side, people protect themselves from litigation. More procedures/policies are introduced and then our children suffer, for example banning kids from playing with balls/Frisbees and not being able to do cartwheels at school.

We are cutting down more trees, creating additional expenses (including insurance) and reducing precious resources. I know I would rather be working with people than boxed in an office chained to a desk. Whether that be teaching, guiding, caring, helping or supporting! Basically all the people that are currently underpaid and treated poorly, that do and can mould our future so we are able evolve efficiently.

What are we doing? We are taking the enjoyment out of life!

For adolescents, how can they find their own direction when everything is controlled or taken away? They need to experience; enabling them to learn and grow, good or bad, to understand the consequences and risks.

If we are basing our life on dollars/possessions, how can any of us find what is real for each of us? (I know I'd like to spit a few coins out of my ass at the moment so I can get rid of a few flies-bills!)

Most people are not satisfied in life because they want material items. As a result, people work more or have to pay off debts adding unnecessary pressure in life. In essence, until we realise that the true value of one self is not based on money and possessions then all challenges we see today in society will remain. This is basic logic and the answer is how to find a happy balance.

Obviously all of us question what the world has become. Many people, past (including centuries before) and present have been able to instigate positive significant changes.

There have also been major negative events such as war, World War II for one. It was frightening to get an appreciation of what transpired over that period of time. Absolutely horrific, makes my skin crawl. How could people be so blind sighted by the actions of one leader? Were they brain washed or tricked? Were they afraid to challenge?

As much as it was inhumane and evil, there was a lesson to be learned. Society had to rationalize, food and products were scarce but they survived. Have we learned from this?

You only have to consider the amount of waste in your own bin, yard and house. Buildings left derelict and empty houses unoccupied whilst others are living in the streets. Shame Shame Shame (as Derryn Hinch would say! – I was always on your channel!)

Why aren't we viewing the environment in the same manner? Are we just taking it for granted, expecting that all will rejuvenate? We are already experiencing the ill effects of an over productive society and the impacts it has on the environment.

I assume the people that faced the Tsunami on Boxing Day 2004 weren't thinking about money and survival would have been first and foremost. Money would have held no value for a period of time. After much devastation, places do rejuvenate; essentially it provides an opportunity to clear the slate! However that is at the detriment to lives, positive and negative, people and nature!

We saw people coming together to assist one another. It was uplifting, one because it is not expected and no material value was placed on life.

It pains me when I hear that people can't seek the correct treatment for themselves or their child because they lack funds. The government basically puts a price on your life without you realising it! They spend exorbitant amounts unaccounted for in different areas. Where it is most needed, medical and education, funds are not allocated appropriately. Even when you have private health cover, you still have to pay more? Why, because they misuse our funds. We pay them to do that? Call me crazy but what society has become is despicable!

I guess that is why I believe we currently live in a cancerous society that is very depressed. Like cancer, our habits have caused mental issues and an environmental disease. Intellectually we are inept to realise it is at our detriment. Don't you think it's time to change our ways? Break the chain and the vicious cycle? One by one, we have the power to succeed and achieve this.

As far as I'm aware, not many have challenged to this degree or we would be living in a better world. There is nothing perfect about the current world. I know I feel ashamed but prior to my realization I had no control over such matters. I was aware but not interested because it was uncontrollable. However with a more positive mindset and different perspective, I can now create awareness which is better than sitting back saying and doing nothing.

Just for the record, I still have little interest in politics. However if there is a plausible option to improve the world we live in, I'm no worse off for trying. At the very least, I can hopefully instigate a review and improve the system for Mental Health patients.

From a simple personal perspective:

Governments have special privileges that we common people don't receive. They receive more pay when others are struggling to survive. They have a greater superannuation fund which they can access earlier. Double standards? What good is that money when you're on your way out? I want to enjoy life, not be stuck in some home thinking about what I could have done! At the moment, that's why my credit card is always maxed out too! I know there is enough super to cover it, if I checkout early. Secondly when it's maxed out it's of no use to potential scammers!

Superannuation is another way for the government to use your funds without you realising it. Why don't they use the funds that we already provide to cater for this, if they deem it to be an issue for the future? When the market does not perform, there are no guarantees on those funds currently held in trust. The government doesn't make up the difference. Some retirees have had to work longer as a result. How is that fair for the aging population who have already significantly contributed to society? Then there is talk of extending the age limit. How many catch a plane before they get to enjoy what they worked so hard for? Criminal really and robbing people of a better way of life!

The government is basically dictating to you when you can spend your hard earned funds, whilst they indirectly play with your money. Any financially astute person knows money holds more value today, than years down the track. Just in basic terms you could invest it now or enjoy it – depends on what rocks your boat! When do you want to spend your money? I know I want mine now!

I also know I would like to pay less tax and free my husband from the exhaustive work that he is currently enduring to provide for the family. This will also allow him to spend more time with us. If we had access to superannuation, people would be able to pay off their house more quickly and not feed the banks. For us personally, we would be able to reduce our mortgage to a quarter of the size and have our house paid off in five years. If extra funds from a reduced tax were evident, it would also provide a better life style. For those that are renting, they may be in a better position to buy and still live a reasonable lifestyle. We could all be living the dream and have security when we are old.

I envisage for the future, that we have the potential to reform this. Tax could be considered a giving, a positive way of helping others. Regaining control of how you wish to spend your money and/or time, instead of the other way around. ("Mama's Happy Giving" as an alternative to tax, just throwing it out there!!)

Power to the people! We need to sort out challenges ourselves, in a constructive manner rather than relying on the government and judicial system. Together we can mould what laws need to change now (short term) and those that will require more time.

These changes should be managed without the red tape (tape to shut your mouth?) Ironic that they cut the red ribbon (ribbon -make it look good!!) (red – signifying blood, sweat and tears!!) Every time the government/council excessively spends our hard earned cash!

We need to break down the walls and stretch the boundaries. I guess it's a matter of time, to review the past and clear the slate for outdated policies/laws so we can prosper! (Pollies don't need any more crackers, they need less cents and more sense!)

Now 'worthy' comes to mind! We are all worthy of a better life no matter who we are or where we come from and it is entirely up to us! Hopefully this provides an insight and outlook of what could potentially be possible, if we are courageous! I might be outrageously out of my mind but there is no harm in trying!

Rome wasn't built in a day, but could come down in one! Just like the economy/financial markets, so due diligence is required to prevent major disruption/upheaval. It is also interesting that in ancient times, empires did clear the slate financially. Rome was the first to discard this notion and built a powerful empire. It did come at the expense of the poor at that time.

Whilst I'm on that train of thought, there is nothing loyal about the royals. It is essentially an empire built over many of centuries but it was the loyalty of the commoners that created the opportunity. Do they still serve a purpose in today's society? Not for me to decide, I actually don't care! Just throwing it out there!

I'm not recommending a communist society either because people take advantage of that too – corruption is rife as seen in some countries. It is more about creating change collectively one by one, helping ourselves and others from a different angle.

(Dr. Hughes, I hope you understand where I'm coming from now! You failed to accept or listen to my honest answers when you asked me about what my thoughts were about world destruction. Would you have had the time to understand? I appreciate you would never have accepted any of my comments based on current practices/knowledge! Just remember, you may miss an important opportunity judging a person or book by its cover!)

In true form, sing it...."I can see clearly now the rain has gone, I can see most obstacles in my way, now that the dark cloud has gone, I'm seeing a bright, bright, bright sunny day!" (Must be the drugs they are forcing me to take or maybe they aren't working! Sorry can't help myself – bad habits!! He he he).

Evolution, revolution or happy compromise to find a new phase in time; nevolution (new revolution for evolution)?

If we are the "Advance Australia Fair" the youngest continent, it only makes sense that we have less to unravel and become innovators of a better world. The lucky country could become luckier! While all the working classman strive to enjoy their real fruits of life! Welcome to the real paradise! Oi Oi Oi!!!

In principal, are we prepared to acknowledge and accept propaganda? And what can we do to change, if we agree? Chugga chugga choo choo...let's explore what we could do!

11. If I could turn back time!

If I could turn back time, I wouldn't change a thing! Firstly as so many have stated, I wouldn't be the happy grounded person that I am today who has the ability to help others. I am able to live an enriching free happy life because of my journey to-date. More importantly, I can't change the past, so why would I entertain something that can't happen? However acknowledging, accepting and evaluating life's lessons as a result of experiences or events are viable and worth considering!

I know I will never get legally married again. I don't plan on getting divorced either! I applaud anyone who does not conform to unnecessary practices. We don't need a piece of paper to prove our love. What was I thinking? I wasn't, I could have publicly declared my love to my husband amongst family and friends without the paperwork or created my own if I felt it was necessary to make it official. I had to pay for a legal binding document. I consumed resources for no real benefit and added to the government coffers. Those who get divorced are forced through the courts and are spending more of their hard earned cash. People who live out of wedlock are not sinners, they are smart! On another angle, how many atheists have married? Why would they seek a license to marry when religion was the catalyst for creating the mechanism for conformity through law? (Well that's the way I view today, everyone else is entitled to their opinion!)

I know that I won't be consuming precious land to dump my lifeless body after my organs have been donated (for me, my body is equivalent to packaging). I don't want to pay for a plot that I will never enjoy or see either! I also hope my family won't be forced to purchase a coffin as we need to save valuable resources! Wrap me up, like a material girl and "Mama-Fry me!" Have a real burn off! While the rest enjoy a Smirnoff, burn baby burn, disco inferno style! If it was acceptable to be mummified in the past, why can't we have the option today?

Ashes to ashes, dust to dust, spread me across my favorite part of the earth's crust! No need to leave a plaque because what I have left should be in your heart! (Sorry just thought I'd share more of my creative side by way of poem!) Where will my remnants reside? I'll give it to you in song……Country road, take me home, to the place I belong, Melbourne, Australia, Mountain Mama, take me home, country road! (Nothing morbid about my farewell party – that's the way I'd like it!)

I will be more considerate of what I purchase and why I need material items. I have been forced to do this recently because of my financial situation. I also try to buy items produced locally or Australian made. I have purchased approximately 5 items of clothing for myself in the last 3 years. Friends have passed on their clothes for the children and I have not needed to buy for them either. But when I did have money, I never considered those that had sacrificed their livelihood. I'd buy impulsively and things would be sitting in my cupboard for years only to be discarded. Excessive amount of toys that I have purchased in the past have ended up as landfill. How many items from Asia or Africa are currently lying dormant or discarded in houses around the world and at what cost to humanity? As a result of my changed buying habits, it has allowed me to spend more money on activities, food, and drink. Basically enjoying life and hopefully in the near future, helping others on my new venture!

I have always purchased furniture of quality with a thought that it will last a life time. I might spend a bit more but I'm not wasting valuable resources by continually buying items that need to be replaced. If I want a change, the décor or setting satisfies me! I may not have the capacity to influence others but at least I know I'm doing the right thing for my children and teaching them. If people are genuinely concerned about the environment, it is a small change.

On another thought, I love my home and the memories it holds, it will not be replaced. I have built additional rooms to cater for a larger family and it is humble. I don't need a 50square house, plus it's not how we want to live! We prefer to spend time together; any excess space would be a waste! If I have the opportunity to buy other properties, it will be for different intentions. We have never aspired to have what someone else has because we are happy.

I plan to grow my own vegetables and spend time in the garden with my children. It will be a rewarding project that will teach them how to be self-sufficient to a degree while we spend quality time together. Items that I am not able to source from my garden, I will purchase from the local green grocer and helping those that find it difficult to survive in a very competitive market. I may pay a little more but I'm helping others. If others adopted this strategy eventually the market would shift and the major retailers would be forced to drop their prices.

I don't buy home-brand items consistently as over time it could affect the way we shop and what is on offer. For example: Some items have been forced off the shelf and some suppliers have become redundant. Logic prevails, once a retailer is able to force other suppliers out of the market by offering cheaper alternatives, there is no other option. The price of home-brand items will increase and we will end up paying more in the future (and in some cases for an inferior product). I tend to mix my shopping up and buy branded items in bulk when they are on sale.

As it is approaching Christmas, I might as well share my thoughts on that too. I dislike the fact that there is an expectation to buy excessively. How much is discarded over Christmas because we buy items that we think people would like or want and don't necessarily need. Don't get me wrong, I like to buy and receive gifts but haven't we lost the essence of what it is all about? It is not about spending beyond your means, becoming stressed, creating waste and fulfilling an expectation. It's about enjoying time with those you love. Have we lost focus? Was the concept introduced to create more business? Easter is not as commercial as Christmas, why would it be different?

That's probably enough at a high level on what I've learned from a personal micro economical perspective. Basically we are all different and the market is driven by our habits. Any consistent change would eventually shift the market over time, the more the better. If you are willing to change and honestly care about the environment and livelihood of others less fortunate, these are just a couple of ideas. There are many other possibilities too. How you choose to live is entirely up to you!

Heading down another track......Labels - we are governed by them! Why does it matter if you are a doctor, professor, labourer, Mr., Mrs. etc. we are all classed like cattle. Shouldn't we be treated the same? The government may claim that it allows them to confirm what society needs and plan accordingly. Why is it then that there is a massive shortfall in resources and facilities? Why are roads upgraded after they are congested for years? Why can government employees have access to their superannuation before the rest of the general public? The list goes on and on and these are only examples that come to mind as I type!

We complete tax returns that provide a great deal of information. There are also associations that capture and provide credibility for professions. All this information, little benefit and just adds to the cost. Do these service providers add credibility or do they provide governments with indirect control? Or access to funds at a deeper level? I didn't need a building surveyor to complete forms, I didn't need mortgage insurance or a solicitor to buy a house but I was forced to comply. Why, because we have accepted that this is how it is or should be? Stamp duty to process a document that costs thousands, criminal! I'm not recommending that we abolish all processes/procedures but we should be simplifying in order to reduce the cost and resources of the current complex world we live in. This would allow us to be more productive in areas that we neglect and essentially become more cost effective on a level playing field.

Locally, we are forced to comply with a plethora of permits. For example: we require a permit for riding a motorbike on our own property or to build a shed or an extension to the house. Why do we need resources to govern what people should be able to do freely? Yes, we need controls to ensure that we are not compromising others or the environment. However wouldn't it be easier to express the standards publicly and make it the responsibility of the individual to adopt/apply the standards? Why should we pay for permission to do what we need or please? Why should everyone be subjected to filling out forms, seeking approval, impeding on resources, cost and time to satisfy the government/local requirements? Are we not trust worthy? Use the resources to reprimand when individuals fail to comply or offer permits when individuals/companies pursue anything outside of the set conditions. That would significantly reduce the cost of doing business for the government and stimulate the economy in other areas. What we are subjected to is forced control and it is becoming extreme! Especially when kids can't fly a Frisbee in their local park or sell lemonade on the corner street! Kill the fun/enjoyment and then spend money on suicide programs? Wake up!!

Our local council is planning a new office development, when there is absolutely nothing wrong with their current offices. They could extend the current building if they needed to. If they reviewed their practices and adopted a different management strategy, I'm sure they wouldn't need extra space! Why are they spending valuable community resources on projects that offer little benefit to the majority? Some of the roads in the area are disgraceful and in urgent need of an upgrade. There is currently a lack of resources for the youth. They roam the streets with little to do. Suicide is becoming more of an issue. In my opinion, create facilities or provide free courses/activities to encourage a more vibrant community! The council shouldn't be spending money on building bigger offices! They need to focus on what will provide an overall benefit to the community. They also need to lead by example when trying to encourage others to change. Most small country towns adopt strategies that assist the community because they can't afford to be frivolous with available funds. If the local country council doesn't offer a reasonable lifestyle, people would move to other places and it would be at the towns own detriment.

I don't want to get too involved into other political agendas and as you can appreciate, there is an enormous amount that can be covered. I just wanted to highlight a few examples of some opportunities locally without boring you!

Some may perceive me as "anti-government" after what I have covered but I'm not. I am merely highlighting flaws to enable improvements to live in a better world. Our primitive mindset and ways have impeded us from evolving to a degree. The government does serve a purpose but under a new management strategy/structure.

Hypothetically we could all create massive change by not complying! If every company and person failed to pay tax, refused to pay fines or seek permits and basically neglected all avenues that support the community through government, we could instigate change. The government does not have the capacity in terms of resources or time to resolve the problem if this situation occurred. There are not enough spaces in court or in prison to control a mass anarchy of this sort! However we wouldn't adopt this approach because it could cripple the economy, create more issues and upheaval than currently present. It would be a no-win situation for all.

Logic prevails, considering there are more of us than the government/local council, we have the potential to re-shape and create change through a different strategy. It is not extreme and is quite feasible.

Primarily we should be voting on projects not people and it should be managed from the bottom up and the top down! This would create the balance that society needs or wants. We have the technology to apply or adopt this approach. Governments and local council should be offering a snapshot of desired changes/projects for the community to accept or reject. A brief summary of the benefits, overall impacts and cost (including opportunity cost) for the masses to vote on.

We have many political parties but in Australia the main ones are Liberal and Labour! There is nothing liberal about the labour in the management of Australian affairs! I guess there is an expectation or perception that one party keeps the other honest and responsible for achieving set goals/targets. Hundreds and thousands of dollars are wasted on resources trying to establish what is right for us. Why wouldn't we collectively contribute to achieve a better outcome overall? By voting on projects rather than people and using the resources more effectively, we could establish a better management approach and achieve more.

We don't need individual parties and conflict in parliament. Lately the leaders of our country having been squabbling over the mismanagement of affairs and have failed to address core problems. It's embarrassing! With this lack of control at the highest level, how can we achieve goals if they don't address or focus on the matters that count?

If the dedicated resources do not deliver their portfolio of projects, they should be replaced. We don't accept inefficiencies in business so why should we in government? By adopting this strategy, it should ensure projects are delivered in a more cost effective manner and timeframe because people will be held accountable.

At present, no-one is held accountable and by default, there is no incentive to deliver. Just blame or make an excuse and everything will be forgotten, seems to be the approach of today. That doesn't help anyone! By changing the strategy and empowering the majority, I'm sure we would experience a more credible and successful government whilst benefiting from the changes. Obviously we wouldn't vote on every project, I recommend it should be the major programs/policies for each faculty of government. Any minor projects could be managed locally under the same structure.

I guess if people support this notion, we will have to vote it in? Will the government accept and be able to make the necessary changes to satisfy the public? Probably not, as some influential people may be displaced or we may receive excuses as to why it wouldn't work! I shouldn't be cynical but I know a change of this magnitude is quite difficult to manage considering the complex structures of parliament. It is also a result of what has been established over time.

If the community believes this is a viable option and the government won't listen or support the change, start locally! Withhold payments to the local council, rates, fines, permits etc. it would have an impact and the community could instigate the change through that option. It won't create massive upheaval but it will force the council to concede (they don't have the resources to reprimand all locals). As a result, the community may be able to influence how their money is spent more effectively. As an optimist, I believe there is no harm in trying if it is of value! This is how we could all be pioneers of change! It seems logical to me!

Shareholders in business could adopt this approach. The members of the board are meant to serve this purpose but there is often a conflict of interest when money is the driver. How many businesses have failed as a result of dishonesty or mismanagement? Or how many could be improved? Remuneration could be addressed more easily for one!

You have to start somewhere if you want to live in a better world and gain some control of the inconsistencies in society. We have created our own demise to a degree but we could have the opportunity to restore a better balance. Not for me to decide but I know what I would prefer! Just laying some different cards on the table for others to consider! My views might be extreme but hey, I'll just add crazy extremist (in a positive light) to my dynamic traits!

I think I've covered enough and it's time to move on. I never entertained politics until recently and I've surprised myself by actually writing about it! I suppose I had to explore this path because basically I have been frustrated and tormented by an unjust system! There was no point whining if I had a potential to create awareness for change!

If we could turn back time, it may provide an opportunity to explore changes but you can't change the past! The true meaning of live and learn, another one of my mum's classical sayings! I'm on a train to somewhere, ooh ahhh (rather than a road to nowhere!) Now we're here, no need to throw Mama off the train just yet! Let's take the track of hope and dreams! Chugga Chugga Choo Choo...

12. Hopes and Dreams

First and foremost, I hope that you can find happiness regardless of your colour, size, race/culture, physical ability, sexuality, beliefs, health and wealth.

I also hope that my philosophies encourage people to enjoy luxuries for good reasons and not at the detriment of livelihoods (animals included). As I continue to prove, knowledge is power and we all have it. Hopefully in the not too distant future, someone will give you a helping hand, if you are in need of one. Never lose touch or sight of hope and be mindful of taking things for granted!

I hope in time people become less self-absorbed by becoming self-less and enjoying life rather than material possessions.

I hope you can appreciate that you will bounce back and forth, while you re-adjust if you choose to change. This is all normal and is required to grow and live an enriching life.

I hope all families and communities become more functional rather than dysfunctional. I have faith that people will happily integrate and enjoy the diversity of cultures rather than causing destruction. Logically if we are individually happy than this will eventuate naturally!

I hope that the Government updates current political program's to ensure Australia (at the very least) can become a better place to live. With foresight, we could economically thrive in a sustainable environment by exploring and implementing the necessary changes previously highlighted. This will allow us to commence our journey in the right direction. (I don't claim to nor do I know it all, many hands/brains make for light decent work!)

I hope that Governments retract from war and address issues in their homeland. Violence creates more violence and the approach is not conducive to anyone. Soldiers return mentally scarred and livelihoods of those and war torn countries don't seem any better off either! Furthermore, too many lives have been sacrificed for what reason and purpose? What goes around; comes around! Karma can be good and also bad!

I hope places of congregation around beliefs become more of a place of soul searching! Providing groups of people with the skills, support and direction that they need to enjoy a better path in life (whilst having fun of course!) Maybe they could offer accommodation for the homeless. (It's not up for me to decide, I'm just throwing out ideas that surface as I type.)

I hope people in their local shires have the courage and tenacity to deploy recommendations, in order to gain greater control and expedite their required changes for their community.

I hope nature's force is kind, if it is a mechanism outside of our control to manage over population and restore the earth to ensure sustainability long term.

I hope we can curb diseases in a more productive manner by focusing less on profit and more on humanity for all species.

I hope everyone realises that my views are based on pure logic and could not be determined without all who are or were in my life. I also would not have been able to articulate this, if it wasn't for all our predecessors /ancestors before our time. For that reason, we could all be a part of this new paradigm of the 21st century and I hope it inspires peace and harmony.

I hope all will see that good does come with bad to keep us in balance so we can continue to grow and learn (vice versa). Understanding, even when we are presented with a negative experience or event, you can turn it into a positive. Essentially evolving through a cycle but also coming full circle in unison (if viewing it graphically, a bit like what sperm looks like hey!). This learning cycle keeps us stimulated and enriched in life.

Personally:

I hope that by some miracle Rose will fully recover from her illness and enjoy a long and happy life! (I hope the cancer never becomes terminal. Ironic that we call places of transport terminals? Arrivals = Birth, Departures = death/catching a plane!?)

I hope I can assist all my mates at P-Block so they can take a more positive journey in life with total care, if they so wish and without being judged!

I hope I get the opportunity to meet Kelly in Philadelphia. I can't wait to meet Punk Rock Mommy's husband and the family! I will be looking forward to seeing what tattoo we'll come up with and where to put it, in honor of those who have suffered and who have inspired others!

I have faith that the Australian Medical Association will immediately review, implement required changes and re-direct resources to provide better care for all patients. It would also be beneficial for the government to initially provide adequate funding to allow further research into mental conditions. I hope that they can appreciate that the short term cost will fundamentally provide a greater return long term for the sake of all on all facets. Particularly as the growing rate of violence, suicide and deaths (murders, road toll, disease etc.) become more evident in society.

My mum has always been longing to find out more about her ancestry and place of birth. I want to take her on the OWL world tour – Outrageous Wise Ladies (and hopefully find her brother) with the rest of the family of course! Maybe some of my other mum's would like to join us too, all expenses paid of course!

My dad loves to gamble and so do I, I'd like to take him and his friends on the Dads On Casino (DOC) world trip! (With a similar entourage I was planning for my mum!)

I hope I can provide my family and friends with the opportunity to fulfill their hopes and dreams. (Fortunate to say there are too many to list but they all know who they are and some have been mentioned in this book!) I will also encourage them to promote or pay it forward so more people can benefit, creating a follow on effect.

I hope Monster Pictures in Australia want to add another genre to their film making business, happy to provide Grant with the rights (no contract required a hand shake agreement will do).

I hope Tracey, Flynn and I can meet up with Bon Jovi and sing a few tunes! I hope I can also get Kenny up to play at a dear friend's shed for a shin dig as well!

I hope I get the opportunity to spend time with Veronica & Ferg's family in Ireland, as I didn't get that far in 2000. I also know it would be authentic travelling with a great Irish soul brother and sister.

I hope I can assist Marky Mark and Noelene in attaining their hopes and dreams. If I get the opportunity, I'd like to at least take them on Ellen with me, as they have a lot to offer and have already put their hands up!

I'd like to invite a plane load of friends to Las Vegas, I have always dreamed of partying with them there! Three days wasn't enough back in 1995, when Mich and I had a ball on our USA/Hawaii Contiki Trip!

I would also like to re-unite Fazel with his parents in London and help him fulfill his hopes and dreams. (Thanks for educating Mick and bringing him home that early morning!)

I'd like to give M Swinge from Random House (UK) the opportunity to assist me in publishing my next book. (She was the only one that had the courtesy to acknowledge my original email).

I hope I get the chance to have a beer with Mal, John and invite Fevola (because I said he'd be coming to the party on that day)! I'm sure we'd have a lot to catch up on and a good laugh! (I hope Fev heads back to the Blues Football club if he still wants to play, because I loved watching him perform!)

I know I'll be able to pay my outstanding fees on my caravan very soon. However I hope that the kind generous and beautiful owners allow me to buy the property if funds become available and they want to sell. So no-one has to pay for any more holidays at that site and it remains as is for my family and friends in the future.

I hope Mary has found true happiness in her life. I'm not sure if I offered any support or comfort when she was subject to abuse just for playing on the monkey bars but I should have defended Mary. Clearly as a child not directly impacted it still left an impression. As I believe in Karma, for all the years of suffering thinking no one cared, Mary, I did and I hope you're still singing a great tune! Hopefully we will reconnect again so we can sing together, you can have the microphone!

I hope I get to meet and sing with a few of my favourite celebrities that I feel are on my mental channel and seem true to their core self (just to name a few):

Home grown:

Derryn Hinch, Anh Doe, Crissy Swan, Fifi Box, Andrew O'Keefe, Karl Stefonovic, John Farnham, Jimmy Barnes, Russell Gilbert, Danni & Kylie Minogue, Delta Goodrem, Klarise Eden, Olivia Newton John, Grinspoon, The Living End, Screaming Jets, AC/DC, Hugh Jackman, Deborah Lee Furness, Paul Kelly, Kyle Sandilands and Ruby Rose (If Michael Hutchence was alive he would have made the list too.)

Internationally:

Ellen, Bon Jovi, Robbie Williams, Pink, Pearl Jam, Green Day, Foo Fighters , Kenny Rogers, Nigella, Chelsea Lately, Oprah, Prince Harry, Adele, Katie Perry, Lady Gaga, Billy Connolly, Mrs Brown, Angelina Jolie & Brad Pitt, Whoopi Goldberg, Eminem, Kiss, Mel B, Matt Damon, Johnny Depp, Madonna, Drew Barrymore, the Maddern Brothers, JLO, Bethenny Frankel, Rod Stewart, Richard Branson

(Maybe the internationals could do an Australian tour, because I haven't traveled as much as I would have liked to, in my own country!)

I hope that due to the controversial and confronting nature of this book, people do not exert a negative path. It would be counterproductive and of no benefit to all and more importantly you! (This includes any personal legal ramifications as a result of me stretching the current boundaries! Someone has to start somewhere or we would all be permanently stuck in this time warp!)

I hope safety is not compromised for me, my family and friends as a result of trying to help others! I don't fear catching the plane early but I have more partying to do for the benefit of humanity!

I was hoping to launch this book at the Monash Medical foyer but given my checkered past, I didn't want to give them the opportunity to lock me up again! (As I haven't received the official discharge notice, they could throw me back in!) I will however be sending a friend in to deliver some books for the bookshelf! That should provide all (including me) with some satisfaction and hopefully it will help commence my journey to improve the care, starting with respect!

On to my dream, I've always dreamed of owning my own pub. In the current world I knew it wasn't possible because I wouldn't have made any money to stay afloat. I would have happily chatted and handed out free drinks, it's me and in my nature.

The beauty about this dream is I may have the potential to develop my ultimate dream (The Mama of all places for the potential new world – "Mama's house of fun!") which was to create a venue, in a shape of a flower or similar. With the huge bud being a place to hold concerts with each petal (circular rooms) depicting a time of the past and celebrating different phases to-date. It would be a compilation of: music, arts, food, theatre, history, architecture, countries, cultures and technology.

For example:

"The Pub" room: bringing a combination of pubs together from the Western worlds (Australia, New Zealand, England, Ireland, Scotland, America and Canada)

"I dream of Jeanie" room: a lounge bar based on the bottle on TV sitcom of the 70's.

"The gold miners" room: where the environment is set in the times of the gold rush and your meal arrives on a cart to your table.

"The techno" room: Sci-fi, robot like décor containing exhibits of bizarre contraptions, advances in technology, also offering astronaut food!

"The Ancient Empire" room: depicting ancient Rome/Greece and getting an artificial feel of what it was like, costumes included, smashing plates etc.

"The Bollywood" room: touch of India bringing music art and food together.

"The Bali" Room: where I had shared some amazing moments with friends. Hopefully set up a new "Sari" Club.

"The psychedelic" room: something similar to the Austin Powers movie, where comedians perform and after dinner, it turns into a night club.

"The Happy Days" room: Iconic of the 60's TV show, Roller skate waiters and all!

"The African" room: where Safari and exotic food would be the theme.

"The Asian" room: celebrating all things extraordinary about their culture and food.

"The European room"; collectively bringing all the countries together!

"The Middle East" room: celebrating the culture, food and arts of those cultures.

"The German" room: set up like the October fest for all year round dedicated to Wally who I've always enjoyed a beer with and to mum of course because of her origin.

"The Theatre" room: for stage performances.

"The Kids" room; massive fun filled family room, like the movie BIG/Willy Wonka, where adults can be kids with their kids, instead of getting stuck in a tube!

And finally my favourite -

"The Casino/Pokies" room: where people can gamble with a new spin to it as well. I imagine we could develop poker machines that include options for extra bonuses or cash. For example: sing and perform the "Chicken Dance" at the time of winning and receive an extra $10, you may receive 5 dares to enrich your life when you win or a voucher to shout a stranger a drink/meal to encourage a chat. I'd also introduce something similar on the gaming tables! (Dedicate this to Donna who I spent many of nights out gambling with!)

And just one more thing, a race track!

(On second thought, I might need a few poppies spread all over the place!)

I envisage that if my dream eventuates, it will be open 24 hours with the opportunity to sing, dance and be merry nonstop! With all the perks a courtesy bus brings too!

It is contrary to the expectations of today's view. With consideration, this is a more suitable or logical approach to resolving some of the issues presented today:

- People not forced out of venue's, less violence or action on the streets
- People can get home safely
- If people are striving to find themselves and be happy, naturally current issues will decline
- Provides more enjoyable work than pushing paper
- Fun approach for integrating society more effectively
- People have more freedom of working hours
- Provides the opportunity to expand demographics and employment rather than densely populate an area. This in turn relieves pressures on an already constrictive infrastructure, roads for one!

Now for any that I develop, I will manage as a non-profit organization because I'm not interested in being wealthy. I prefer to give and feel the rewards of love, life and happiness whilst enjoying time with my family and friends. In fact, I will be leading by example and after I have resolved my current financial situation, all funds will be redirected to help others in some shape or form. I'll manage the financial aspect as required, hope to have a team if it gets that big! (Start small, think big! Or it could be Start big, think small after considering this book.)

Hopefully others will share this dream and help me on my quest so other countries can enjoy a similar place. Sharing is caring to get the job done!

I'm also mindful that there may be critics questioning why I would want to build more and impacting resources. My main reasons are:

- It is symbolic of massive change, compromise and monumental significance for our time (that we would have all communally contributed towards).
- It provides a vision of what could be achieved if we are prepared to jump on board.

Purpose:

- Rewards all that step outside their zone to achieve a common goal in a fun and happy environment for mankind

I guess that's enough hopes and dreams for the moment (and if I have forgotten any that I have mentioned previously in this book, those too). I'm sure the list will have to adapt over time – just call me the dream weaver, day dreamer or day dream, dream weaver!

"Mama's world" would be a great fun place for all to enjoy!

Attention passengers we have almost arrived at the designated place to depart. I hope you have enjoyed the journey and are able to embrace my hopes and dreams! More importantly, I hope you can achieve your dreams, there's no harm in trying!

13. Que Sera' Sera'

Now at the start of this book, I advised that you didn't have to buy a ticket but you obviously purchased my book. Thank you for helping me and hopefully in return, I have helped you. If all goes well, we could all be pioneers of massive change! We can all use our intellectual property more effectively, because whilst we are breathing, we can make a difference! The only thing that prevents us is fear! A life lived in fear is a life half lived! In addition to this, regrets are opportunities we fail to take! You can make a difference to your life and those around you! With an open mind, actions do speak louder than words and speaking from experience, it is very rewarding to find your inner-self and explore what is important to you; truly divine in fact! We are all a diamond in the rough that deserves to shine like a star!

Collectively, we do have enormous power to find a healthy compromise with appropriate philosophies/strategies whilst avoiding major upheaval. We could all have input in what I have previously highlighted at the lowest level, just by changing how we manage our daily lives. A peaceful and constructive Armageddon of the modern day 21st century! While the top (government) re-align to meet us in the middle. Effectively negotiating and identifying the changes that are required for a brave new savvy world for all of us to define and live an enjoyable enriching life!

Ultimately it would be a step closer to provide sustainability for our growing population and future generations, with an aim for peace and serenity. These changes could be brought into effect quite quickly with the redirection of resources and positive mindset. No such thing as can't because we have an approach to make a start! I guess it is one for all and all for one – I believe it has more credit and logic than what we are presented with today! Optimism hasn't failed me to-date and if you believe, anything is possible! No harm in trying to create awareness. Some may have found this book confronting. Is it because I brought matters to the forefront and attempted to remove the con (confront)? It's not for me to decide but I know where I stand!

For those that are still not convinced, it's your choice and your journey! I know I'd rather be a part of a better world than stick my head in the sand like an emu!

Locally, if I am able to provide the assurance for residents of my shire (who fear to step outside the boundaries) I will be happy to put my money where my mouth is, if or when it rolls in! Time will tell!

My main objective was to create awareness and help those in desperate need who had no capacity to help themselves. I will actively advocate for changes in the Psychiatric ward at the Monash Medical Clinic. With any luck, they could be innovators of changes that may have the potential to be deployed nationally or internationally, turning the negative into a great positive.

Personally, the 21st date or number has been significant throughout my discovery for many reasons. I also believe it will mark some important milestones for me in December and maybe years to come. I'm hoping it will be the date I submit my book to commence the publishing stage (if that's the way it's meant to be). Other reasons you will have to find out when I publish my next book on Connections and Coincidences (CC). Depending on interest of course, let's CC what we can see, see, see!

See - as one, See – together, See - for the world, for the next station on my train of thought as I proceed on my journey! (Inspired by the nursery rhyme, a sailor went to sea, sea, sea, to see what he could see, see, see but all he could see was the deep blue sea! For me; the reference to the deep blue sea is delving deeper into my mind!) If I gave you everything I explored in those two months, not many would understand me or the book and we'd be no better off! This is only the tip of the iceberg or pyramid depending on how you want to view it! (Plus if you all have an epiphany like I did, there wouldn't be enough beds to go around!)

It's my life, it's now or never, I'm not going to live forever! I just need and want to be me!! I guess I have ticked many things off my list to do before my 40th birthday in a very short time– I never in my wildest dreams thought I would, it just happened! Oh what a ride!

For the meantime, I will continue to live in the moment! I will be enjoying each day (going with the flow), spending precious time with my family and friends. I don't consider my life as a job, it is a journey! With minimal expectations, minimal fears, minimal inhibitions and emotionally in check with a positive balanced mind!

On reflection, I opened "Mama's box"............ of all sorted chocolates. I'm content on being free, living as me! So call me crazy, I don't mind. I view it as a compliment and testament to how I've lived my "crazy normal, normal crazy" life!

This was my key ("MYKI") to find my inner self! Hopefully you are able to find the treasure in you! "For those disembarking at the first stop to explore, please mind the gap as you land on platform AA!" (Signifying - Acknowledgement & Acceptance or Alcoholics Anonymous! Maybe it will be a happy combination of all elements, HAAAA! I will be enjoying a decent drink after writing this book!) I know one thing for sure (other than catching a plane); I won't have to bore people at any of my future parties with formal speeches!

Wishing you all a life time of love and happiness! Que Sera' Sera' whatever will be, will be!

"Thank you very much!" (Said in true Elvis style!!)

In the event you identify any errors including grammatical, you have a sharp eye! I was limited to resources and thought it was more important to help people in a reasonable timeframe rather than seek perfection.

Just a final reminder, life in more ways than one, always comes full circle, the circle of life! Karma will serve you well if you remain positive and act accordingly! It works in the reverse too - trust me!

I trust that you enjoyed the read at the very least and it made you think! Thanks again,

Mama, Nettie, Stef, Tripper, Annette or any other name you wish to call me! xx

Social Media Services

If you would like to express your view, seek advice through questions and answers or communicate your issues/opportunities, please feel free via the following:

info@madazmama.com

www.ingramcontent.com/pod-product-compliance
Lightning Source LLC
Chambersburg PA
CBHW050330230426
43663CB00010B/1810